NOTES FROM THE FORTUNE-TELLING PARROT

NOTES FROM THE FORTUNE-TELLING PARROT

ISLAM AND THE STRUGGLE FOR RELIGIOUS PLURALISM IN PAKISTAN

DAVID PINAULT

Equinox Publishing Ltd

London   Oakville

Published by

UK: Equinox Publishing Ltd., Unit 6, The Village, 101 Amies St., London SW11 2JW
USA: DBBC, 28 Main Street, Oakville, CT 06779

www.equinoxpub.com

First published 2008

Library of Congress Cataloguing-in-Publication Data
A catalogue record for this book is available from the Library of Congress

ISBN-13   978 1 84553 345 8   (hardback)
            978 1 84553 346 5   (paperback)

Typeset by Forthcoming Publications Ltd
            www.forthpub.com

Printed and bound in the UK by Antony Rowe

For Jody, with love

CONTENTS

INTRODUCTION:
PLURALISM AND RELIGIOUS IDENTITY IN PAKISTAN

Inspiration to write this book first came when I encountered Liaqat Husain Bitalvi and his homemade shrine.

A retired jeweler and poetry reciter, Liaqat is originally from Amritsar. He emigrated from India to Pakistan after Partition in 1947. Now he lives in a neighborhood of Lahore called Islampura (many residents still refer to it by its old pre-Partition name, Krishannagar, "the abode of Krishna"). There, in 1974, as an act of piety, he undertook to build one of the more unusual Shia worship places I've ever seen in South Asia: what he calls Imambargah-e Qiyamgah-e Shabih-e Zuljenah ("the Imam-chapel of the lodging of the likeness of Zuljenah").

On the right as one enters is a *zarih* (cenotaph) honoring Hazrat Zaynab (the Imam Husain's sister, who was present at the fateful seventh-century battle of Karbala). Neighborhood women come here Thursday nights to honor her. On a wall nearby is a display of *'alams* (copies of the battle-standards carried into combat by the Karbala martyrs; they feature prominently in Shia rituals). Such things are common in Shia shrines.

Less common is what one sees on the left as one enters: stalls housing two stallions. Each horse is big and well-groomed, its mane hennaed a brilliant auspicious red. "There are five *imambargahs* in Islampura," Liaqat told me proudly when I visited in 2002, "but this is the only one where Zuljenah horses actually live."

Zuljenah is the name of the battle-steed ridden at Karbala by Husain, the prophet Muhammad's grandson. Folk Islam in localities throughout India and Pakistan includes veneration of *shabih-e Zuljenah* ("the icon/semblance of Zuljenah"), a stallion chosen as a living likeness of Husain's horse.

As we admired the animals, children gazed down at us and waved from an upper-story concrete-block balcony. His brother's boys and girls, explained my host. When he constructed this shrine, Liaqat included several upper floors to house family members in the same complex.

His horses, explained Liaqat, are busiest during Muharram (the annual season for commemorating Husain's death), when he organizes neighborhood processions. The horses take turns being caparisoned as Zuljenah and paraded through the streets. But throughout the year Liaqat also uses his horses for private "home visits." Families where an individual is sick, for instance, will ask Liaqat to bring a horse to their home. Family members then pray in Zuljenah's presence for God to grant the patient health, and they make a cash donation to support Liaqat's shrine.

This is an example of what I'd call improvised Islam, a form of the religion that is localized, entrepreneurial, and unsupervised, an Islam that is attuned to the day-to-day spiritual needs of a given neighborhood. It's also an Islam that irritates the clerical hierarchy. Both Sunni and Shia religious authorities I interviewed expressed disapproval of Zuljenah rituals, though for varying reasons, as will be explored in this book.

My goal first of all is to document some of Pakistan's many local and improvised forms of Islam, whether involving sorcery, self-flagellation, parrot-oracles, or pariah-kite rituals. Despite the monolithic connotation of the title "Islamic Republic" in the nation's official designation, Pakistan is rich in religious diversity, a legacy of its pre-Partition past, when Hindus, Sikhs, and Christians coexisted in large numbers with Muslims under the aegis of British India.

Since the creation of Pakistan as an Islamic homeland in 1947, its citizens have grappled with the question: What does it mean to be Muslim? The issues that emerge in this book—blasphemy laws, decrees against specific rituals, Sunni–Shia conflicts, Hudood ordinances pertaining to women's status, the persecution of the Ahmadiyyah—can be understood as attempts to define and circumscribe Islamic identity.

As Islamic societies confront the challenges of modernity—urbanization, deracination, the diffusion of global communications, etc.—defining what it means to be Muslim becomes increasingly urgent. Despite appearances, confrontation between Islam and the West is not the prime locus where this is being played out. Instead, definitions of Islamic identity are being contested in tensions between local forms of worship (as in my Lahori friend's horse-shrine) and forms of the faith that are exclusivist, transnational, and pan-Islamist. For years, preachers and militants shaped by the ideologies of Wahhabi Saudi Arabia and Khomeinist Iran have competed for influence in Pakistan. These ideologues disagree on many things, but the Wahhabis and Khomeinists are alike in their hegemonist drive to eradicate the unruly diversity of religious practice in Pakistan and replace it with a standardized and homogenized Islam that is easier to control.

In writing about Pakistan's religious diversity I hope to encourage its survival. This will entail the cultivation of pluralism, a concept described by scholar Wade Clark Roof as "a recognition and acceptance...of the legitimacy of religious and spiritual alternatives, which is something considerably more than a group simply tolerating another."[1]

I would take the idea of religious pluralism further. It entails the notion that spiritual paths alternative to one's own have value; that these alternatives have something to teach us, even as they challenge us by their difference; and that our own religious identity and spiritual life are deepened by the self-reflection triggered in the encounter with diversity.

Lest what I say sound hopelessly Western and alien to the nation under discussion, let me cite the example of Dara Shikoh, a figure from Pakistan's own Moghul history. Crown prince and son of emperor Shah Jahan, Dara certainly had his faults; like many autocrats, he was impractical, impulsive, and at times violently self-indulgent. But he was fascinated by Hinduism and believed ardently that the study of Hindu scripture enriched his understanding of the Quran. Controversial even today, Prince Dara insisted he was a true Muslim even as he was targeted with a fatwa condemning him as an apostate. This book's last chapter examines how progressive-minded Pakistanis draw on Dara's legacy today in their struggle to create a religiously pluralist society.

Portions of several chapters appeared in preliminary form in various publications. Part of Chapter 1 was published in *Pakistan Studies News* 8.1 (Fall 2004), 15-18. Part of Chapter 3 appeared in two issues of the Jesuit magazine *America*, 187.4 (August 12, 2002), 18-20, and 194.13 (April 10, 2006), 8-10. Part of Chapter 4 was published in the *Journal of South Asian and Middle Eastern Studies* 26.3 (Spring 2003), 62-84. And part of Chapter 11 appeared in *Amphora* 6.1 (Spring 2007), 12-13, 16. I thank the publishers for permission to use this material.

I have many individuals to thank for the information and courteous help they provided in my research: in Lahore, the Most Reverend Lawrence Saldanha, Diocesan Archbishop; Mr. Khaled Ahmed, consulting editor of the *Daily Times*; Mr. Nasir Husain Zaydi, of the Anjuman-e Imamia Lucknavi; Mr. Amarnath Randhawa, general secretary of Lahore's Hindu Association; Mr. Iqbal Hussain, proprietor of Cooco's Café; and the staff of the Berkeley Urdu Language Program in Pakistan, especially Mr. Mohammed Razzaq (the Lahore office's director) and Mr. Qamar Jalil (a superb Urdu tutor and delightful road companion). In Peshawar, the following persons provided outstanding assistance: Dr. Ihsan Ali, Director of Archaeology and Museums for the North-West Frontier Province; Allama Javad Hadi, director of the 'Arif al-Husaini Madrasa;

---

1. Wade Clark Roof, "Pluralism as a Culture: Religion and Civility in Southern California," *The Annals of the American Academy of Political and Social Science* 612 (2007): 84.

and the faculty of the Department of History at the University of Peshawar, especially Professor Syed Minhaj-ul-Hassan, Mr. Zahid Ali, and Mr. Waqar Ali Shah. In Islamabad, Mr. Nadeem Akbar, Center Director of the American Institute of Pakistan Studies, undertook skilful troubleshooting on my behalf; and Mr. Pervaiz Masih, Member of the National Assembly, guided me through his nation's political history. And in Rawalpindi, I was privileged to make the acquaintance of Mr. Anwar Kamal Azim Khan, parrot-master of the Ganjmandi Bridge. I thank them all.

Closer to home, research grants from the American Philosophical Society, Santa Clara University's College of Arts and Sciences, and the Bannan Institute for Jesuit Education and Christian Values at Santa Clara University facilitated my work in Pakistan. I acknowledge with thanks their support. Mr. Elwood Mills of SCU's Media Services provided invaluable help in formatting the photograph that appears on the cover of this book. For many years Dr. Wilma Heston of the University of Pennsylvania has furthered my work; I'm grateful for her encouragement. And I thank Janet Joyce of Equinox Publishing, and Dr. Duncan Burns, my copy-editor, for their care in guiding the Parrot manuscript through the stages of production.

My biggest thanks, as always, go to my wife, Dr. Jody Rubin Pinault. Without her none of this would have been possible.

Santa Clara, California
August 2007

1

MY FORTUNE-TELLING PARROT
TRIGGERS TROUBLE IN LAHORE:
STREET RITUALS AND THE LEGACY
OF RELIGIOUS PLURALISM

Introduction:
How I Learned Not to Laugh Too Fast at Oracles

I'm standing on the footpath outside Data Darbar. This is Lahore's biggest Sufi shrine—in fact it's one of the biggest in Pakistan—and Data Darbar draws Muslim pilgrims from all over the country. These pilgrims—like spiritual journeyers in every part of the world—bring with them hearts full of petitions, worries, questions. So the sidewalk outside the shrine is a good place for fortune-telling parrots to set up shop.

I push through the crowd, pay my five rupees, crouch by the cage and get an oracle-card from the parrot. Passers-by want to know what the oracle has to say to the American. The men serving as my escorts—a Shia Muhajir, a Sunni Punjabi, and a Pashtun from the NWFP (North-West Frontier Province)—squat beside me before the parrot cage. Partly they're shielding me from the crowd. Mostly they just want to look over my shoulder as I read.

The contents are ho-hum. I've been to Pakistan five times in recent years, and I've had parrots divine my fortune on umpteen occasions. This one follows the usual pattern. I've been facing hardship, I've been unjustly targeted by enemies, but Allah will soon lift my burden and transform my life for the better. Et cetera. It ends with the usual Urdu-Arabic formula: *Aur kaho in sha' Allah ta'alla*— "And say: If God most exalted wills it."

Rafiq is dismissive. He's the rationalist, the educated guy in my group, and he doesn't altogether approve of my interest in folk Islam. He says the parrot-masters are always savvy enough to offer only the kinds of pronouncements people want to hear. He's too polite to say all this is a waste of time, but I get the idea.

But Rafiq doesn't manage to discourage Imtiyaz Yusuf. Imtiyaz is my driver, a Pashtun from Peshawar, and this stuff fascinates him. He was supposed to stay with our car—a tiny box-shaped Hyundai—but he doesn't want to miss the fun. He pays his money and the parrot plucks another card from the outspread deck. Imtiyaz smiles as he gets his card.

The smile fades fast. "Through your own ignorance and neglect," the card warns, "you've spoiled your affairs. Now is the time for work. If you don't learn a lesson from your past mistakes, then a new worry will assail you soon."

Well. Rafiq is starting to say that's what Imtiyaz gets for consulting a parrot, and I'm trying to think of something to say to cheer up my driver. I know he'll be fretting all day over the form this new worry will take.

Turns out we don't have to wait long to find out. A shout from behind makes us turn around.

The Hyundai is somehow suspended in mid-air, six feet above the ground. Punitive magic from the parrot? Hard to see clearly, with these throngs of people pressing in close. I have a moment of mental vertigo—common enough in Lahore, where I get reminded daily that life knows no limits in the surprises it can spring—and then I see what's happened.

A forklift—operated by the city, as a way to penalize illegal parking—has scooped up our Hyundai. Policemen, pilgrims, onlookers all converge. The show's too good to miss.

One of the cops says the car will be impounded. My driver will have to appear in court and answer for his reprehensible carelessness in blocking the entrance to a holy shrine. Rafiq and Imtiyaz protest.

To no avail. The forklift, its steel tongues holding our Hyundai captive, begins to nudge a path through the crowd. "Appear in court," the policeman says again, and my guys turn to me with apologies.

"Unless," says the cop, "you prefer to settle the fine now." He holds out a hand.

I ask how much. The cop says 200 rupees. That's a little over three dollars.

I pay the three bucks. The forklift lowers our Hyundai and sets it back on the ground. Imtiyaz looks relieved his predicted new worry came and went so fast.

As we leave I try for another glimpse of my ominous parrot. But it's too busy picking a card for its next client to spare me a look.

"Powerful as an Enchanted Steed":
Parrot-Oracles in Singapore and India

Since 1989 I've done research on Shia self-flagellation rituals and Sunni–Shia relations in the subcontinent. Interesting work, but—to put it mildly—emotionally demanding. Wandering the streets for distraction is a way to unwind. That's how I met the parrots.

My first encounter with a fortune-telling parrot took place in India. This was in the city of Hyderabad. I saw an elderly Hindu (his forehead marked with the paste-stripes of a Vishnu devotee) seated on the sidewalk in a busy commercial district. Beside him was a large shrouded cage. When I approached, he removed the shroud, revealing a handsome brilliant-green parrot. On a mat before the cage was arranged a long row of overlapping envelopes.

The parrot-master explained that for five rupees his bird would select an envelope the contents of which might offer me wise counsel or a glimpse of my future. For five rupees this sounded like a good deal, so I said all right.

By way of sample the man opened several envelopes and showed me what was inside. Each envelope contained a devotional card picturing Shiva, Lakshmi, Krishna, or one of the other Hindu gods.

The master took my five rupees and asked me my name. He opened the cage door, showed his parrot the money, and repeated to it my name. The bird hopped out and paced three times back and forth over the line of envelopes. Then it paused and made its choice. With its beak it tugged free an envelope and fluttered to the shoulder of its master. The man opened the envelope.

It held two cards. One showed a copy of the Quran, surmounted by Arabic lettering that proclaimed "the glorious Book." The second card depicted a familiar scene from Christian iconography: Christ on the cross, flanked by the sorrowing figures of Saint John and the Blessed Virgin Mary.

As a Catholic who happens to be a researcher in the field of Islamic studies, I found the parrot's choice of cards to be a good summary of my religious identity and my professional life. I was impressed.

But it was during a trip to Pakistan that included a stopover in Singapore that I learned more about the world of fortune-telling parrots. This world is extensive, ranging from the Pakistani Punjab to India and Southeast Asia. From other travelers I've also heard of fortune-telling parrots as far afield as Calcutta and Kuala Lumpur—basically, the realm of Indian culture and the Indian diaspora. For convenience I use the term 'parrot' to describe this creature, but the bird most typically used by fortune-tellers (to judge by those I've seen) is one of the smaller members of the parrot family, the rose-ringed parakeet (*Psittacula krameri*).

In Singapore the best place to go for fortune-telling parrots is the neighborhood known as Little India. I saw several at work on Serangoon

Road, in the vicinity of the Sri Veerama Kaliamman Temple. All the parrot-masters I encountered there were Tamil Hindus, whose families originated in India's Tamil Nadu State.

As in Hyderabad, the bird's technique was to select a fortune from a row of envelopes. But in Singapore each envelope contained not only a Hindu-deity devotional card but also a slip of paper bearing a fortune printed in Tamil on one side and in English on the other.

This bilingualism seemed necessary, given the clientele, which included local Malays, Chinese, and Indians, as well as tourists from around the world. In fact, various 'Visit Singapore' websites and tour groups in Singapore promote 'parrot astrologers' as one of the advertised attractions and must-see items in itineraries to the island.

My first parrot-fortune in Singapore read as follows: "The wheel of fortune turns to the phase of a yogi, abiding only in his prayer. Whatever will be your wish, it will be granted. Your enemies will vanish and you will be as powerful as an enchanted steed, because of the merit of the prayer."

The next card selected for me announced, "You are currently worrying about a specific problem. In fact your life in the recent past has been full of hardships." It went on, however, to offer the reassurance that these problems were "mainly due to the unfavorable position of your star" and that "all your worries will soon become things of the past." A third card suggested that I "avoid quarreling and gambling." "In the long run," it promised, I would be "very happy."

Despite this warning against gambling, Little India's parrots can also be induced to help with the selection of "lucky numbers." The birds pick a card from specially marked decks to help individuals play their hunches in Singapore's lottery or in off-track racecourse betting.

Talismans and Palmistry:
On the Varied Skills of Parrot-Masters

The fortune-telling parrots of Pakistan's Punjab function similarly—up to a point. In Lahore they can most easily be found in the neighborhood where Imtiyaz nearly lost his Hyundai—Ravi Road, near the Data Darbar (vendors and beggars gather here because of the volume of pilgrim traffic to this Sufi site). They also cluster in the vicinity of Minar-e Pakistan, opposite the entrance to the shrine of Hazrat Sher Shah Vali, on Circular Road. I interviewed eight parrot-masters at these sites in the course of a few days. In the city of Rawalpindi I encountered members of this profession who had set up their business on the Ganjmandi Bridge, in the vicinity of Raja Bazaar.

Like their counterparts in India and Singapore, the parrot-masters I met in Pakistan have trained their birds to select a fortune from a row of envelopes arrayed before prospective clients on the footpath. In Lahore most such vendors advertise their presence via Urdu-language placards, each of which typically is illustrated with a brightly painted parrot that holds in its beak an envelope. One such placard I saw stated, "Islamic book of oracles/omens (*Islami fal-nama*). Parrot oracle, five rupees. Quranic oracle, ten rupees."

The term *fal-nama* links the parrot-masters of Lahore with the centuries-long history of divination in popular Islamic culture. In the medieval era *fal-nama* ("book of omens") referred to a genre of texts that guided diviners in interpreting dreams, taking auguries from the behavior of animals, finding the mystical significance of numbers and letters, and so forth.

One placard-advertisement I saw in Lahore made the claim that this practice of "Islamic divination" was created by the "holy prophets and noble companions of the Prophet Muhammad." Another assured customers that the oracles on offer were "free of any taint of frivolous matters (*jo fazool baton se pak hayn*)." Such advertising hints at a certain anxiety and defensiveness concerning the religious orthodoxy of divination and parrot fortune-telling in contemporary Pakistan, a point to which I return below.

As the placard described above indicates, the more expensive service available in Lahore involves a *Qur'ani fal*. This entails an oral consultation, wherein the fortune-teller refers to a "Quranic oracle book" in guiding the client.

The two texts I saw most in use are Iqbal Ahmad Nuri's *Shama'-e Shabistan* and the *Fal-nama-ye Qur'ani* of Maulana Arshad Sahib. Very inexpensive editions of both texts are currently sold in Lahore's Urdu Bazaar.

Another text I found in Lahore's Urdu Bazaar, an anonymous pamphlet entitled *Qur'at al-Qur'an* ("The Quranic Oracle"), offers thirty-two different "prophetic" oracles, each listed beneath the name of an Islamic prophet. Preceding these oracles is a chart tabulating the names of these same thirty-two prophets. The chart arranges these names one beneath another in a diagram comprising four columns, with eight names in each column. The fortune-teller, after performing the *wudu'* (ritual ablution), invoking God's name, and reciting the *Fatihah* (the Quran's first chapter) three times, closes his eyes and taps the chart of names with his index finger. The prophetic name thus chosen at random indicates which oracle is to be read out loud to the client. The *Qur'at al-Qur'an*'s anonymous author assures readers that this form of divination was invented by the Muslim prophet Daniel.[1]

If the client opts for the *tota-fal*, then the oracle is chosen by the parrot rather than by human agency. As mentioned above, the bird selects a fortune from a row of envelopes. Each envelope contains a slip of paper comprising a photocopy of a divinatory pronouncement from one or another Urdu oracle-book.

Here's an example of an oracle that a Lahori parrot offered me outside the Data Darbar shrine: "Your situation is certainly complicated, but God will make it easy. No harm will come to you from any enemy. But you, for your part, should not stir up any conflict or quarrel. If you comply with this and are patient, your heart's desire will be fulfilled."

Another oracle I received from a Data Darbar parrot went like this: "O holder of the oracle, you are afflicted with great grief and sorrow, but soon your cares will be over. Your poverty will change to wealth, your problems to joy. Although you consort with pure-hearted people, certain individuals harbor enmity for you. But they will not be able to harm you. Your star is about to shine with prosperity."

And a third Data Darbar parrot offered a card warning me my current situation in life was "not good." But the text went on to advise me, "Endure these days with patience and gratitude and do not neglect your acts of worship."

Like the parrot-fortunes I encountered in Singapore, the oracles I've been offered in Lahore follow a certain pattern. They refer in general terms to the client's current difficulties but are melioristic in tone: they offer an optimistic view of the future, coupled with common-sense advice as to behavior (be patient, don't pick fights, etc.). A few oracles—like the one given to my driver outside the Sufi shrine—take a harsh tone; but these are exceptional. Generally the Pakistani divinatory texts remind clients to fulfill their religious obligations ("do not neglect your acts of worship") while reassuring them of Allah's ultimate protection. Overall, the language is formulaic, the tone one of orthodox Islamic piety.

The parrot-masters I encountered in Pakistan came from a variety of backgrounds. One man I met in Rawalpindi is a middle-aged Pashtun from the NWFP. He learned his trade, he told me, from his father. A sixty-year-old I spoke to near Lahore's Data Darbar lost his first job due to illness and was advised by friends to take up the oracle-trade because, so he told me, it would allow him to earn money "without having to move around too much." An eighteen-year-old near the Minar-e Pakistan

---

1.　Anonymous, *Qur'at al-Qur'an ya'ni fal-nama-ye Qur'an-e majid* (Lahore: Idara-ye Raushna'i, 2001), 31-42.

monument in Lahore told me that the parrot-work was his "second job." He also worked in an office, he said, and he had learned the oracle craft from other footpath practitioners.

What all the parrot-masters I met have in common is the ability to read. This, they agreed, is the most important skill needed for the job, as many of their clients are illiterate and unable to read the oracles offered to them.

But this is not the only skill possessed by the parrot fortune-tellers. Some read palms; others make amulets. Many fortune-tellers offer advice in choosing one's "lucky number," "lucky day," or a propitious gem-stone to be set into a ring. One parrot-master I met in Rawalpindi sells small plasticized holy cards that depict various talismanic motifs: Ayat al-kursi (the Quranic "throne verse," famed for its power to avert evil), Dhul fiqar (Imam Ali's sword), and Zuljenah (the horse of Imam Husain). Dhul fiqar and Zuljenah—both associated with Shia devotionalism—are known as icons of protection and healing. They suggest how parrot fortune-telling reflects an eclectic South Asian tradition that is willing to borrow from any source—Muslim, Hindu, astrological, magical—and make use of it to address the fears and needs of streetside clients.

Pierced Hearts and Scorpions:
What the Parrot Had Available in the Way of Tattoos

There is yet another trade—one widely frowned on in Islam—that some parrot-masters pursue: tattooing. One fortune-teller—a pleasant young Lahori resident named Iqbal, who commutes with his caged bird by bus every day from Islampura to Minar-e Pakistan, where he does his side-walk oracles—told me many of his customers are men in their teens and twenties. Some of these customers, he explained, want a tattoo in honor of their girlfriends—but there's a potential problem.

"Here in the Punjab," said Iqbal, "some people will kill each other over a family's reputation or a girl's honor. Young men have to be careful." What this means, he added, is that his customers are forced to be discreet in how they immortalize their love—so they prefer to be tattooed with the mere initials, rather than the too-revealing full name, of their sweethearts.

Iqbal said he also tattooed men's arms with images of various sorts, and he showed me a placard that illustrated the designs he did: a rose, an eagle, a scorpion, an arrow-pierced heart, and (my favorite) a whimsi-cally curlicued centipede.

And the tool he used for this work? A battery-powered gun, lying about for the moment on a dirty tarpaulin by his parrot's cage. The tattoo-gun's needle-tip was sludged thick with oil and grease. The thing looked capable of giving clients some dread disease faster than you could say Tetanus.

Tattoo-work contributes to the poor reputation parrot-masters have in the minds of pious-minded Pakistanis. Conservative Muslims are quick to link tattooing with the customs of the ancient *Jahiliyah*—the "time of ignorance" among the pagan Bedouins of pre-Islamic Arabia. The practice is associated especially with Bedouin women, who are said to have spent much time adorning their bodies in various ways.

One Muslim critic I met in Lahore directed me to a website called Islamweb.net, which offers an online fatwa on the subject of tattooing. The fatwa cites a pronouncement attributed to Muhammad: "The Prophet...cursed those ladies who practiced tattooing and those who get themselves tattooed." Another Islamic website rationalized the prohibition by classifying tattoo artistry as a form of harm to the human body, justifying this stance by quoting another moral ruling by Muhammad: "The Prophet...forbade mutilation (or maiming) of bodies."[2]

On the Orthodoxy of Oracles: Criticisms of Parrot Fortune-Telling

All the parrot-masters I met insisted on the antiquity of their trade. One of my Lahori informants claimed that parrot fortune-telling in the Punjab "dates back to the time of the English, to the Moghuls." He said that he himself had been doing this work for over forty years. The Pashtun I met in Rawalpindi told me that he remembered his father using a parrot for oracle-giving in the 1940s, in the days before independence and the partition of the subcontinent.

But I have not been able to find specific textual evidence to document how far back the use of parrot oracles goes. One of the first books I checked was a text published in London in 1891 called *Beast and Man in India*. Its author, John Lockwood Kipling, worked in Lahore for many years (his son Rudyard became the celebrated story-teller of British India). Kipling discusses the public entertainments offered by Delhi's "performing parrots" but says nothing of parrots as fortune-tellers.[3]

2. Mufti Abdulla al-Faqeeh, "Tattoos in Islam," Fatwa No. 8383, www. islamweb.net; Osama Abdallah, "Are Tattoos Allowed in Islam?," www.answering-christianity.com/tattoos.htm. See also a pronouncement on tattooing by Yousef al-Qaradawi, cited in www.sakkal.com/Graphics/Calligraphy/Custom_Arabic_ Tattoos.html.

3. John Lockwood Kipling, *Beast and Man in India* (London: Macmillan & Co., 1891), 16-22.

But I have come across various texts from the Middle East and the Indian subcontinent in which parrots are characterized as more than mere entertainers. Medieval story-tellers are fond of describing parrots as counselors and household spies. An example is the *Arabian Nights* tale of "The Jealous Husband and the Parrot." A suspicious-minded merchant wants to find out about his wife's extramarital liaisons. He buys a talking parrot and commissions it to monitor his wife's doings while he's away on his business trips. Loyal to the husband, the parrot does so, and in fact it catches the wife bringing a lover into the house while her husband is gone. But then the wife devises countermeasures to neutralize the bird's ability to engage in domestic espionage.[4] This tale has a long history. Thematically it's linked to Ziya al-Din Nakhshabi's fourteenth-century Persian *Tuti-Nama* ("Parrot Book"), which in turn was derived from the ancient Sanskrit *Shukasaptati* ("Seventy Tales of a Parrot").[5]

Another example is Rajab 'Ali Beg's nineteenth-century Urdu work, *Fasana-ye 'aja'ib* ("Tales of Wondrous Things"), which features a wise parrot that "knew how to converse with courtesy and good taste." In this narrative the parrot gladdens the heart of a young prince named Jan-e 'Alam with "fascinating tales and marvelous stories." And when Jan-e 'Alam preens himself on how handsome he is, the parrot is the only member of the prince's court brave enough to speak the truth and reprove the young man for his vanity. Thereafter the bird acts as Jan-e 'Alam's guide in the prince's quest to find the realm of the beautiful princess Anjuman-e Ara.[6]

Pakistanis with whom I spoke varied in their reactions when they learned of my parrot-interests. Islamist-revivalist types generally disapproved, saying that parrot fortune-telling was justified by neither scripture nor prophetic *sunnah* (the exemplary lifestyle of the prophet Muhammad). Self-styled Deobandis (adherents of the puritan ideology that spawned the Taliban) told me that Lahori Muslims borrowed this custom of parrot fortune-mongering from the Hindus. (The linkage with Hinduism was most certainly not intended as an endorsement.) Parrot-masters I interviewed in Lahore complained that their business has dropped off in recent years, due to what they described as criticisms by preachers and Muslim reformers.

4.   Muhsin Mahdi, ed., *The Thousand and One Nights (Alf layla wa-layla) from the Earliest Known Sources* (Leiden: E. J. Brill, 1984), vol. 1, 98-99.

5.   David Pinault, *Story-Telling Techniques in the Arabian Nights* (Leiden: E. J. Brill, 1992), 56 n. 42.

6.   Rajab 'Ali Beg, *Fasana-ye 'aja'ib* (Lahore: Ferozsons, n.d.), 8-17.

One parrot-man I spoke to pointed to the painted sign he uses as advertising. He read the text aloud: "*Tota-fal. Islami fal-nama*" ("Parrot oracle. Islamic oracle-book").

"See?" he said. There was defiance in his voice; fear, too, I thought. "'Islamic,' it says. I use Quranic verses for my amulets. I cite the Quran in the advice I give people. I'm a good Muslim."

When I repeated this argument later to a Lahori mullah, the cleric let me know he wasn't impressed. "That kind of talk," he frowned, "doesn't change the fact that all this parrot-business is Hindu."

Prospects for Survival:
On the Future of the Parrot-Oracle Trade

The fortune-tellers I met in Lahore and Rawalpindi said that their customers tend to be one of two sorts. The first are "villagers," impoverished individuals burdened by family and work problems. The second are individuals who are more educated and more sophisticated. "Such people," as one informant told me, "take the *fal* and consult the parrot just for fun."

This leads in turn to the question: how long will the custom of parrot fortune-telling survive in a region such as Pakistan's Punjab? One possible answer is suggested by something I received as a present in Islamabad during a recent visit—a calendar published by a Pakistani non-profit organization called the "Asian Study Group." Among the calendar's photos—which are intended to highlight the historical and cultural attractions of Pakistan—is a picture from Rawalpindi of a parrot-master and his fortune-telling parrots.

Who knows? Perhaps in years to come Pakistani entrepreneurs will follow Singapore's lead in marketing parrot-oracles for the tourist trade.

2

BEING HINDU IN PAKISTAN: LEGACY AND SURVIVAL

Introduction:
Abandoned Temples and Displaced Statues—
On Discarding a National Heritage

A good rule for sightseers: spot something that intrigues you? Get a close look now. Don't put it off till next visit; it might be gone by the time you come back.

I learned that the hard way in Lahore.

June 1991, and my first visit to Pakistan. Not the best time of year: my memories of that trip include hostile sun-glare and a mix of dust and gritty car-exhaust that made breathing raspingly hard.

But I wanted to see Lahore, and the Punjab Tourism Corporation promised a one-day excursion—"in air-conditioned comfort"—to catch all the sights. Turned out the tourist van's a/c didn't work; but I did manage to see what I wanted. Jahangir's tomb and the Badshahi Mosque; Lahore Fort with its tilework pictures of angels, swordsmen, and Bactrian camels; Shalimar Gardens, where families strolled and fountains splashed and shrieking children jumped into the pools.

The tour included the welcome twilight and coolness of the colonial-era Lahore Museum, where Rudyard Kipling's father was once curator. I wanted to linger over the gallery of Gandhara Buddhas. But my driver-cum-guide—a young prayer-capped Pashtun from the NWFP—said he had to show me his favorite display in the museum.

I followed him to another room, anticipating some masterpiece of Islamic calligraphy or exquisite arabesque in red sandstone.

Wrong. He pointed with enthusiasm to a pair of Spandau machine-guns that had been captured from the Germans on some European battlefield in World War One. His comment on this armament made me realize he must have been thinking of the recent mujahideen campaign in Afghanistan. "Now these," he said glowingly, "would have been useful against the Soviets."

But something else on display in the same room caught my attention: a bulky bronze statue of an enthroned Queen Victoria, depicted broodingly deep in thought over her Empire. Substantial presence; massive lady.

My guide wasn't so impressed with the piece. He said only that in the time of the English the statue had been displayed in a marble pavilion in a park off the Mall in the heart of Lahore. Near where the Summit Minar is now, he said.

And in fact I passed the Summit Minar on a walk later that same day. I was out strolling after dinner, glad for the evening breeze that stirred the stale air. That's when I noticed the park near the Mall and the marble pavilion mentioned by my guide. No Massive Lady in residence; but an indeterminate substitute was there instead, positioned beneath the pavilion's stone cupola. I stepped closer for a better look.

That's when I saw something else, something I all but tripped over, right at my feet. Something large, big as a giant raccoon, moving fast in the dark and close to the ground. Gave me a shudder; and then I realized what it was: a ragged legless man, seated on a square of cardboard, scooting along the sidewalk with quick thrusts of his arms.

With a cheery cry of "Peace be upon you," he held up his hand. I gave him five rupees and was rewarded with a smile. He wished me peace once more before hurrying on his way and leaving me alone beside the pavilion.

Where the bronze Queen once sat something else now presided: an oversized Quran, adorned with gold-leaf lettering, housed in a glass case. The message seemed clear enough. Victorian imperial identity was gone. In its place was an icon of the region's new identity: national solidarity symbolized in the scripture of the Islamic faith. Shared homage to the Empress of India had been replaced by shared veneration of the Quran. The implicit proclamation: to be Pakistani is to be Muslim.

One problem. 97% Islamic though it is, Pakistan still numbers among its citizens several million Christians and Hindus. What about their national identity?

Which brings me to the most poignant and troubling monument I saw during that first visit to Lahore in 1991.

Part of the sightseeing package offered by the Punjab Tourism Corporation was an escorted excursion through Anarkali Bazaar. We did a tour of the neighborhood and the nearby tomb of Sultan Qutb al-Din Aibak. I confess I remember nothing of the tomb, but I do recall something I noticed in the distance as we stood outside: an elegant tapering steeple or spire of some kind, towering over the buildings to either side of it.

Just an old Hindu *mandir* (temple), was the driver's reply when I asked what that was. In his words, "Not worth seeing"—the ultimate condemnation from a tour guide.

The place was abandoned, he said. Its worshippers had left in 1947, at the time of Partition and the formation of Pakistan. The *mandir* had been converted to some other use, he said, or so at least he had heard. In any case the Hindus were gone.

An abandoned temple; a marker of Pakistan's religious diversity and neglected spiritual legacy. I felt an impulse to see it.

Not part of the itinerary, came the reply. Not included in the package.

I should have insisted, should have offered extra baksheesh. But I was tired and told myself I'd seen enough for one day. I glanced at the steeple again and gave it a silent salute. Peace be upon you, as the legless beggar said. I could always see it another time. It wasn't going anywhere.

Which was a mistake. Years went by before I returned to Lahore and made the time to seek out the *mandir*. By then it lay in ruins, demolished by a population that wanted no reminders of its Hindu past.

Idols Vomit Jewels:
Tasty Burgers, Golden Monkeys,
and the Hindu Legacy in Old Lahore

Some Muslim chroniclers of Lahore start their history with the conquest of the region in the early eleventh century by the Afghan warlord Mahmud of Ghazna. He established Islamic control over Lahore and launched a number of raiding expeditions deep into India.

A telling anecdote survives concerning one of Mahmud's wars in search of plunder. This involved his capture of the Hindu city of Somnat.

After he'd won his victory, Mahmud ordered Somnat's temple destroyed. Brahmin priests rushed forward to save the shrine's chief idol, offering the sultan gold as ransom if he would spare the statue.

His officers were inclined to accept. But Mahmud prided himself on his Islamic orthodoxy. He had the idol thrown onto a fire. While the flames jumped high he declaimed virtuously that the merit-yielding fight against idolatry weighed more with him than gold. Worldly loot, he boasted, meant less than the reward in paradise Allah would grant him after death for his act of pious arson.

Yet as the idol burned it cracked open from the heat, revealing a cache of jewels that spilled forth at Mahmud's feet. So now the onlookers knew: one could fulfill the jihad-obligation of fighting paganism and still be rewarded here in this life for the effort.[1]

---

1. Farid ud-Din Attar, *The Conference of the Birds*, Afkham Darbandi and Dick Davis, trans. (Harmondsworth: Penguin Books, 1984), 160-61.

This is the image of the subcontinent's history some South Asian Muslims cherish to this day: the clash of Hinduism and Islam, and the erasure of Hindu monuments. They forget that Muslims and Hindus often coexisted amicably enough, and that Islam spread throughout much of India not only via conquest but through the peaceful preaching of Sufi saints and miracle workers.

Things change; things topple and vanish. But even when suppressed from view, they're not entirely gone. In the 1950s, archaeological surveys unearthed traces of Lahore's buried pre-Islamic past. Excavations extending to a depth of fifty feet beneath the rampart-foundations of Lahore Fort unearthed a wealth of artifacts—a pot depicting cows and peacocks; figurines of goddesses and a thunderbolt-wielding Indra: traces of Lahore's Hindu legacy.[2]

Yet little of this legacy is readily visible to the casual visitor. Tourists are most likely to notice the physical remains of more recent dynasties. A few gurdwaras survive, a reminder that the Sikhs held dominion here in the late eighteenth and early nineteenth centuries. They were ousted by the British, who in turn left their mark on the city in the form of "Indo-Saracenic" architecture—an appealing fantasia-confection of Victorian and "Moorish"-Islamic building styles.

But the British held Lahore for scarcely a century. Much more pervasive is the lingering heritage of Muslim rulers like Jahangir and Aurangzeb, in the form of gardens, mosques, and palaces.

Much of this heritage, unfortunately, is now obscured by the smog-blasted ephemera and grime that characterize Lahore as one over-stretched city among countless others in South Asia. A journal-jotting from the 1991 visit summed up my impression of Lahore from that initial trip: "Dust-blown Moghul glory, gummed over with ads for 7-Up."

Fifteen years and four more trips later, that description of the city's appearance largely still holds true for me, except for one emendation. The 7-Up ads are now layered over with blurbs for cellphone services and Kentucky Fried Chicken and McMaza Burgers from McDonald's ("McMaza" being a clever way, I can't help but note, for this globalized chain to insinuate itself down Pakistani throats: *maza* is an Urdu-Hindi word that connotes both tastiness and fun).

But it would be wrong to trust what's visible today as an accurate index of how vibrant Lahore's Hindu community was before 1947 and the tragedy of Partition.

---

2. Muhammad Wali Ullah Khan, *Lahore and Its Important Monuments*, 2d ed. (Karachi: Department of Archaeology and Museums, 1964), iii-iv.

One measure of the dynamism of the city's Hindu presence can be found in a book from 1892 entitled *Lahore: Its History, Architectural Remains and Antiquities*. The author, Syed Muhammad Latif—a district judge, employed by the government of British India, and a fellow of the Royal Geographic Society who also happened to be Muslim—provides a detailed description of no fewer than 31 major Hindu temples in Lahore that were active in his day.

Note the following sampling of descriptive comments by Muhammad Latif in his catalogue of Lahori *mandirs*:

The "Bawa Thakurgir" shrine: "This dome is surmounted by a golden pinnacle, which gives the temple a picturesque appearance."

The "Raja Dina Nath" temple:

> The walls fronting the street are tastefully decorated with paintings of Devatas [gods] and Avatars [incarnations or earthly manifestations of the god Vishnu]... In the western outer hall are placed the big kettle-drums, trumpets, shells and bells to summon the congregation to worship, at the appointed hours of service and at other times. In the midst of the court-yard, on a raised platform of stone, is the *mandar* [alternate spelling of *mandir*], in which is kept a beautiful image of Shiv Ji Maharaj ["the great king Lord Shiva"]... The floor inside the *mandar* on which the Shiv Ji takes his seat on an eminence, is of pure marble. When the time of service arrives, the musical instruments that are blown and beaten create a deafening noise, which, however, is indispensable for the service.

The "Bakshi Bhagat Ram" temple: "The *mandar* contains a large number of beautifully chiseled stone idols of different sizes, which are worshipped by the votaries."

The "Thakurdwara of Raja Teja Singh": "The walls inside are decorated with stone carvings, and in a niche of marble are gracefully placed the images of Sri Karishna Ji Maharaj and Radhika Ji, dressed in rich cloths."

The "*Mandar* of Hanuman Ji" [Hanuman, a monkey-god known for his loyalty to the great god Rama, is the object of numerous cults in contemporary India]: "On the eastern wall is a large image of Hanuman Ji, colored with red lead."

The "Thakurdwara of Bankey Behari": "Tastefully decorated... The entire building looks like some beautiful ornament, or crystal palace, and is, architecturally, a success."

The "Pandit Radha Kishan" temple: "On the top of the tower is placed a golden image of Hanuman, instead of a pinnacle, which gives it a picturesque appearance."[3]

3. Syed Muhammad Latif, *Lahore: Its History, Architectural Remains and Antiquities* (Lahore: Syed Muhammad Minhaj-ud-Din, 1956), 234-38, 241.

Two things in Muhammad Latif's comments are remarkable—breath-takingly so, when one considers the status of religious minorities in Lahore today.

First is how highly visible and audible the city's Hindu presence used to be. A golden statue of the monkey-god perched proudly in the open air atop a tower. Paintings of gods and divine avatars were displayed on the street for passers-by of any faith to see, instead of being hidden away in the recesses of a *mandir*. Conches, drums, and trumpets were so loud as to be "deafening." Latif's account is an implicit attestation of the con-fidence and vigor of Lahore's nineteenth-century Hindu population.

The second point worth remarking is how respectful this author is in his descriptions of non-Muslim places of worship. Rather than designate Hindu deities by their bare names alone, he is careful to include the titles that reverent Hindus themselves would use in referring to the gods: Maharaj ("great king"), Sri and Ji (the latter words are honorific terms that convey the sense of "sir" or "lord"). No Muslim I met in any of my trips to Pakistan was so deferential in referring to India's gods.

Notice, too, the vocabulary employed by Latif in referring to the *man-dirs*: "tasteful"; "beautiful"; "graceful"; "a success." True, his repeated use of the term "picturesque" and his "crystal palace" comparison (a reference intended, perhaps, to recall London's own 1851 "Crystal Palace" exhibition) give his work a bit of the condescending tone of a guidebook for British imperial tourists. But his open-mindedness and tolerance are a far cry from the anger with which I have heard some Muslims insist on the need to eradicate what they regard as the con-taminating presence of Hinduism from Pakistani society today.

And if Muhammad Latif occasionally shows exasperation—as in his acknowledgment that Hindu temple music can be "deafening"—he's also quick to excuse and defend the practice: the noise, he explains, is "indis-pensable for the service." This was a man who wanted folks to get along.

Unsurprising, perhaps, to learn that Syed Muhammad Latif was a passionate supporter of British India. He reminded his readers that during the reign of the Sikhs (a time still within living memory for many readers in his audience), Raja Ranjit Singh had used Lahore's greatest mosque, the Badshahi Masjid, as an ammunition dump and as a place to stable horses. The British, however, restored the mosque to Muslim custodians.

He also credited British India with restraining tensions among the principal Muslim denominations, recalling for his readers the kind of sectarian violence that had once stained its places of worship.

Nowadays, he asserted, Muslims of any and every sectarian loyalty could peacefully pray in the Badshahi Mosque—in contrast to a notori-ous spectacle he recalled for his audience from the Moghul era involving this same mosque: "From the high pulpit…had been seen rolling down the floor the head of a Shiah pontiff that had been cut off by an infuriated Sunni congregation, for his daring to utter an offensive expression."[4]

This Muslim loyalist of the British Indian Empire also offered an optimistic assessment of interfaith relations in Lahore:

> In the same streets of Lahore where bloody feuds were the order of the day, we see both Muhammadans and Hindus, holding friendly meetings for the furtherance of national causes. Having forgotten their mutual broils in common subjection to the British, they vie with each other in loyalty to the Crown which has given peace to all; and they have been attached to the British Crown by a conquest over their minds, which is by far the most durable, as well as the most rational, mode of dominion.[5]

This last point is worth pondering as Western nations try to win hearts and minds in Islamic societies in this post 9/11-world we inhabit.

"Like the Crunch of Termites":
Hindu-Muslim Violence in the Punjab
on the Eve of Independence

"Having forgotten their mutual broils": well, not entirely. Newspaper accounts of the period describe the Hindu–Muslim violence that would sometimes erupt during the annual Muharram season, when Muslims staged lamentation processions (as they still do in the twenty-first century) in the streets of Lahore's Old City neighborhoods to honor the martyrdom of the Imam Husain.

In the 1880s Rudyard Kipling, at that time a young news reporter for Lahore's *Civil and Military Gazette*, wrote two articles and a short story describing the Muharram celebrations. The first of these articles, published in October 1885, described a "Hindu–Mussulman fracas…on the part of the very scum and riff-raff of the City of the Two Creeds" that flared during Lahore's Muharram observances. Kipling praised the local British District Officer for the precision with which he authorized the police and military to use just enough force to quell the rioters without triggering further violence.[6]

The job of covering the Old City's Muharram processions was an assignment Kipling loved. This locality stimulated the storyteller in him, an instinct which colored even the nonfiction pieces he wrote for the

---

4. Latif, *Lahore: Its History, Architectural Remains and Antiquities*, x.
5. Latif, *Lahore: Its History, Architectural Remains and Antiquities*, x.
6. Roger L. Green and Alec Mason, eds., *The Readers' Guide to Rudyard Kipling's Work* (Canterbury: Gibbs & Sons Ltd., 1961), vol. 1, 582-90.

Gazette. Consider, for example, the article he published in October 1887 describing the Old City neighborhoods where he wandered at night as he followed the chanting crowds: "The yard-wide *gullies* [alleys] into which the moonlight cannot struggle," he wrote, "are full of mystery, stories of life and death and intrigue of which we, the Mall abiding, open-win-dowed, purdah-less English know nothing… Properly exploited, our City, from the Taksali to the Delhi Gate, and from the wrestling-ground to the Badami Bagh would yield a store of novels."[7]

The 1887 Muharram season reported on by Kipling passed peacefully in Lahore, with no outbreak of communal riots. After a long cramped night of studying "the crush and smother and blaze of the last night of the Mohurrum," the twenty-two-year-old Kipling felt ready to return to the Mall, "the wide boulevard that runs from the European quarter to the old walled city."[8] In his *Gazette* article he summed up the night as follows. "There had been no trouble, the City was quiet and another Mohurrum had been safely tided over. Beyond the city walls lay civili-zation in the shape of iced drinks and spacious roads."[9]

Kipling wrote both fiction and nonfiction pieces that referred to Hindu–Muslim violence in Lahore. A theme common to all these writings is that it was only the presence of the British that ensured some measure of harmony between members of the "two creeds." His story *On the City Wall*—published in 1888, the year after the *Gazette* article described above—portrayed the latent communal tensions among the Hindu and Muslim residents of Lahore's Old City:

> You must know that the City is divided in fairly equal proportions between the Hindus and the Musulmans, and where both creeds belong to the fighting races, a big religious festival gives ample chance for trouble. When they can—that is to say when the authorities are weak enough to allow it—the Hindus do their best to arrange some minor feast-day of their own in time to clash with the period of general mourning for the martyrs Hasan and Hussain, the heroes of the Mohurrum.[10]

Worth noting is that the practice of using Hindu festivities to confront Muslim neighbors has recurred in recent years in India. In the city of

7.   Thomas Pinney, ed., *Kipling's India: Uncollected Sketches 1884–88* (New York: Schocken Books, 1986), 267.

8.   Charles Carrington, *Rudyard Kipling: His Life and Work* (London: Macmillan & Co., 1955), 36-37.

9.   Pinney, *Kipling's India*, 268-69.

10.   Rudyard Kipling, *A Kipling Pageant* (New York: Halcyon House, 1942), 52. For a fuller discussion of this story, see David Pinault, *The Shiites: Ritual and Popular Piety in a Muslim Community* (New York: St. Martin's Press, 1992), 69-72.

Hyderabad, Hindu nationalist organizations have routed processions in honor of the gods Ganesha and Kali through Muslim localities so as to assert communal identity. Hyderabadi Muslims have responded with religious processions of their own that are timed to coincide with Hindu holydays. The result: confrontation and violence.[11]

Kipling documents how British colonial authorities dealt with such problems:

> Gilt and painted paper presentations of their tombs [i.e. of the Muslim martyrs] are borne with shouting and wailing, music, torches, and yells, through the principal thoroughfares of the City, which fakements are called *tazias*. Their passage is rigorously laid down beforehand by the Police, and detachments of Police accompany each *tazia*, lest the Hindus should throw bricks at it and the peace of the Queen and the heads of Her loyal subjects should thereby be broken.[12]

In Kipling's Lahore, Hindu–Muslim tensions were held in check by a government that had the will and power to supervise and intervene.

But with the departure of the British in 1947 and a Partition that split the Punjab between Pakistan and India, that supervisory intervening power was gone. In newly independent India, Sikh and Hindu mobs butchered defenseless Muslims. Lahore, which fell within the boundaries of the freshly created state of Pakistan, held a sizable minority population of non-Muslims—all of whom were now endangered. By 1947, Muslims in the crowded Old City outnumbered Sikhs and Hindus three to one. Penderel Moon's Partition memoir *Divide and Quit* identified Lahore as one of the Punjab's worst centers of rioting.[13]

Larry Collins and Dominique LaPierre, who gathered eyewitness accounts of Partition in their book *Freedom at Midnight*, describe what happened: "Almost a hundred thousand Hindus and Sikhs were trapped inside Old Lahore's walled city, their water cut, fires raging around them, mobs of Moslems stalking the alleys outside their *mahallas* [neighborhoods], waiting to pounce on anyone venturing out."[14]

Robert E. Atkins, a British officer from a Gurkha regiment that tried to protect Lahori minority communities, saw the city tear itself apart. Collins and LaPierre recorded his impressions:

11. Pinault, *The Shiites*, 155.
12. Kipling, *A Kipling Pageant*, 52.
13. Penderel Moon, *Divide and Quit: An Eye-Witness Account of the Partition of India* (Delhi: Oxford University Press, 1998), 81.
14. Larry Collins and Dominique Lapierre, *Freedom at Midnight* (New York: Avon Books, 1975), 298.

> The gutters of Lahore were running red with blood. The beautiful Paris of the Orient was a vista of desolation and destruction. Whole streets of Hindu homes were ablaze while Moslem police and troops stood by watching. At night, the sounds of looters ransacking those homes seemed to Atkins like the crunch of termites boring into logs.[15]

Collins and LaPierre conclude their description of Lahore's 1947 Partition riots with a detail that reminded me of my own visit to the Summit Minar and the park that once housed the Massive Lady of bronze:

> In late August, as the violence reached a crescendo, anonymous hands performed before fleeing a gesture that was an epitaph to Lahore's lost dream, a silent and bitter commentary on what freedom's first hours had meant to so many Punjabis. Someone laid a black wreath of mourning at the base of the city's famous statue of Queen Victoria.[16]

The Prince and the Guru:
A Muslim–Hindu Friendship in Old India

Slaughter; black wreaths; gutters running with blood. But the idealist in me prefers to linger over a pre-Partition image, a more hopeful image, from seventeenth-century Lahore: two men, one Muslim, the other Hindu, seated in friendship, discussing their religious traditions. They do so not to convert each other or score theological debate-points but to pursue the shared spiritual interests that help make them—and us—human.

I am thinking of Dara Shikoh and Baba Lal Das, two of the most intriguing visionaries that ever resided in Moghul-era Lahore. Dara Shikoh (1615–1659), eldest son of the emperor Shah Jahan, crown prince and commander of his father's armies, was widely expected to inherit the imperial throne. But his real interests lay elsewhere. A Sufi initiate and philosopher, he sought the company of spiritual questers and wanderers—Muslim, Hindu, and Christian alike—who came to Lahore from all over the world. So strong was Prince Dara's interest in the non-Muslim faiths of India that he studied Sanskrit and collaborated with Hindu pundits in translating scriptural texts such as the *Upanishads* into Persian.

One of Dara Shikoh's most influential Hindu companions was Baba Lal Das, a shaven-headed ascetic and a member of the Kabirpanthi school. The latter comprised followers of a celebrated fifteenth-century Muslim Sufi known as Kabir. Syncretistic in his tastes, impatient with the formal doctrines and religiously mandated social hierarchies that defined and segregated Hinduism and Islam, Kabir strove to combine the

---

15. Collins and Lapierre, *Freedom at Midnight*, 330.
16. Collins and Lapierre, *Freedom at Midnight*, 344.

best aspects of the two faiths in his teachings. Kabir in turn had been a disciple of Ramananda, a Hindu mystic who espoused the *bhaktimarga* (the "devotional path" focusing on the cultivation of an intimate personal connection with immediately accessible forms of the Supreme Divinity).[17]

Dara Shikoh encountered Baba Lal Das in 1653, after a year of active military service beyond the frontier of the Moghul realm. The emperor had assigned his son Dara the task of attacking fortresses in the vicinity of Kandahar (at that time these forts were held by the Safavid dynasty of Iran). The army Dara led included artillery, war elephants, archers, horsemen, and infantry armed with matchlock rifles.

The campaign was long and frustrating, the fighting intense. (The royal Moghul chronicler of the expedition noted that the defenders of the Afghan forts "rained down quantities of fireballs" on Dara Shikoh and his troops, of whom "many quaffed the *sharbat* [drink] of martyrdom."[18]) Dara returned to Lahore from the ten-month Afghanistan campaign ready for rest and relaxation.

R-and-R for this prince-mystic, however, meant chatting at his ease with the Hindu Baba Lal. The two met several times over a period of three weeks at various venues in Lahore, including a hunting park, a palace, and a garden belonging to a royal courtier. The conversations were in Urdu; a Hindu scribe who was present translated them into Persian, preserving them in the form of a manuscript known as the "*Mukalama* (Dialogue) of Baba Lal and Dara Shikoh."[19]

Readers of this *Mukalama* will perceive at once that these two men were familiar with Persian poetry, Sanskrit epics, and the religious vocabulary of Hinduism and Islam. In the dialogue Dara asks a wide range of questions—about the transmigration of souls and *moksha* (release from the cycle of reincarnation), about Hindu cremation versus Muslim burial of the dead, about the power of chanting the sacred syllable OM, and about the significance of the ten avatars of Vishnu.

The questions give us the impression of a freewheeling intellect, inquisitive, interested in everything. His queries are direct and uninhibited, as in this request for clarification concerning what for many Muslims constitutes the most offensive part of Hinduism—its practice of idolatry: *But-parasti dar 'alam-e Hind chist va-farmudah kist?* ("Idol-worship in the world of India: what is it, and who mandated this practice?").

17. S. M. Ikram, *Muslim Civilization in India* (New York: Columbia University Press, 1964), 126-27.

18. W. E. Begley and Z. A. Desai, eds., *The Shah Jahan Nama of 'Inayat Khan* (Delhi: Oxford University Press, 1990), 487, 492.

19. Claude Huart and Louis Massignon, "Les Entretiens de Lahore," *Journal Asiatique* 209 (1926): 288.

Baba Lal takes the question in stride, providing an answer that draws on a category of thought he knows will be familiar to Dara in his capacity as a Sufi—the distinction between apparent/external forms and internal/hidden significances:

> The meaning of this is that it [i.e. idol-worship] was established in order to fortify spiritually the [human] heart. The person who understands the inner significance has no need for the external form that corresponds to this inner sense. But anyone lacking knowledge of the image's *batin* [i.e. its hidden mystical dimension] remains bound to the external form.[20]

Of all the points discussed in this dialogue, the most interesting is the one in which Dara asks his Hindu mentor about the challenge of being simultaneously a yogi-ascetic and a ruler who must exercise worldly sovereignty—a poignant question for a crown prince who is temperamentally and instinctively drawn to contemplative seclusion.[21]

The conversations of Baba Lal and Dara Shikoh represent what I would call the interaction of Hinduism and South Asian Islam at their best: each enriching the other, each offering fresh perspectives on how spiritual pilgrims may live their lives.

A precious moment in history, soon to be eclipsed. Dara's philosophical friendships with non-Muslims, and his attempts to reconcile Muslim doctrine with Hindu teachings, gave his rivals at the Moghul court an opening. Ultimately he found himself gazing down the business-end of a fatwa that targeted him as an apostate and a danger to Islam.

But that's a story to be continued in a later chapter of this book.

Babri Masjid and Lahore's 1992 Anti-Hindu Riots.
The Weight of Fallen Temples: Violence, Regret, and Memory

In the late 1980s and throughout the 1990s, my research took me to India, where I focused on ritual practices among Shia communities. It wasn't until 2002, eleven years after my first trip to Pakistan, that I returned to Lahore. Muharram self-flagellation and Shia–Sunni relations preoccupied me in 2002 and 2003. But in March 2004, on my fourth trip to Pakistan, I set out to learn what I could about Lahore's Hindu community and present-day Pakistani Muslim attitudes to the country's pre-Islamic past.

20. Huart and Massignon, "Les Entretiens de Lahore," 287.
21. Huart and Massignon, "Les Entretiens de Lahore," 298, 320-21.

I decided to begin where I'd left off, with the Hindu temple I'd glimpsed in the distance during my tour of Lahore back in 1991. I described its location to my Muslim friends. They told me this must have been the Jain Mandir, located in a neighborhood called Purani Anarkali, not far from the campus of Punjab University.

Too late to see it now, my friends warned me. Along with a half-dozen other temples, it had been destroyed in a wave of anti-Hindu riots that gripped Lahore in December 1992.

Lahore's riots amounted to retaliation for what had befallen India's Babri Masjid. The latter was a mosque built by the sixteenth-century emperor Babur, founder of the Moghul dynasty. Hindu agitators claimed that Ayodhya, the site of the mosque, was the ancient birthplace of the god Rama. Mobs goaded by Hindu militants demolished the Babri Masjid, triggering Hindu–Muslim riots that killed hundreds throughout northern India.

But this connection with the Babri Masjid violence made me all the more convinced that the story of the Jain Mandir and Lahore's other Hindu temples was important and merited piecing together.

I thought I'd begin by interviewing surviving members of the city's Hindu population. But this proved none too easy. All my Muslim friends said yes they were sure some Hindus still resided in Lahore; but no one knew any personally or knew anyone who did. It took considerable time before I developed my first contact with Lahori Hindus.

In the meantime, however, I interviewed local Muslims who remembered the Jain Mandir from the days before its destruction. One informant was Khaled Ahmed, consulting editor of Lahore's best newspaper, *The Friday Times*.

Born in India near the end of the British colonial era, Khaled moved with his family to Lahore at Partition and grew up in Purani Anarkali, not far from the temple. He recalled that the shrine had been built in the 1930s and that during his childhood it stood deserted—abandoned by its worshippers during the riots of 1947. Nevertheless, empty and desolate though it was at the time, it made an impression on Khaled. "I remember how beautiful the Jain Mandir was," he told me, "especially its steeple."

Sometime in the 1960s, Khaled said, it was turned into an Islamic school for local orphans—making it all the more ironic that Muslim demagogues later had it destroyed in 1992.

Khaled Ahmed wasn't the only person I met who recalled the temple's beauty. Another old-time resident of Purani Anarkali, an educated Muslim in his 60s now resident in Lahore's Cantonment, said Anarkali's skyline was impoverished without the Jain Mandir. He remembered it

had a spire shaped "somewhat like an obelisk." Its façade included ele-
gantly carved flower-petals. He said much of the rubble had never been
cleared away after the temple's demolition in 1992. If I was lucky, he
said, I might be able to see the toppled spire.

"It won't be hard to find," he promised. "Just go to Jain Mandir
Chowk [*Chowk* is the Urdu word for crossroads or public square.] The
Chowk keeps the name of the *mandir*, even if the *mandir*'s been knocked
down."

He also repeated an allegation I heard from many sources, that the
municipality had colluded in the temple's destruction. Government officials in Lahore provided tractors and bulldozers, he said, to help the
rioters tear the building down.

The impression of government collusion is corroborated by the
account of the attack published immediately after the event in *The New
York Times*. "In Lahore, Muslims used a bulldozer, hammers and hands
to demolish the Jain Mandir temple near Punjab University. The police
did not intervene. Nor did they act when a crowd stormed the Air-India
office." The article also notes the cries chanted by the mob: "Crush
India!" and "Death to Hinduism!"[22]

These interviews increased my desire to see what was left of the site.
One afternoon in March 2004, accompanied by my Urdu tutor, Qamar
Jalil, I set out for Jain Mandir Chowk.

A snarl of traffic—not unusual for Anarkali—greeted us when we
reached the site: buses, gravel trucks, horse-drawn tongas, and a tiny
valiant donkey hauling a piled-high cartload of metal scraps.

We got out of our car and looked about. Across the street were weathered apartment buildings with rickety wooden balconies. One rooftop
held a large wire-mesh cage within which birds fluttered from perch to
perch. A boy standing about saw me glance at the roof. "Pigeons. They
belong to my uncle." He added proudly, "He races them."

On the near side of the street was what I'd hoped to see: the remains
of the Jain Mandir. My Anarkali informant was right: the steeple had
never been removed. It lay tilted on its side, partially obscured behind a
six-foot-high whitewashed brick wall that separated the street with its
traffic-whirl from the grounds of the old temple.

Even lying in its ruin, the steeple was impressive, rising up at least
five feet above the perimeter wall. Before its destruction it must have
towered up a good thirty feet or more in height. From where I stood in

22. "Pakistanis Attack 30 Hindu Temples," *The New York Times*, December 8,
1992.

the street, I saw my informant had been correct—the spire did look a bit like an obelisk.

At first it seemed Qamar and I wouldn't be able to get a closer look. A padlocked iron-barred gate blocked the entrance to what must once have been the temple courtyard.

Nor did we have the site to ourselves. Men lounged on charpoys by the gate. Parked in front of the perimeter wall was a line of broken-down auto-rickshaws (one three-wheeler had its back painted with a tropical-idyll scene: a palm-tree-lined lagoon, sailboats and a rose-pink sky, beneath the words *Khosh amadeed*—"Welcome"). Pipes and wrenches littered the ground. Tires lay stacked atop the wall. The footpath in front of the temple had been converted to a rickshaw repair yard.

We learned this from the charpoy-men, who told us they were just taking a break from working on a particularly troublesome motor. Hospitable, these individuals. One—a smiling young man, bone-thin, with twitchy long fingers and spindly long legs—got up and asked if we'd like to go inside and have a better look at the temple.

I pointed to the heavy padlock securing the gate. Did he have a key, I asked.

He told me no need. He showed me where one bar of the gate's grill-work was missing and had been replaced with a thick twist of taut wire. Crouching, he pulled the wire aside, producing the narrowest of open-ings. It gave just enough for him to squeeze adroitly through—first his head, then his shoulders, then the rest of him, as supple as a snake. He made it look easy.

From inside he held the wire aside and gestured an invitation as if wav-ing me into his home. "*Tashrif laie,*" he said politely. "Please come in."

So I did, stooping and wriggling and contorting myself and banging my knee and wondering for a moment whether like Peter Rabbit I'd get stuck in the grill. From behind a workman gave me a helpful push. I was in. My tutor Qamar managed his entrance with more dignity.

Worth the effort, this squeeze. We admired the *mandir*'s decorations from up close. Carved flower petals, just as my informant had said. Plus scrolled pillars, scalloped niches, and leaf-patterns in stone. We had to cock our heads sideways to imagine the original effect, since the tumbled steeple now lay on its side. Saplings grew weedlike in the yard. Heaped up on the ground was trash of various sorts. Plastic bags and old water bottles. Crushed cigarette packets ('Gold Leaf King Size'). A dead crow.

My reaction? A line from my journal-entry for that day conveys it all: "Great sadness wells up; lost heritage and wasted legacy."

Just as well I didn't get to linger in that mood. Our host led us around to the upended base of the fallen tower. The snapped-off base stood eight feet high and was shrouded in a dirty tarpaulin. From behind it came the sound of voices.

Our host lifted a corner of the tarpaulin and told us we could go inside. We ducked beneath the tarp.

Resting on a mat, stretched out at their ease within the hollow of the spire, were several chatting men—more mechanics, we learned, from the rickshaw yard. They'd rigged the tarp as an awning and made the interior of the fallen tower into a makeshift rest-spot and cave-retreat from the sun.

They invited us to sit and were glad to talk. I asked them about the December 1992 riots that resulted in the destruction of this temple. At first they were cautious—uncertain, no doubt, how to respond to a foreigner about the issue of communal violence. One man volunteered that as a boy he'd attended school here before the *mandir*'s demolition.

More hesitation, and a lull in the talk. To provoke a response I showed them something I'd brought with me: a photocopy of a picture from *The New York Times* dated December 8, 1992. It showed a mob of Muslim protesters crowding around one of Lahore's Hindu temples as it crashed to the ground.

The picture did its job. Everyone started talking at once. One man reminded me of what Hindus had done so unjustly to the Babri Masjid. Then he interrupted his flow of Punjabi (which Qamar was translating for me into Urdu) with a pithy two-word phrase in English: "Action, reaction." He savored the words, repeating them for effect with evident satisfaction: "Action, reaction."

The implied logic was clear: they tear down our mosques; we tear down their *mandirs*. I heard this same English phrase several times from Muslims when I asked them to explain Lahore's anti-Hindu riots: Action, reaction. The jingly rhyming quality of the phrase seemed to confer on these words an incantatory coercive authority of their own, as if no further explanation were needed.

It reminded me of another phrase I've heard some Pakistanis use to explain the source of all their nation's problems: *Yahood aur hunood, yahood aur hunood*: "The Jews and the Hindus, the Jews and the Hindus." For some individuals, it seems, the rhymed *hood–nood* provides all the euphonic evidence one needs of a linked conspiracy of foreign powers.

One of the rickshaw mechanics described the demolition of the Jain Mandir's tower in terms that made it clear he saw it as a great accomplishment: "To be able to knock down a brick and concrete and stone temple that was three stories high: that wasn't easy! It required a lot of work."

Months after this interview, back in the States, I found a BBC News article filed by a Muslim reporter who'd driven by the Jain Mandir the night of the 1992 riots and been forced to join in on the "work" for which the rickshaw mechanic voiced such admiration. "I was stopped by a mob on the road," wrote the BBC reporter:

> There were some 200 men armed with clubs, axes, and hammers. They were gathered at Jain Mandir, a blackened, weather-beaten Hindu temple that had not been in use since 1947... My part was to keep the car engine running and direct the headlights towards the temple so they could see better. I tried in vain to tell them that whatever they were doing was not sane, civilized or even Islamic. They just told me to shut up.[23]

Our own encounter at the ruined Jain Mandir gave me and my tutor Qamar much to talk about. Careful to offer no comment while we interviewed the mechanics, Qamar made his disappointment with their mentality plain later. As we continued our interviews with residents of neighborhoods where two of the temples had been destroyed, we gained an impression of prevailing attitudes towards the events of December 1992:

In the immediate aftermath of the Babri Masjid violence, most Lahori Muslims seem to have felt that destroying Lahore's temples was a good thing, and a very appropriate retaliation for the loss of the historic mosque in India. Anger was the prevalent mood in Lahore at the time.

But there were some Muslims—admittedly a small minority—who felt that such retaliation was completely wrong-headed. They were capable of distinguishing between Hindu perpetrators in Ayodhya and innocent Hindus in Pakistan. As Qamar himself said during one of our interviews: "The Hindus who live here, it wasn't their fault. Besides, these temples in Lahore were part of our heritage. Why destroy them?"

But much more common among Lahori Muslims in 1992 was the attitude: Mosques belong to Muslims. *Mandirs* belong to Hindus. The *mandirs* have nothing to do with Pakistan. They belong to the Hindus, and the Hindus—regardless of where they happen to live—are part of India, not Pakistan. We're not doing Pakistan any harm if we destroy

---

23. Aamir Ghauri, "Demolishing History in Pakistan," *BBC News World Edition*, December 5, 2002 (news.bbc.co.uk/2/hi/south_asia/2546373.stm).

these temples. Such talk—revanchist in its ideology—reflected an utter failure of religious pluralism.

More recently—at least during intervals when relations have improved, if only sporadically, between Pakistan and India—some Pakistani Muslims have voiced regret for the loss of their pre-Islamic national heritage.

This regret has come out obliquely, it seems to me, in quarrels over names. An electronic webforum chat-site called *Gup Shup* (Urdu for "gossip" or "idle talk"—the site deals with various Pakistani controversies) posted a Lahore *Daily Times* news article that generated a great deal of online response. The article (from June 2005) announced that the city's District Government had issued a resolution calling for the "Islamization" of street names that sounded (to judge by the names being targeted) too British, too Sikh, or too Hindu.

Chat-room responders heaped scorn on the idea. One correspondent noted previous attempts to do away with the name Krishannagar ("the town of Krishna," one of Lahore's oldest neighborhoods) and replace it with "Islampura." These attempts, as the correspondent remarked, "failed miserably."

Another chat-room member wrote about the locality Qamar and I visited:

> There was (is) Jain mandir chowk in Lahore, people tried to change the name to Babri chowk (after babri masjid incident) but still every one knows it as JAIN mandir and people will give you blank face at babri chowk. There are Dayal singh college and dayal singh mansion at the Mall road and so many more. These names are part of [the] rich culture of Lahore.[24]

Typical of the online responses was this: "There is no need to change the hindu names. They are sweet and easy to remember."

And in fact some Lahori bus conductors, I was told by informants in Anarkali, tried renaming Jain Mandir Chowk by announcing the stop as Babri Chowk (thus continuing the mentality of tit-for-tat retaliation and eradication at the level of nomenclature). But it didn't catch on: everyone I talked to in Lahore called the place Jain Mandir Chowk. Old names, as the chat-room writer wrote, "are sweet and easy to remember."

A few days after our discovery of the Jain Mandir's ruined steeple, Qamar and I set out to locate the site of another temple that had been destroyed in the 1992 riots. This is the one known as Moti Lal ("the radiant red pearl"). A picture of this *mandir* appeared in *The New York*

---

24. "All Hindu Street Names of Lahore to be 'Islamised'," *GupShup Forums*, June 2, 2005 (www.gupistan.com/gs/showthread.php?t=184302).

Times at the time of the riots. The photo captures the moment when the rioters and arsonists have just completed their work: the tower cracks apart and begins its sliding crash to the ground.

We'd heard that the Moti Lal Mandir had been housed in a neighborhood called Shalmi (the local nickname for Shah Alam Chowk). We went from street to street asking for directions—first from a fruit vendor, then from some tinworkers, then from a roadside construction gang. The road crew squatted in the street, their heads covered with rags to shield them from the sun, chipping with mallets and lengths of pipe at a pile of rocks. One man straightened and pointed his crowbar across the street. There, he said, was where it used to be.

No trace of Moti Lal survived that I could see. In its place stood a long arcade of interlinked shops. The specialty of those employed in these shops: calligraphic engraving on tombstones. Freshly chiseled stones stood stacked against the walls. The topmost one read, in spidery Urdu script: "Haji 'Abd al-Rahim, son of Haji Nur Muhammad."

But we'd come to the right place. A half-dozen carvers gathered around us, all eager to have their say, when they found out we were interested in the old temple. They seemed to agree: destroying the *mandir* had been wrong.

One carver—elderly but with a foreman's self-assurance—invited us into his workroom. He said he had something to show us. His hands were chalked with white stone-dust. He wiped them on a cloth and then carefully lifted down something he kept displayed on a wall of his shop.

It was a framed black-and-white photograph of the Moti Lal Mandir, *purane zamane se*, "from the old days," before its destruction.

Two towers are visible in the photo. The nearer looks huge, perhaps five stories high. In its design it resembles the Jain Mandir—a tapering obelisk rising from a massive square base. At the foot of the *mandir* huddle small shops with awnings. Above the shops, propped against the second floor of the temple, and blocking its windows, is a pair of billboards: Urdu lettering and smiling young women advertising some product or other. The photo must date from the 1950s.

The carver said he kept this picture to remind himself of better times, "before everyone hated each other." This had been a beautiful thing, he said, pointing to the *mandir* in the picture; and it had done no one any harm. It should not have been destroyed. The other workers voiced their agreement.

Then he brought out a second picture, a color snapshot. This was from 1992, and it displayed a moment I recognized from *The New York Times*: the demolition of this same temple. The color photo shows hundreds of onlookers, crowding together on rooftops, in the streets, perilously close to the shrine's tower, as it comes crashing down. They seem to be competing to get the best view of the spectacle.

"The government," he said, remembering, "did nothing. If even one policeman—and there were plenty of policemen there—had fired a warning shot, the whole crowd would have dispersed. If one policeman had raised a rifle and said 'Beware,' everyone would have run away. But the government had a hand in this."

In his voice, sadness and anger. He put back the pictures, picked up a hammer, stooped over a gravestone. He said something about the unfinished inscription. These letters here would be inked in black. Those words below would be in red. I pocketed my notebook, thinking the interview was over.

I was wrong. He put down his hammer and twisted about to face Qamar and me. "We all worship the same God—Bhagvan, Allah, whatever you call Him. It doesn't matter if you're a Muslim or Hindu or Sikh or even if you're an *Angrez*" ("an Englishman"—and here he smiled and patted my knee).

The last thing he said to us was, "We're all human. So what was the point of destroying that temple?"

Then he went back to carving his gravestone.

Being Hindu in Twenty-first-Century Pakistan:
Strategies for Survival

In all this searching about for *mandirs*, I'd yet to meet a Lahori Hindu. I'd seen my share of crushed and lifeless ruins. Didn't the city have any shrines that were alive and actively functioning?

My friend Muhammad Razzaq came up with a lead. Somewhere he'd heard about a site that had celebrated a Hindu festival within the past few months. He didn't know where it was located, but he thought it was called the Krishna Mandir.

That was enough to get me started. Qamar Jalil and I heard the temple was located on Ravi Road, in a neighborhood called Bhatti Chowk. But the building wasn't easy to find. Most people shrugged and turned away when we asked. One man referred to it as the Kali Devi Mandir. He spoke the name with distaste. (We learned later this was the shrine's former title—and we also learned why the name had been changed.)

On Ravi Road we hailed a teenager on a bicycle and asked for the temple. "Destroyed. Gone," was his reply. Qamar said in that case please point us to the rubble. The boy said even the rubble was gone. "Carted away." He peddled off on his bike.

But we persisted and found the place. From the outside there wasn't much to see: a small cement-and-stucco building, locked and shuttered. Little here to identify the place readily as Hindu. Its only distinctive architectural feature was a diminutive and unadorned pyramid-like structure rising from the roof. We found a very small sign with the words "Krishna Mandir," and a tiny insignia representing the syllable OM. Another sign in Urdu prohibited parking in front of the *mandir*.

I thought of Muhammad Latif's book and his description of Hindu shrines in nineteenth-century Lahore, with their painted gods exuberantly visible from the street, and with a golden Hanuman monkey perched confidently on high for everyone to see. Compared with the Jain Mandir and the five-story Moti Lal, this Krishna-site seemed a shrunken thing.

No one in the street; no response when we knocked. Not the most auspicious start.

Other research topics intervened, and I postponed my work on Lahori Hinduism. But on my next trip to Pakistan, in December 2005, I finally met a representative of the city's Hindu population.

The meeting came about through Shia acquaintances of mine in Lahore's Inter-Religious Affairs Council, a group that is charged with facilitating relations among the region's various faith communities. The council member with the title of "Vice-President for Hindu Minorities" is an individual named Amarnath Randhawa (who, as I learned later, is also general secretary of the Lahore branch of the Pakistan Hindu Dalit Welfare Society).

I first met Amarnath when I asked my Shia acquaintances in the council to arrange for a Hindu community leader to escort me to the Krishna Mandir. We agreed on a rendezvous point on Mall Road. My Muslim friends Muhammad Razzaq and Reza offered to come along as well.

The street was crowded, and as we stood outside waiting for Amarnath, I wondered if I'd be able to pick him out among the hundreds of passers-by. Would he wear anything that might identify him as a Hindu—caste-mark, wrist-amulet or medallion with an image of Ganesha, paste-stripes on the forehead to show he was a devotee of Vishnu or Shiva? Given the religious tension that buzzes in Lahore of recent years, it seemed unlikely.

This I pegged right. A young man dressed in *shalwar-qameez* (baggy trousers and tunic) like a thousand other men around him came up and introduced himself as our guide to the *mandir*. Trim and studious, with a discreet black mustache and clothes that were a muted neutral beige, Amarnath Randhawa was the ideal escort for guiding guests through the streets without attracting unwanted attention.

On our way he talked about the life of religious minorities in Pakistan. There are some two hundred Hindu families still residing in Lahore (about two thousand persons, he estimated, out of a total urban population of well over five million for all of Lahore). The Hindus are concentrated especially in the Anderun Shahr (Lahore's Old City quarter), especially the Mochi Darvaza and Bhatti Darvaza localities, as well as in another neighborhood, Bibi Pak Daman.

I asked about the types of jobs held by Lahori Hindus and was told most are shopkeepers or run small businesses of their own. He himself works with his brother, who owns an auto-parts shop.

As we reached Ravi Road, Amarnath said the Krishna Mandir was the only temple available to Lahore's Hindus for worship. Because of damage to the *mandir* during the Babri Masjid riots in 1992, he explained, the temple was currently undergoing renovation. To demonstrate its commitment to the welfare of Pakistan's religious minorities, the government had recently agreed to contribute 1.2 million rupees to the project.

I asked where Hindus prayed while these renovations were underway. "Currently we do *puja* [worship rituals] in our homes, at private altars," he said. For social gatherings and bigger events during holydays, they used a building on Lower Mall Road called Agarwal Ashram.

The ashram has another function as well. It serves as a guest house for *yatris* (pilgrims, both Hindu and Sikh) who come from India to visit the surviving *gurdwaras* and other sites in Pakistan that are sacred to these two faiths.

For Hindus, he said, the primary pilgrimage goal in Pakistan is Ketas, situated in the Margalla Hills, near the Jhelum River. Ancient myths state that when the god Shiva was separated from his wife Sati, he came to Ketas, sat there and wept for her. His flood of tears formed Lake Ketas. Hearing this tale reminded me that this country possessed a sacred topography far older than Pakistan or the advent of Islam, a topography that transcended national boundaries.

At the Krishna Mandir, in contrast to my attempt at a visit the year before, we found a hive of activity. Construction crews were busy on each floor. Were the workers Hindu?, I asked. No, Muslim. Amarnath added that the workmen and the Hindu supervisors and architects were all getting along just fine.

My friends Muhammad and Reza seemed pleased to hear this. During our visit the two of them went out of their way to raise discussion points that emphasized what Hinduism and Islam share in common.

When our guide said something about the Hindu belief in Brahman, and how Brahman is everywhere, subsuming all deities and other lesser beings in one divine Reality, my Muslim colleagues seemed delighted. "So," exclaimed Reza, "our two communities share respect for *tawhid* [the monotheistic assertion of God's oneness]." Amarnath said yes that was so.

Reza had told our guide he was a Shia, so Amarnath added that just as the "women of Karbala" once wept for Husain, so too Shiva wept for Sati. "Many points in common," he said. "Many." Everyone looked happy.

But Amarnath understood very well that plenty of Muslims in the neighborhood might not be so happy at the prospect of the temple's reopening, and he explained the precautions the community would undertake.

First, the temple would have no *murtis* (statues) or other images of deities visible from the street, so as not to offend Islamic sensibilities.

Second, raucous celebrations like Holi (a spring festival, where people splash each other with dyed water and powder) would be held indoors rather than out on the street. ("Otherwise our Muslim neighbors will think this is just some troublesome *tamasha* [spectacle].")

Third, the temple's former name—Kali Das ("Servant of Kali") or Kali Devi ("the Goddess Kali")—which dated back to before 1947, had long since been dropped. "Muslims hear the name Kali and they think of things they don't like—black body, red tongue sticking out. Krishna they don't mind so much." (In the chapter on Lahore's pulp fiction magazines, we'll see how these prejudices play out in stories addressed to Pakistani Muslim reading audiences.)

While Amarnath explained the ways in which Lahore's Hindus tiptoed around Islamic sensibilities and took care to make themselves as nearly invisible as possible, the *azan* (the Muslim call to prayer) sounded, first from one mosque nearby, then from a second and a third. Each muezzin, it seemed, was in a competition to be loudest. The *azans* were loud-speakered and amped-up and backed by uninhibited levels of wattage. As a display of religious domination it was hard to beat.

Before we left, Amarnath showed us what would be the focal point of worship on each floor of the temple—an *'ibadat-khana* ("house of worship"), an alcove-shrine the size of a big closet with doors that could be closed and locked for safety. The *murtis* would be housed there, he said. As part of the renovation, the community was arranging to import statues of Krishna and Mata Rani ("the queen mother-goddess") from India.

(I'm glad to report that reconstruction at the Krishna Mandir was finished in time for the spring Holi celebration to be held there in March 2006. Later the same year, in August, the *mandir* hosted a weeklong *Janamasthamy*—a festival in honor of the god Krishna's birthday. Lahore's *Daily Times*—which, together with its sister publication *The Friday Times*, constitutes the country's most progressive source of news—reported on both celebrations in detail, commenting on the latter: "A large number of Hindus, Sikhs, Christians and Muslims participated in the ceremony."[25])

Before we said goodbye, I asked our host what was the most pressing issue that Lahore's Hindus wanted the local government to address. Without hesitation he replied, "Authorization for a *shamshan ghat*." The *shamshan ghat* is a cremation site, traditionally located on a riverbank, where Hindus burn their dead and scatter the ashes in the water in accordance with ancient custom.

Before the creation of Pakistan there were eleven such sites in Lahore. Now there are none. With Partition and the exodus of Hindus from the city, newly arrived Muslims from neighboring India claimed the land for themselves.[26]

In the current situation, I asked, what sort of funerary options are available to Lahori Hindus?

Families that can afford it, I was told, arrange for their dead to be taken to a cremation ground on private property owned by a well-to-do Hindu. The site is in the Punjab, a two hours' drive from Lahore. After cremation the ashes of the deceased are scattered into either the Ravi or Jhelum rivers.

This option entails some expense, however, and is simply beyond the means of the city's poorer lower-caste Hindus. The solution: many such persons are buried in Lahore's Christian cemeteries.

Given the circumstances in which Pakistani Hindus live, this is a logical and pragmatic solution. "Here, Hindus and Christians have good relations," explained Amarnath. "Many Hindus attend Christian services." At the same time, he acknowledged, many church-going Hindu Christians still maintained altars at home for their favorite deities.

25. Shahnawaz Khan, "Drenched in Red," *The Daily Times* [Lahore], March 15, 2006; and Shahnawaz Khan, "Weeklong Janamasthamy Comes to an End," *The Daily Times*, August 17, 2006 (www.dailytimes.com.pk).

26. Emmanuel Yousaf Mani, ed., *Human Rights Monitor 2006: A Report on the Religious Minorities in Pakistan* (Lahore: National Commission for Justice and Peace, 2006), 30-31.

This view was corroborated in my many conversations with Khaled Ahmed of *The Friday Times*. "In our city, most Hindus have assumed Christian names for protection," he said. "They go to church but have *murtis* in their homes." He added that church-going Lahori Hindus have definite preferences with regard to the various Christian denominations available to them. "They're drawn to the richness of Catholic ritual," according to Khaled. Catholic statues and incense and bells, after all, have something in common with what one encounters in Hindu shrines. "Protestantism," he said, "they tend to find too austere."

Christian–Hindu relations in Pakistan can be contrasted with the situation across the border in India. Plenty of Hindus are drawn to churches there just as they are in Pakistan. The difference is that in India, Hindu demagogues frequently score political points by fomenting hostility to Christianity and accusing Christian missionaries of enticing Hindus away from their ancestral faith.

In Pakistan, on the other hand, many Hindus see membership in Christian churches as a refuge against Islamic persecution. It's true, of course, that Pakistani Christians suffer persecution too; and in Lahore's churches I met individuals who complained that to be a Christian in a Muslim country generally means being at the bottom of the heap. But based on what I've seen, I'd say Pakistani Hindus have it worse. This is for several reasons.

Hinduism of course is associated with the perennial enemy India. And—monotheistic assertions about Brahman notwithstanding—Hindus after all are widely regarded in Islam as *kuffar* (*kafirs*, or pagan unbelievers). Christians at least have some status as *ahl al-kitab* ("People of the Book," or recipients of a scriptural revelation associated with the Abrahamic tradition), even if Christianity is held to be inferior to Islam.

Moreover, Christian churches maintain an educational system and run a network of schools that are respected throughout Pakistan. Finally, to be Christian in Pakistan is to have the sense of belonging to a global organization that takes an active interest in the welfare of all its adherents worldwide.

In fact I would go further and say that the most outspoken champion of Hindus in Pakistan is the Catholic Church. This can be seen in the courageous work of the National Commission for Justice and Peace, established in 1985 by the Pakistan Catholic Bishops' Conference.

Annually it publishes a book called *Human Rights Monitor: A Report on the Religious Minorities in Pakistan*. The Catholic Bishops' Conference documents violence and discrimination against not only Christians but also members of other minority communities, most notably Hindus and Ahmadis.

The *Monitor*'s reports for 2005 and 2006 itemize numerous human rights violations. Many involve women: abduction, rape, and acid throwing directed against Hindu and Christian girls and young women; violence against non-Muslim women and girls working as servants in Muslim households.[27]

The 2006 edition of the *Monitor* devotes considerable attention to what could be called systematic ideological warfare against Hindus in Pakistan. State-run schools still use textbooks authored during the regime of General Zia ul-Haq (1977–1988), under whose leadership various "Islamization" programs were initiated. Here is the *Monitor*'s evaluation of religious bias in Pakistani school texts:

> The curriculum of Social Studies in Pakistan as both the product and propagator of the "Ideology of Pakistan," derives its legitimacy from a narrow set of directives... From the government-issued textbooks, students are taught that Hindus are backwards and superstitious, and if given a chance would assert their power over the oppressed, especially the Muslims... In their Social Studies classes, students are taught that Islam brought peace, equality, and justice to the Subcontinent and only through Islam could the sinister ways of Hindus be checked. In Pakistani textbooks "Hindus" rarely appears in a sentence without adjective[s] such as politically astute, sly, or manipulative.[28]

Hindus I met in my visit to Lahore's Krishna Mandir praised President Pervez Musharraf and the government for allocating money for the temple's restoration. They interpreted this as the government's attempt to fight back against the pervasive presence of Islamist bigotry among Muslim preachers, mullahs, and educators.

But it's an uphill battle. The *Monitor* documents Hindu complaints of their children being forced to take "Islamic studies" programs at school. The report also enumerates instances where individual Hindus are subjected to forced conversion to Islam.[29]

Some of the most alarming examples of anti-Hindu sentiment involve allegations of insults to Islamic scripture. In the town of Naushera, in the NWFP, a Muslim mob desecrated a Hindu temple and then set it afire—along with the nearby homes of Hindu families—after a servant was accused of burning pages of the Quran in a trash-fire. In another NWFP village, a Hindu husband and wife, Lal and Krishna Chaman, had to flee

27. Mani, *Human Rights Monitor 2006*, 84-91. See also Emmanuel Yousaf Mani, ed., *Human Rights Monitor 2005: A Report on the Religious Minorities in Pakistan* (Lahore: National Commission for Justice and Peace, 2005), 53-62.
28. Mani, *Human Rights Monitor 2006*, 49.
29. Mani, *Human Rights Monitor 2006*, 29, 41-42.

for their lives while "a mob chanting anti-Hindu slogans gathered in front of Chaman's house and destroyed it."

The reason? A Muslim passer-by claimed to have seen a copy of the Quran lying sacrilegiously in a field adjacent to the house. This was enough to foment a rumor that this Hindu couple must have maliciously desecrated Islam's scripture. The day after their home was burned down, the couple were arrested by the police and put in jail.[30]

The legislation used to justify such arrests is Ordinance 295 B-C, known in Pakistan as the "blasphemy laws." I examine this legislation in my discussion of Pakistani Christians—the subject of my next chapter.

30. Mani, *Human Rights Monitor 2006*, 27, 59.

PAKISTANI CHRISTIANS
AND THE PROSPECTS
FOR INTER-RELIGIOUS RESISTANCE
TO THE BLASPHEMY LAWS

Golden Light, Shattered Glass:
Attending Church in a Time of Terror

Sunday, March 17, 2002: what would turn out to be a day of sectarian killings, directed against Christians in one of Pakistan's biggest cities. But—ignorant of what was coming—I decided to attend a church service that morning at Lahore's Anglican Cathedral of the Resurrection.

I'd gotten my schedule wrong and arrived an hour early. Not a problem: it was a beautiful day, the sun not yet scorching, the air still cool, the courtyard quiet. I stood about outside and admired the church. Lancet windows, twin bell towers, massive Victorian brickwork: a survivor, solid and reassuring, from the nineteenth century.

For company I had my guide Nasir and my driver Imtiyaz Yusuf. Bored with gawking, they withdrew to the car and sat and smoked.

Inside the church, deacons readied the altar. Otherwise I had the place to myself for half an hour. And for someone with a taste for colonial history, there was plenty to see. Brass plaques, one after another, mounted on the walls and pillars of the cathedral's interior, gleamed yellow in the morning light.

The first plaque I saw bore the likeness of a gold cross and crown and an inscription that began: "Erected in memory of the officers, NCOs, and men of the Punjab Rifles who gave their lives for their king and Empire in the Great War." Then came a long roster of names. A Lieutenant J. North, killed in 1916 in German East Africa. A 2nd Lieutenant Barrett, who died in Mesopotamia. A Captain Giles: Kashmir. Volunteer Pinto: North-West Frontier Province. And many, many names listed as fallen in France. A stained-glass window nearby showed a knight in armor together with a text explaining that the artwork was meant to honor one "James M. McKain, Captain, 34th Sikh Pioneers, killed in action in France November 1914. Aged 29 years."

The geography of death reminded me of the vast reach and sweep of the old British Empire, and of the sacrifices that went into maintaining it. No American in Pakistan in 2002 could see such a list without thinking of our soldiers in Afghanistan and the sacrifices made by them in fighting the Taliban and al-Qaeda. (And as I pen these words now, five years later, I think of our many dead in Iraq.)

My thoughts shifted as I studied another plaque, this one illustrated with a Masonic compass and ruler, honoring an Englishman who had died in Lahore in 1901 after serving for years as secretary to the District Grand Lodge of the Punjab. "This memorial tablet," concluded the text, "was erected by his brother Masons."

Standing there in this Pakistani Anglican cathedral, I was reminded of the Punjab's most famous Mason, the Anglo-Indian storyteller Rudyard Kipling. On a nearby wall hung another reminder of this poet of Empire: a sculpted wall plaque, also from 1901, depicting a celebrated British military figure, Sir Samuel Browne. The sculpture was very much in the style of the artist John Lockwood Kipling (the poet's father) and perhaps came from his studio. John Lockwood Kipling, after all, had been principal of the Mayo School of Art as well as curator of the Lahore Museum, and both institutions were located just down the Mall from this church.

For me the mood of nostalgia continued as the cathedral filled with worshippers—mostly Punjabi Christians, to be sure, but also Africans, Canadians, Australians, and Brits. The prevailing air was one of calm, of order. The neo-Gothic vaulting overhead, the hymns sung by the choir from an old Church of England repertoire, the tea served afterward in the rectory: these things were lulling and made it easy to sentimentalize the morning as part of some bygone heyday from the imperial Raj.

The next day's news headlines were a jarring wake-up to present-day realities. That same Sunday terrorists had attacked the Protestant International Church in Islamabad's diplomatic enclave. They hurled grenades inside the church while morning services were going on. The result was devastating: "Blood flying across the simple hall where worshippers were listening to the sermon," according to news accounts, "glass... blown out of every window, and huge holes...punched in the ceiling." The attack left dozens wounded and five dead, among them a Pakistani as well as an American woman and her high school-aged daughter.[1]

1. Raymond Bonner, "Two Americans Killed in Attack on Pakistan Church," *The New York Times*, March 18, 2002.

The assault wasn't the first in Pakistan on a Christian place of worship. On October 28, 2001, three weeks after the United States began bombing Taliban and al-Qaeda targets in Afghanistan, an attack on a church in Bahawalpur left 15 Pakistani Christians dead, together with a Muslim policeman who tried to guard them.

In the weeks after the Islamabad attack, I talked to many Pakistani Christians—Catholics, Protestants, and Anglicans—in private homes and at dinners and church socials. Several discerned what they described as a larger pattern of violence directed not only at Christians, but at other religious minorities throughout the country. Among these targets of hatred is the Shia Muslim community. A minority in Pakistan (they comprise some 15 percent to 20 percent of the population), Shias are viewed with suspicion by many of Pakistan's Sunni majority, who regard Shia beliefs and rituals as heterodox. Militantly minded fundamentalists among the Sunnis go further. For example, leading members of an anti-Shia organization known as the SSP, the Sipah-e Sahaba Party ("Soldiers of the Prophet's Companions"), have labeled Shias *kafirs*—that is, infidels —and hence legitimate objects of attack by "orthodox" Muslims. The SSP has been implicated in numerous attacks on Shia places of worship.

Despite the fact that in January 2002 President Musharraf's government announced a ban on the SSP and other militant sectarian groups within Pakistan, attacks on Shia shrines persist. Eleven worshippers at prayer died on February 26, 2002, when gunmen fired on a Shia mosque in Rawalpindi. Twelve more Shias died when a bomb exploded later that year on April 25 in the women's section of a Shia prayer hall in the city of Bukker in the eastern Punjab.

Among the Pakistani Christians and Shias with whom I spoke, there was a shared perception that violence against minorities has worsened in response to the presence of the U.S.-led coalition in Afghanistan. Initial American and coalition victories in Afghanistan in 2001–2002 had forced hundreds of Taliban militants to retreat across the border into the autonomous Tribal Areas and Pakistan itself (where many of the Taliban have homes and families). As Hamid Karzai's Western-backed government has continued its struggle to achieve stability for Afghanistan, these militants have been using Pakistan and the Tribal Areas as staging points for cross-border attacks on coalition forces.

In the days when they still held power in Kabul, the Taliban, whose ideology derives from the most conservative and stringent forms of Sunnism, had imprisoned Christian missionaries and persecuted Afghan Shias. Now that they are back in Pakistan, as one Christian from Lahore told me, "The defeated jihadis seem to be picking easy targets" as a way of venting rage—rage at the West in general, at the United States in particular, and at President Musharraf personally, for siding with America against the Taliban and al-Qaeda.

Pakistan's Christians constitute an especially vulnerable target. In such a country, which was founded as a homeland for the subcontinent's Muslims, where 97 percent of the population is Islamic, to be Christian is to be susceptible to the charge that one's patriotism and national loyalty are somehow deficient. The charge is unfair—Pakistan's Christians have contributed to society at large in many ways, most notably in education, medicine, and health care—but Muslim suspicions linger.

Caste, Dhimmitude, and the Status of Christians in Pakistan's Social Hierarchy

Central to any understanding of Christians' status in contemporary Pakistan is the role played by caste. In South Asia the legacy of Hinduism's hereditary system of unyielding social stratification has been rancorous and enduring. Most Muslims and Christians of the subcontinent are descended from impoverished lower-class Hindus. Embracing Islam or Christianity was a way of escaping the rigid confinements of Hinduism's caste system. "There is no longer Jew or Greek, there is no longer slave or free," as Saint Paul reminds us, "...for all of you are one in Christ Jesus."[2] As with Christianity, so, too, with Islam. Muslims are justifiably proud of their faith's insistence on the absolute equality of all humans before God.

But the past has a way of asserting itself, and Hinduism's caste legacy has by no means disappeared in today's Pakistan. Lahori Muslims I interviewed rated Pakistani ancestral backgrounds as follows: best of all were Sayyeds (a title conferred on descendants of the prophet Muhammad's family), followed by those that could claim Arab, Persian, or Turkish bloodlines—what one informant called "the Muslim conquering races." Least prestigious was a genealogy rooted in Hindu India.

Explicitly or implicitly, the vocabulary of caste surfaced frequently in conversations I had with Pakistani Muslims on the subject of Islam in South Asia. In March 2002, a Lahori researcher named Amir Rana accompanied me on a visit to Lahore's National College of Art, where I interviewed an anthropologist and art historian by the name of Nadeem Omar. In describing the religious customs of the Muslims of the Punjabi town of Chiniot, Nadeem referred to these Punjabis as *musalli*. This is an Arabic term with the literal meaning of "one who performs the *salat*"

2. *Epistle to the Galatians* 3.28.

(the Islamically mandated five-times-a-day ritual prayer). But a glance at my Urdu dictionary yielded these additional meanings: "a sweeper; convert to Islam."[3]

My friend Amir explained that the term *musalli* is used in Pakistan to refer to "new Muslims." He added, "These are tribals, former Hindus and Christians. They're poor. But if one of them manages to become rich, he's no longer called *musalli.*"

Amir added further that *musallis* have a reputation for being "Wahhabis during Ramadan, Shias during Muharram, Barelvis during an *'urs.*" That is, these "new Muslims" are eclectic in their religious practices. In the month of Ramadan, they'll fast along with the puritani-cally observant; during Muharram, they'll honor the Imam Husain by mourning with the Shias; and during the many *'urs-melas* (celebrations in honor of deceased Sufi masters) held throughout the year, they'll throng to the shrines where music and ecstatic dancing honor the wonder-working Muslim saints. (The term Barelvi is used to characterize those Sunnis who admit the orthodoxy of Sufi practices.)

Caste-vocabulary is often used to stigmatize Pakistan's Christians. In one town in the Punjab (I leave the place unnamed in deference to my informant's wishes), I met an elderly gentleman in 2002 who told me he had become Christian in the early 1960s. When his Muslim neighbors heard of his conversion, they shunned him. As word spread, shopkeepers refused him business. Neighborhood boys harassed his daughters by calling out "sweepers!" whenever the girls ventured onto the street.

The insult is telling. Muslims I asked about this account reacted defen-sively and said simply that many Christians are poor and therefore take menial jobs like sweeping floors. But a Christian from Lahore offered a different perspective. He reminded me that a huge percentage of his country's Muslim population is descended from menial-class Hindus. What easier way to forget one's own servile origin, he suggested, than to scorn someone even lower on the social scale? "Being Christian in a Muslim country like ours," he said, "generally means being at the bottom of the heap. In the eyes of some in my country, to be a Christian is to be a sweeper, that is, low-caste."

Sweeper. The Hindi-Urdu term is *chuhra*, defined in old Hindustani dictionaries as "scavenger" and "the lowest caste of village servants."[4]

---

3. M. Raza ul-Haq Badakhshani, ed., *Gem Practical Dictionary: Urdu to English* (Lahore: Azhar Publishers, n.d.), 688.

4. *The Student's Practical Dictionary: Containing Hindustani Words with English Meanings* (Allahabad: Ram Narain Lal, 1940), 242; S. W. Fallon, ed., *A New Hindustani–English Dictionary* (Benares: Medical Hall Press, 1879), 552.

Despised but indispensable, the *chuhras* of the colonial-era Punjab did the jobs that higher castes found repugnant and polluting—disposing of human excrement, cleaning out trash, removing—and sometimes eating—animal corpses left on roadsides to rot.[5]

In her study of Pakistan's Christians, the scholar Linda Walbridge notes that it was precisely rural low-caste Hindu *chuhras* living in impoverished villages who responded most enthusiastically to the Gospel preached by foreign missionaries during British domination of the subcontinent. But with the social dislocations and violence that marked the end of British India and the creation of Pakistan in 1947, many of these converts took refuge in Christian ghettoes in cities such as Lahore.[6]

Since 1947 Pakistani Christians have had to deal with recurrent Muslim suspicions that they aren't 100% Pakistani. To compensate for this, Christian leaders—Catholic, Protestant, and Anglican—take advantage of every chance they get to emphasize that, like other Pakistanis, Christians, too, are good citizens. Thus during my various visits, I occasionally saw public announcements by church organizations proclaiming their solidarity with the national government in deploring the plight of the Palestinians and expressing support for the people of Kashmir—both of which are issues where the country's Christian minority might hope for common ground with Muslims.

Walbridge notes that at rallies where Pakistani Christian activists gather to call for social justice on behalf of the country's religious minorities, speakers frequently cite a 1948 speech by Muhammad Ali Jinnah, the politician revered by Pakistanis as the founder of their country: "You are free, you are free to go to your temples, you are free to go to your mosques or to any other place of worship in this State of Pakistan. You may belong to any religion or caste or creed—that has nothing to do with the business of the State."[7]

This sounds like a reassuringly secular vision of government. But another speech by Jinnah offers a different—and less auspicious— perspective on the prospects for Christians in newly created Pakistan. As the Pakistani scholar A. S. Ahmed points out in his biography of Jinnah, Lord Louis Mountbatten, the last viceroy of British India, suggested in a speech in Karachi in 1948 what might serve Pakistan as the model of "a tolerant Muslim ruler": the reign of the sixteenth-century Moghul emperor Akbar the Great.

---

5. Linda S. Walbridge, *The Christians of Pakistan* (London: Routledge, 2003), 16.
6. Walbridge, *The Christians of Pakistan*, 15-47.
7. Walbridge, *The Christians of Pakistan*, 43.

One of the most controversial figures in India's history, Akbar is—depending on one's politics—either a hero of interfaith goodwill or an apostate who coddled infidels. Akbar lifted from Hindus the burden of paying the *jizyah* (the Quranically mandated discriminatory tax levied on non-Muslims); he promulgated *sulh-e kull* ("universal reconciliation"), a policy of state-sponsored religious tolerance; and he instituted the Sufi-influenced *din-e ilahi*, the "divine religion" that synthesized Islamic belief and Hindu wisdom.[8]

Jinnah was not impressed with the British viceroy's suggestion. In his public response to Mountbatten, the founder of Pakistan offered a different—and to conservative ears, a resoundingly orthodox—model of Islamic statecraft for dealing with non-Muslims:

> The tolerance and goodwill that great Emperor Akbar showed to all the non-Muslims is not of recent origin. It dates back thirteen centuries ago when the Prophet not only by words but by deeds treated the Jews and Christians, after he had conquered them, with the utmost tolerance and regard and respect for their faith and beliefs.[9]

Note that in Jinnah's reading of Muhammad's life the Prophet tolerated Christians and Jews and let them keep their faith—but only "after he had conquered them." Jinnah's speech echoes the sentiment to be found in Quran 9.29: "Fight those who do not believe in Allah or in the Last Day, and who do not forbid what Allah and His Messenger have forbidden, and who do not profess the religion of truth, from among the People of the Book, until they pay the *jizyah* and have been humiliated and made servile."

Dhimmi is the term used in Islamic law to describe this category of unbeliever—"People of the Book" (usually understood to be Jews and Christians, though at times the designation has been extended to other non-Muslims as well)—who acknowledge Islamic rule, pay the *jizyah*, and accept their humbled status in Islamic society in exchange for the privilege of keeping their identity as Jews or Christians.

In other words, Jinnah's speeches from 1948—so often cited by today's human rights activists as a model of religious egalitarianism (at least by comparison with the rantings of militant Muslim hardliners)—already prefigure an Islamist mindset that would only harden with time: religious minorities can be tolerated in Pakistan—as long as they know their place, as *dhimmis*.

8. Bamber Gascoigne, *A Brief History of the Great Moguls* (New York: Carroll & Graf, 2002), 71.

9. Akbar S. Ahmed, *Jinnah, Pakistan and Islamic Identity: The Search for Saladin* (London: Routledge, 1997), 176.

The Head Bathed in Light:
Shia–Christian Solidarity in Suffering?

March 24, 2002, exactly one week after the Islamabad church bombing, was Palm Sunday. That day I returned to Lahore's Cathedral of the Resurrection for morning services. Guards were very much in evidence, patrolling the entrance gate and the high brick walls surrounding the church grounds. I'd wondered whether fear of more terrorist strikes would make parishioners stay away. (I confess I myself had hesitated to go.)

But in fact the turnout was good. There were not many foreigners, true: a few Brits, some Africans. But local Christians there were, several hundred of them, more numerous even than on the previous Sunday, as if Lahore's Christian community wanted to show pride in its identity. The choir led us in singing "Rock of Ages." This week the words of the old hymn, "Let me hide myself in Thee," seemed neither nostalgic nor sentimental, but instead charged with pathos and the power of catharsis.

The sermon that morning began by recapitulating a familiar story, how Christ's entry into Jerusalem became a path that led to his sufferings on the cross. The preacher recalled the persecution undergone by the early followers of Jesus; and this, too, was familiar. But then the sermon became explicitly topical. The preacher spoke directly of the Bahawalpur and Islamabad massacres. "We don't know if such acts will continue," he told the congregation, "but we have to remember we are not walking this path alone." Christ, too, journeyed along this road, as did his early followers. And Christ journeys now, he said, with the members of this parish. "This is what enables us to endure any persecution."

A moving sermon; but interesting, too, for what it left unsaid. No talk of retribution, communal self-defense or the need to capture and punish terrorists. I read into the sermon the implicit message that the protection of the Christian community must be left to the Pakistani government. This conforms to the classical Islamic concept of the *dhimmi* described above: the non-Muslim minority living under Muslim rule. *Dhimmis* are not permitted to use force to defend themselves, but rather are required to rely on Muslim governors for their protection.

Has any good come out of this recent violence against Pakistan's minorities? A Catholic woman from Lahore told me that after the Bahawalpur church killings in October 2001, Shia Muslim neighbors came to her house to convey their sympathies. They told her stories sacred to their own tradition. Fourteen centuries ago, at the Iraqi site of Karbala, soldiers of the caliph Yazid killed the Imam Husain and beheaded him. Individual local Christians of the desert did what they could to honor

Husain and show reverence for his corpse after his martyrdom. A pious priest guarded the Imam's severed head for one night in his chapel and saw the head bathed in light. "Christians tried to help Imam Husain," the Shias told my Lahori informant. "We remember that to this day."

In the martyrdom of Husain, Shia Islam's history shares some affinities with Christianity: the voluntary self-sacrifice of a salvific figure, a narrative of spiritual victory arising from a death that in the eyes of the world initially seemed to represent only humiliation and defeat. Perhaps the violence to which Pakistan's minorities have been subjected will lead to further exploration of what they share in common.

Loser's Vengeance: Muslim–Christian Relations and Pakistan's Blasphemy Law

Gambling often produces sore losers. In November 2005, in the town of Sangla Hill in Pakistan's Punjab province, it served as the trigger for something worse: religious riots and violence against members of Pakistan's minority Christian population.

Yousuf Masih, a forty-year-old Christian, won several thousand rupees playing cards with a Muslim neighbor. The angry loser retaliated by filing an allegation with the local police that Masih had set fire to a copy of the Quran—a punishable offense under Pakistani law. Within hours rumors that a Christian had insulted the Islamic scripture were circulating throughout town. Local Muslim clerics used mosque loudspeakers to call on the faithful to avenge the insult.

The result: the next day, November 12, 2005, a mob of over 2,500 men (some from Sangla Hill, others from nearby Punjabi villages) attacked buildings belonging to the town's minority Christian community. They torched three churches and vandalized a Catholic convent and a Christian elementary school. Local Christian families were forced to flee or go into hiding. Police did nothing to restrain the violence—but they did arrest the luckless Christian card-player Yousuf Masih.

When I visited Lahore the following month, local Christians showed me photographs detailing the destruction at Sangla Hill: a marble altar smashed to rubble, a tabernacle lying dented on the ground, a statue of the Virgin Mary that rioters had defaced with hammers.

I was also shown a copy of a letter of protest dated November 14, 2005 that had been sent to President Musharraf immediately after the violence in Sangla Hill. Signed by prominent Pakistani Catholic and Protestant church leaders, the letter identified a salient factor in the recurrent violence against the country's religious minorities in recent years: Ordinance 295 of the Pakistan Penal Code.

Ordinance 295—commonly referred to as the "blasphemy law"—dates back to the 1980s and the reign of military dictator General Zia ul-Haq. Zia sought to legitimize his dictatorship by indulging the fundamentalist-minded mullahs of Pakistan's various religious parties. 295 gave them what they wanted.

The law's roots go back to the colonial era: the British Indian Penal Code provided two years' jail time for persons convicted of religious insults or acts of desecration against any faith whatsoever. Zia's regime "updated" this legislation by adding provisions designed specifically to "safeguard" Islam. Section 295-B of Zia's law mandates life imprisonment for Quran desecration. Section 295-C goes further: it stipulates the death penalty for anyone who defames or insults the prophet Muhammad.

A progressive-minded legislator from Pakistan's National Assembly whom I interviewed in Islamabad listed what he called "three substantive legal problems" with Ordinance 295. First, no evidence is required in filing a blasphemy complaint. The word of anyone claiming to be a witness is enough. Second, the alleged blasphemer is arrested and imprisoned as soon as the complaint is lodged. Defendants often remain in jail for months awaiting trial. Third, plaintiffs can make false accusations with little worry of punishment or any other legal repercussion.

The third factor is especially important in light of recent data assembled by the National Commission for Justice and Peace (a human rights advocacy group established in 1985 by Pakistan's Catholic Bishops Conference). The Commission demonstrated that in over one hundred cases where defendants in recent blasphemy trials were found innocent, the accusers were shown by the court to have been motivated by personal grudges or hopes of financial gain.[10]

Despite the manifest injustice associated with Ordinance 295, President Musharraf—who has evinced a commitment to protect his country's religious minorities—has been unable to repeal the blasphemy law. Why? 295 is simply too popular.

Based on interviews with Muslims and Christians in both the Punjab and the NWFP, I would say this law is widely accepted by many Muslims—especially in rural areas—because it is seen as a useful weapon for the defense of Islam.

A Muslim professor in Peshawar explained to me that when rumors of blasphemy or Quran desecration circulate, many mosque preachers warn their congregations that *Islam khatar mayn hay*: "Islam is in danger."

---

10. Information provided during interviews in Lahore with Archbishop Lawrence Saldanha, December 12-13, 2005.

This sense of endangerment comes from a widespread perception among numerous Pakistani Muslims: they are a beleaguered minority.

This might sound surprising, given that 97% of Pakistan's population is Muslim. But it makes sense if one takes into account the feeling many Pakistanis have that they are overshadowed and threatened by neighboring India—a country that is not only much bigger than Pakistan but is also overwhelmingly non-Muslim and Hindu.

For many Pakistanis, what keeps their country from being swallowed up, from disappearing, is its Islamic identity, symbolized by reverence for the Quran and devotion to the prophet Muhammad's honor. Ordinance 295 is popular because it is seen as safeguarding both these things. Many fundamentalist-minded Muslims question the loyalty of Pakistani Christians and other non-Muslim minorities, who are often accused of serving as agents for the U.S. and other foreign powers.

A Pakistani Christian friend who used to be active in interfaith dialogue characterized for me Muslim attitudes toward the country's religious minorities: "The whole society is mobilized to be on the lookout for potential Christian and Hindu conspiracies against Islam." Disappointment and frustration embittered his voice. "Such minorities are thought to be allied with outside powers."

Outside powers: a favorite culprit in the Pakistani political imagination. The theme appears in a recent newspaper essay by Hafiz Idrees, head of the Punjabi branch of Jama'at-e Islami (one of the political parties belonging to the Islamist MMA coalition currently holding power in Baluchistan and the NWFP). Idrees disseminates stereotypes of Hindus as "cunning" and Jews as "clever" and then refers to the hostile forces said to be encircling Pakistan: a "triangle of evil" consisting of America, MOSSAD, and RAW (the latter two acronyms designate the national intelligence agencies of Israel and India).[11]

The Good Samaritan at the Madrasa:
A Try at Interfaith Dialogue

Given this climate of suspicion, most Pakistani Christians who attempt interfaith dialogue favor a low-profile approach that is as conciliatory and non-confrontational as possible. One man who works in this difficult field is Father Francis Nadeem, a young Catholic priest I interviewed in December 2005 at Saint Mary's Church in a Lahori neighborhood called Gulbarg.

11. Mani, ed., *Human Rights Monitor 2006*, 47-48.

A member of the Islamabad-based National Council for Interfaith Dialogue (NCIFD), Father Francis said he works with Muslims in three different venues. The first involves conferences he organizes where Muslims and Christians meet to define projects on which they can collaborate (this is reflected in the list of NCIFD "objectives" he handed me: "To create an atmosphere for the people of good will to work at the grassroots levels on common issues to advance social harmony"). At such conferences, he said, he emphasizes what he calls a "dialogue of life" or *insaniyyat* (this Arabic-Urdu term—which I heard repeatedly in talks with progressive-minded Pakistanis—can be translated as "humanity" or "universal values" or "basic human decency in one's dealings with others").

The second venue in which he works: madrasas (Islamic religious schools) where cooperative mullahs allow him to visit their classrooms and talk with the pupils (typically, Father Francis told me, these are boys between the ages of 10 and 14). Madrasas in Lahore are more likely to be open to such visits than in the much more conservative NWFP.

I asked him what a Catholic priest talks about at a Pakistani Muslim seminary. "Bible stories," he smiled. "Stories are always good for getting young people's attention. But one thing I avoid," he added, and here his smile vanished, "is any explicit talk of Christian doctrine."

What would happen, I asked, if he brought up such things as Christian doctrine?

"There'd be an argument, and I'd be accused of trying to convert Muslims, and the maulvis [mullahs] would get angry." He added quietly, "And then I could get shot."

Instead, he said, he offers biblical parables. He outlined his pedagogy: tell a story; identify its theme; apply it to contemporary life in Lahore. He offered an example. "So I'll tell the Good Samaritan story from the Gospel of Luke." He then draws the students' attention to the biblical verse encapsulating the parable's theme: Luke 10.29, where the lawyer interrogating Jesus asks, "And who is my neighbor?" Then, said Father Francis, he offers an answer for the benefit of the madrasa students: "My neighbor is not only the person living next door to me, but anyone in need, regardless of their religion. This is what Jesus showed by the story of the Samaritan helping a stranger." The fact that Jesus is revered in the Quran as a healer and prophet helps make such stories more acceptable to Muslim audiences.

The third setting in which priests like Father Francis interact with Muslims is social events. In his office he showed me a photo taken during a local Ramadan *iftar* (the communal meal at which Muslims break their day-long fast). The picture shows him with a mullah and the mullah's eight-year-old son. As the Muslim cleric looks on, the priest and the boy both dip bread into a bowl of yoghurt. "Muslim and Christian," said Father Francis proudly, "eating from the same plate." For him, this was clearly a good moment and a good memory.

True, some of his Christian colleagues are cynical about all this. "He's always meeting with the same small circle of like-minded Muslims," complained one skeptic. "They're always cutting cake together. It makes a good impression on the foreigners, on visitors." But I couldn't help admiring Father Francis's gentle idealism.

But it's an idealism tempered by a somber awareness of the limits to such dialogue. As I left his office the priest reiterated that whatever the interfaith venue—conferences, or madrasas, or Ramadan socials—he always avoids theological discussions of any kind. "We're always afraid of 295-C," he said, referring to the blasphemy law and the risk of saying something someone could choose to construe as an insult to the prophet Muhammad.

Christ Crucified Everywhere:
The Murder of Javed Anjum
and the "Crime of Being Non-Muslim"

Despite the ongoing threat posed by such legislation, in recent years Pakistan's Christian community has begun to speak out, collectively and publicly, and with an increasing sense of urgency, against sectarian discrimination. On December 20, 2005, Christians throughout the country observed a nationwide day of prayer and fasting to condemn the violence at Sangla Hill and the persecution of minorities in the name of religion. Additional nonviolent protests continued throughout 2006 for the purpose of drawing attention to the injustice of Pakistan's blasphemy law.

Pakistani advocacy groups such as the Catholic National Commission for Justice and Peace have argued that such legislation violates the spirit of Pakistan's own Constitution. The 2006 edition of the commission's annually published *Human Rights Monitor* quotes Article 20 of the Constitution of Pakistan: "Every citizen shall have the right to profess, practice and propagate his religion."[12] The *Monitor* documents numerous recent examples of how Pakistani Christians and other non-Muslims have been subjected to violence in retaliation for refusing to convert to Islam.

12. Mani, *Human Rights Monitor 2006*, 23.

One brutal instance from among many: the case of Javed Anjum. On May 2, 2004, this 18-year-old set out on foot to visit family members in a nearby Punjabi village. Along the way he paused to drink water from a tap outside the Jamia Hassan madrasa in the district of Toba Tek Singh. Confronted by some of the seminary students and accused of being non-Muslim, he refused to deny his faith and instead confirmed that yes in fact he was Christian.

Things turned ugly fast. With the assistance of one of the madrasa's teachers, the students detained Javed by force and accused him of trying to steal the school's water pumps and faucets. They kept him locked up for five days, beating him with iron pipes and trying to force him to become Muslim.

The young Christian refused, insisting on adhering to his faith. After five days of torture, the *madrasa* students dumped him at a police station, calling him a thief. A week later he died of his injuries.

The *Monitor*'s report includes a photo of Javed Anjum from his student days: a handsome young man who looks right into the camera, poised, proud, and self-aware. The *Monitor* provides another photo as well, showing a rally by Christian protesters in Lahore denouncing his religiously motivated murder. One protester carries a placard shaped like a black tombstone. The tombstone reads: "Javed Anjum. Age: 18. Profession: Student. Crime: *Ghair Muslim Hona* (Being Non-Muslim)."[13]

Crime: being non-Muslim. This ironic and bitter comment highlights a recurrent motif in Pakistani Islamist politics: an inability to tolerate religious diversity, and the use of violence to maintain ideological conformity and communal identity—motifs that underlie attempts at forced conversion to Islam (as in the tragedy of Javed Anjum) as well as legislation such as the blasphemy law.

How do Pakistani Christians find a way to live with such threats of persecution? The question was on the mind of Marie-Ange Siebrecht, an official with the Catholic charity group *Kirche In Not* ("The Church in Need"). She reports from a recent trip to Pakistan: "On my journey I asked one poor Christian how he could endure it all. He told me, 'When I look at Christ on the cross, then my sufferings seem small to me.'"[14]

One need spend only a short time in Pakistan to see Christ crucified everywhere.

13. Mani, *Human Rights Monitor 2005*, 22-23.

14. "Archbishop Demands Protection for Pakistani Christians," *EWT News*, May 22, 2007 (www.ewtn.com/vnews/getstory_print.asp?number=79000).

The Logos Confronts Talibanization:
Benedict's Regensburg Speech and Freedom
of Conscience in an Islamic Context

Relevant to these issues is Pope Benedict XVI's controversial Regens-burg speech of September 12, 2006. So fixated did some become on whether he did or did not insult Islam that they lost sight of the pope's larger message. The use of violence and coercion in the name of religion contradicts divine nature and God's plan for humankind. "The decisive statement in this argument against violent conversion," argues Benedict, "is this: not to act in accordance with reason is contrary to God's nature."[15]

Benedict contrasts religious violence with Logos ("the Word"—a Greek term familiar in Christian theology as a way of describing Jesus as the second member of the Trinity). The Logos that characterizes Divinity, he asserts, should also inspire human interactions. "Logos," the pope explains, "means both reason and word—a reason which is creative and capable of self-communication."[16]

Thus with God's nature as a model, according to Benedict, we should share our beliefs via reasoned debate, discussion, and dialogue—a notion espoused by yet another controversial figure loathed by many Muslims today: Ayaan Hirsi Ali. The ability to subject religious ideas to the test of reason, for Hirsi Ali, is essential to civilized life in the ideologically diverse landscape of our twenty-first century. "Religion is related to a body of ideas," she argues, "and people have the right to debate and criticize other people's ideas."[17]

Hirsi Ali is reviled by Islamists as an apostate; but the concept of freedom of conscience that she advocates is likewise supported by intellectually daring Muslims who are closer to the Islamic mainstream. The Tunisian scholar Mohamed Talbi states, "[R]eligious liberty is not an act of charity or a tolerant concession… It is a fundamental right for everyone." He correlates his own duty as a Muslim who is commanded by Allah to undertake *da'wah* (the "call" or "summons," that is, the obli-gation to engage in missionary efforts to convert others to Islam) with the rights of non-Muslims in how they react to Muslim evangelizing:

15. Benedict XVI, "Faith, Reason, and the University," speech delivered at the University of Regensburg, September 12, 2006 (www.vatican.va/holy_father/benedict_xvi/speeches/2006/september).

16. Benedict XVI, "Faith, Reason, and the University."

17. Ayaan Hirsi Ali, *The Caged Virgin: An Emancipation Proclamation for Women and Islam* (New York: Free Press, 2006), 174.

"My right, and my duty also, is to bear witness, by fair means, of my own faith, and to convey God's call. Ultimately it is up to each person to respond or not to respond to this call."[18]

Unfortunately current political trends in many parts of Pakistan amount to a repudiation of Talbi's enlightened viewpoint. In the spring of 2007, journalists reported on the ever-increasing Talibanization of Pakistan's North-West Frontier Province. Islamist mullahs are using madrasas as bases for indoctrinating young men with a violently intolerant form of the faith. These "students"—armed with rifles and rocket-propelled grenades and a confrontational vision of Islam—roam unchallenged from town to town, imposing a pitiless version of Quranic law on ordinary people throughout the province.[19]

Such a pattern has already established itself in Waziristan and other parts of the Tribal Areas on the Afghan–Pakistan border. What is alarming observers about this latest trend, however, is that such militants operate with impunity in the NWFP, a region that—unlike the Tribal Areas—is supposedly under the direct and undisputed control of Pakistan's central government.

As might be expected, this Talibanization trend has worsened interfaith relations in the province. In May 2007 CNN and other news agencies reported on threats directed by "pro-Taliban militants" against the Christian minority community in the North-West Frontier Province town of Charsadda. "All Christians are informed," ran the text of a warning delivered to a local Christian politician, "either become Muslims within ten days and shut down churches, or leave Charsadda. Or else you will be executed." The group delivering these threats identified itself as Anjuman-e Taliban Dhamaka Khez ("the Taliban Bomb-Setting Association"). Local government officials downplayed the threat, claiming the province's Christians "are safe and well protected." The bishop of Islamabad, however, held interviews to highlight the crisis: "I appeal to the world to help us in this dangerous struggle against fundamentalism." In June 2007 similar threats were made against Christians in the Punjabi village of Shantinagar: "[C]onvert to Islam or face dire consequences." Shantinagar had already experienced sectarian violence: in February 1997, after allegations that a local Christian had desecrated a copy of the

18. Mohamed Talbi, "Religious Liberty," in Charles Kurzman, ed., *Liberal Islam: A Sourcebook* (New York: Oxford University Press, 1998), 167-68.

19. David Montero, "Pakistan Losing Territory to Radicals," *Christian Science Monitor*, May 29, 2007; Munir Ahmad, "Convert or Die? Pakistani Christians Seek Help," *Associated Press*, May 18, 2007 (http://news.aol.com/topnews/articles/_a/convert-or-die-pakistani-christians-seek/20070517).

Quran, mobs of angry Muslims set fire to homes and churches, driving out 20,000 Christians and rendering them homeless.[20]

Another sign of creeping Talibanization is newly proposed legislation introduced in May 2007 by the Islamist MMA coalition. Called the "Apostasy Act," this proposed bill would mandate life imprisonment for women and the death penalty for men who abandon Islam. Apologists for the bill note that the law would give apostates the chance to repent: "Section 5 stipulates that the 'offender' must be granted 3 to 30 days to recant the conversion and return to Islam." Nevertheless, the bill imposes a two-year jail sentence even on penitent apostates. Moreover, under this law apostates would forfeit their property and custody of their children to Muslim relatives. The mind boggles at the ways in which such a bill could be abused by opportunists of all kinds.[21]

Opportunistic abuse also features in some of the most recent cases involving the blasphemy law. In May 2007 an 84-year-old Lahori Christian was jailed after being accused of burning pages of the Quran. But defense lawyers pointed out that those who filed the blasphemy charge were colluding with Muslim businessmen who had unsuccessfully tried to pressure the elderly Christian into selling them his land at below-market prices. Another case arose in April 2007 when an 11-year-old Punjabi Christian boy was charged with blasphemy after he got into a fistfight with a Muslim boy. The Muslim child had been wearing an amulet containing a Quranic inscription; the amulet is said to have been damaged in the fight. Hence the blasphemy charge, which has led to Muslim retaliatory violence against Christians throughout Punjab's Toba Tek Singh district—the same region where 18-year-old Javed Anjum had been beaten to death with iron pipes three years earlier by a thuggish madrasa teacher and his pupils.[22]

20. "Pakistani Christians Live in Fear," *CNN*, May 16, 2007 (http://edition.cnn.com/2007/WORLD/asiapcf/05/16/pakistan.christians.ap/index.html); "Bishop Requests Prayers for Threatened Pakistani Christians," *Catholic Online*, May 23, 2007 (www.catholic.org); "Christians Threatened: Convert to Islam or Die," *Asia News*, May 11, 2007 (www.asianews.it); Asher John, "Shantinagar Christians Getting Threatening Letters," *Daily Times* [Lahore], June 23, 2007 (www.dailytimes.com.pk).

21. Qaiser Felix, "New Apostasy Bill to Impose Death on Anyone Who Leaves Islam," *Asia News*, May 9, 2007 (www.asianews.it).

22. Qaiser Felix, "84-Year-Old Christian Accused of Blasphemy to Force Him to Sell Land," *Asia News*, May 10, 2007 (www.asianews.it); Ecumenical News International, "Blasphemy Charges Heighten Easter Tensions for Pakistani Christians," *Ekklesia* (World Council of Churches), April 6, 2007 (www.ekklesia.co.uk).

Given the threats these days directed against anyone who falls foul of Pakistan's blasphemy law, it's understandable that most of the individuals I interviewed on this subject preferred to remain anonymous. One exception is Lawrence John Saldanha, the Catholic archbishop of Lahore. Currently the president of Pakistan's Catholic Bishops Conference, Archbishop Saldanha is spearheading a movement for the repeal of Sections B and C of Ordinance 295 of the Pakistan Penal Code (recall that these are the sections governing Quran-desecration and dishonoring the prophet Muhammad).

I first met the archbishop in December 2005 at his office in Lahore's Catholic Cathedral. A peaceful setting for discussing grim topics: as we talked, birds flitted among the pillars of a stone portico and called from the trees in the Cathedral courtyard against the last light of a winter sky. Cloistered tranquility, evanescent and precious.

I was impressed with Archbishop Saldanha at once—for his bluntness, his honesty, his energetic way in conversation of driving straight at topics that make others dive for cover. The man is fearless—a word with meaning in Pakistan, where life tests people's courage every day.

I started the interview by asking him about his background. Of Portuguese descent, his family is from south India, where his father once worked in the Telegraph Department of the British Indian railway system. In 1942 the family was transferred to Lahore, which is how the future priest became a resident of Pakistan.

I learned many things from our talk. How so many Pakistani Muslims hold local Christians responsible for everything America does. How Muslim converts to Christianity frequently have to flee Pakistan because of persecution by their families and neighbors. How zealots who murder non-Muslims are garlanded and hailed as heroes by mullahs in their home villages.

But one issue topped the archbishop's take-action list. When I asked what he thought were the prospects for productive Christian–Muslim dialogue in Pakistan, he said at once that the most useful form of interfaith dialogue would be for Christians and Muslims to collaborate on working to repeal 295 B and C. Overturning 295, he said, should be a top priority—for Christians, for Muslims, for everyone who wishes Pakistan well.

He is fighting for the repeal, he told me, because this harmful ordinance—which is worded so as to encourage slander against anyone designated an "enemy of Islam"—has provided a legal rationale for inciting religious violence and the persecution of minorities. 295 rewards religious hatred.

I returned to California and wrote an essay on 295 and the harm it causes. Once the piece had been published, I mailed copies of the essay to the archbishop's office. Then I went back to the professorial round of teaching courses and grading papers and explaining to querulous undergrads why their tests merited only a C-plus instead of a B-minus.

But in June 2006 I received an unexpected call. Archbishop Saldanha was briefly in the States, in San Francisco in fact, meeting with Catholic officials on humanitarian issues. He had a car and a driver and a few hours free at his disposal, and he wanted to know: how far from San Francisco was my university?

In fact, not that far; and we had a pleasant reunion on the campus of Santa Clara University. One thing in particular he wanted to share with me: a copy of the text of the "Charter of Demands" presented in April 2006 to the government of Pakistan in Islamabad by leaders of the All Pakistan Minorities Alliance (APMA). The latter is an umbrella organization representing the various social justice groups and non-Muslim communities from throughout Pakistan.

The Charter of Demands is comprehensive in the abuses it identifies—not only Ordinance 295 B-C, but also forced conversions to Islam and the fearsome Hudood ordinances dating from General Zia's time that have made life a torment for so many Pakistani women.

Worth quoting in full is article 16 in the APMA's Charter of Demands:

> All the [proposed] laws and enactments should be made in conformity with the Universal Declaration of Human Rights dated 10th December 1948 and as envisaged under the Declaration on Rights of Persons Belonging to Religious Minorities adopted [by the] General Assembly of UNO [United Nations Organization] through resolution no.47/135 on 10th December 1992. These Declarations are legally and morally binding on the Government of Pakistan.

I'm glad to report that Pakistan's APMA is not the first to apply criteria established by the United Nations to Islamic societies. The Sudanese legal scholar and social-justice activist 'Abdullahi Ahmed An-Na'im compares the UN's Declaration of Human Rights with the codes of social conduct stipulated in *shari'ah* (Quranically derived legislation). His conclusions challenge every Muslim-majority society that is accustomed to regarding *shari'ah* as the ultimate source for structuring the legal framework of modern social life.

An-Na'im makes the following claim (a claim that accords well, I would argue, with the Logos-model of religion and reason presented by Pope Benedict). Wherever Islamic law conflicts with basic freedoms—whether in issues involving religious identity, gender discrimination, or enslavement—traditional interpretations of *shari'ah* must yield to recognized principles of universal human rights: that is, the concept that individuals are entitled to a fundamental dignity not because of their religious affiliation but because they are human beings.[23]

When it comes to religious minorities in Islamic countries, both An-Na'im and Pakistan's APMA are in effect arguing for the same thing: a shift from dhimmitude to pluralism. Such a shift would mean renouncing the repressive and contempt-flavored "tolerance" extended by Muslim societies such as Pakistan towards their religious minorities. This would be replaced by a mentality that regards divergent worldviews as potential sources of wisdom and religious diversity as worthwhile in itself rather than as something to be feared.

Pakistan is not there yet and may never choose to go there. But thinkers like An-Na'im and advocates like Archbishop Saldanha and groups like the All Pakistan Minorities Alliance have shown the way.

A Concluding Note. Dragging Traitors Through the Streets: How the Blasphemy Law Affects Muslims

Worth emphasizing is that Christians are not the only ones who have suffered because of Pakistan's blasphemy law. The Catholic Bishops Conference has pointed out that 54% of the individuals imprisoned under Ordinance 295 are Muslims. They were denounced as apostates by fellow Muslims—whether out of religious zealotry or sheer opportunism—on charges of questioning the Quran or showing insufficient reverence for the prophet Muhammad's legacy. (The other prisoners are Christians, Hindus, and Ahmadis.)[24]

After being charged under 295 B-C and publicly identified as having "insulted the faith," at least 20 persons in recent years have been snatched from the authorities by angry mobs and dragged through the streets and beaten to death. Of these 20 identified victims of extrajudicial killings, 6 were Christian—and 14 Muslim. Those labeled "traitors" to Islam are regarded with far more hatred, and as far worse, than mere non-Muslims.[25]

---

23. 'Abdullahi Ahmed An-Na'im, "Shari'a and Basic Human Rights Concerns," in Kurzman, ed., *Liberal Islam: A Sourcebook*, 222-38.

24. Mani, *Human Rights Monitor 2005*, 38.

25. Information provided during interview in Lahore with Archbishop Lawrence Saldanha, December 13, 2005. See also the statistics cited in a leaflet entitled "The Blasphemy Laws in Pakistan," which was published by the National Commission for Justice and Peace and circulated in Lahore in 2005.

The fact that Muslims have used Ordinance 295 to indict fellow Muslims points up the larger harm inflicted on Pakistan as a whole by this legislation. A Lahore-based Muslim intellectual told me, "295 makes it impossible to think out loud about Islam freely. We're at risk of paralysis, both as a nation and as a religious tradition."

For the good of all its citizens, it's time for Pakistan to repeal its blasphemy law.

4

RITUAL AND COMMUNAL IDENTITY: SHIA–SUNNI RELATIONS IN PAKISTAN

To start with, two anecdotes—one from a lecture in the North-West Frontier Province, the other from a visit to a Muslim saint's shrine in Islamabad—to illustrate the themes at play in this chapter.

Who's Right, Who's Wrong:
Bad Moments on the Interfaith Dialogue Circuit

Peshawar, December 2002. I'd been invited to give a lecture at the University of Peshawar's "Shaykh Zayed Islamic Studies Center" (an institute funded by sources in the United Arab Emirates). Professor Qibla Ayaz, the Zayed Center's chairman, told me the center's purpose is *tabligh*: the evangelical dissemination of Islam. In Pakistan *tabligh* refers especially to missionary efforts by conservative Sunnis to reform the faith of fellow Muslims—particularly those Muslims deemed deficient in their orthodoxy or insufficiently rigorous in their ritual life. Before my lecture the chairman introduced me to the Zayed Center's professors, and a number of them displayed a forthright anti-Shia bias.

Problematic, this, given my lecture topic: Shia–Sunni relations and the prospects for sectarian reconciliation in Pakistan. Aware of the (to put it mildly) climate of religious conservatism in the NWFP, I came prepared for some mental recalcitrance when I hit campus.

My first warning that the topic might be a hard sell came when Doctor Ayaz took me aside ten minutes before my talk to say no students would be allowed in to hear me speak. "The subject is too sensitive." He was apologetic. The campus mood of anti-Americanism made my presence provocative.

Would I have anyone at all, then, in the lecture hall?

Not to worry, he said: I would address the faculty of the Zayed Center. And all fifteen professors filed in and found seats.

Oh well: educate the educators, and let them spread the message. I began by briefly reviewing things all of them must have known: caliphal history, the imamate, the pernicious effects of medieval sectarian polemics. I came quickly to my theme: the opportunity for Muslims to learn from the mistakes made by Christians during the violent history of the Church. For centuries Catholics and Protestants refused to recognize each other as Christians and instead killed each other in the name of God, convinced as they were that religious truth must be limited to one sect alone. Only in recent years has ecumenism taken hold. Protestants and Catholics, I said, have gradually come to acknowledge that each denomination has something important to say. Protestantism, with its emphasis on the need for individual believers to encounter God directly in Scripture, and Catholicism, with its emphasis on God's physical and sacramental presence in the world, together offer complementary aspects of the same message. The two complete each other.

I've offered variations on this talk at interfaith venues aplenty over the years, so I've had practice in gauging my audience. Fifteen blank faces. Eyes empty and non-committal. A hard sell. My host Doctor Ayaz gave me a nod I took for encouragement. I plunged on.

So, too, I said, with Islam. Shiism and Sunnism differ, but as the old Arabic saying insists, *Al-Ikhtilaf rahmah min Allah*: Disagreement in viewpoint is a blessing and mercy from God. Rather than judge each other, rather than engage in *takfir* (declaring a fellow believer to be a *kafir* or infidel), Shias and Sunnis could choose instead to acknowledge each other as Muslims. Pluralism, I said, means not merely tolerating the existence of diversity, but welcoming divergent worldviews as a stimulus to one's own spiritual growth. I rounded off my talk with a quote from the Quran (5.48): "If Allah had wanted, He could have made you a single community. But he did not… Therefore compete with each other in good works. Unto God is your return, all of you. Thereupon He will enlighten you as to those things concerning which you once differed."

There. No one had stormed out. Not too bad a job, I thought. Were there any questions?

Just one. A Zayed Center professor stood up, turbaned, bearded, unsmiling. For a non-Muslim, he said by way of praise, I seemed to know a good bit about Islam. So he would like my opinion on simply one thing: which is the truer form of Islam—Sunnism or Shiism? "In other words," he asked, "which of the two is right, and which is wrong?"

So much for my try at sectarian reconciliation. A Roadrunner cartoon image flashed at me: Wile E. Coyote hits a brick wall.

Cave, Tree, Monkey-Thief: At the Saint's Shrine

Anecdote number 2:

Islamabad, March 2004. A tense and unpleasant moment at a book-shop downtown. I wanted to see if the latest *Newsweek* was available but I had trouble getting the clerk's attention. He and a knot of other young men were staring at a TV blaring the latest update from CNN.

The clerk spotted me and jabbed his hand at the screen. Look, he told me, look. His voice shook with anger.

CNN was broadcasting the funeral of slain Hamas chief Shaykh Ahmad Yasin. The screen showed crowds of Palestinians thronging the streets of Gaza in grief—a grief that radiated out into this Islamabad bookstore.

"Killed by Israel," said the clerk. He and his friends turned from CNN to me. "Killed by America."

Time for a quick smiling exit. I could make do without *Newsweek*.

One of the men followed me out into the street as my driver Imtiyaz started our car. "Killed by the Jews," said the man as we pulled away. "Killed by America."

I met a better welcome at my next stop, a saint's shrine called Bari Imam at the northeast edge of the city. The site is consecrated to a seventeenth-century miracle-worker, Syed Abdul Latif Shah. Pilgrims come here from all over Pakistan to ask the saint for favors.

Boys sold rose petals—flowers of paradise—at five rupees a packet. Visitors sprinkled the petals over the saint's grave. Inside the shrine, near the grave, grew a big banyan tree, its upmost limbs piercing the mosque's roof. Strips of cloth, torn from worshippers' clothing, fluttered from the sacred tree's branches. A friendly man standing beside me—he told me he'd driven here with his father from Lahore, a five-hour trip—said pilgrims fix the cloth to the tree to leave a token of their visit so the saint wouldn't forget them or their requests. I nodded. I'd seen the same practice at Hindu temples in India. The Bari Imam custodians also offered for sale a more enduring forget-me-not: padlocks that one could murmur over in prayer and then lock to an upright metal grate between the tree and the grave.

Plenty of business went on while I was there. Vendors sold glass bangles. Numerologists and "astro-palmists" offered to tell my fortune. An old man displayed posters showing the names of the twelve Imams and the words *Ya 'Ali Madad*—"O Ali, help me"—inscribed on the palm of a hand. Iconography dear to Shias.

"Lots of Shias come here," explained Imtiyaz. Also Sunnis and Sufis, I learned: an easy mingling of Muslims of all kinds.

My driver asked if I wanted to do what all the other pilgrims do and visit the *chillah ghar* ("retreat-house")—the cave where the saint Abdul Latif used to meditate and pray.

I hesitated, feeling conspicuous—no other foreigners were to be seen—and remembering the unpleasantness at the bookshop. But the mood here was relaxed and I said sure.

I'm glad I did. It was a pleasant hour's hike to the cave, uphill over stony uneven ground, with hot sunlight, a strong cooling breeze, and the highrise blocks of Islamabad below us in the distance. A steady stream of pilgrims, preceding us and following, made their way to the cave. Everyone I spoke to—and many people were eager to chat—was friendly.

With the exception of the monkeys.

Imtiyaz was ahead of me on the trail, his head turned, warning me about the thievish wildlife—creatures that might jump from the pathside bushes and snatch my sunglasses or camera—when a three-foot-tall monkey blocked our path and grabbed a fistful of my friend's shirttail. It did nothing else, just stood there and looked up at Imtiyaz and gripped his tunic hard. My driver did his best to look stern and growled the Urdu for Scram—*Chelo*—but the thief wouldn't budge.

Imtiyaz sighed and reached into his pocket and pulled out a waxed-cardboard box of fruit juice he'd been saving for himself.

Acceptable baksheesh: the monkey snatched the box and let Imtiyaz go and bounded aside. It bit into the box and tipped back its head and chugged the juice down.

At the hill's summit I watched pilgrims crowd into the saint's cave and thought: This is the old Islam, a faith of rock and soil, rooted in the local landscape, a comfortable blend of ancient Hindu and Muslim practices.

But some can't live with this kind of Islam. A year after my visit, in May 2005, a suicide bomber walked up to the mosque and detonated himself inside the Bari Imam shrine. 19 persons dead, nearly 70 wounded. News analysts noted that the attack was timed to coincide with "an annual festival at the shrine that brings together Shiite and Sunni followers of Islam." Shia survivors of the blast wailed, "This is the work of the enemy of Husain."[1] But it might be more precise to say: This was the work of those who want to polarize denominations and break apart the religious commingling that once characterized Pakistan's traditional forms of Islam.

1.   Somini Sengupta and Salman Masood, "Blast Kills 19 at Pakistani Shrine During Muslim Festival," *The New York Times*, May 28, 2005.

Historical Background:
Shia Theology and the Death of the Imam Husain

Before discussing the status of sectarian politics in present-day Pakistan, it's worth summarizing the events of fourteen centuries ago that inspired the Shia denomination of Islam.

Shiism arose from a political dispute concerning leadership of the *ummah* (the "community of believers") after the prophet Muhammad's death (AD 632). Most Muslims accepted the notion that the caliph (the Prophet's successor as leader of the *ummah*) would be elected via a process of consultation and voting among a council of Muslim elders. Such Muslims were later identified by the name Sunni (i.e. those who follow the *sunnah* or "exemplary custom and lifestyle" of Muhammad). Sunni Muslims today constitute 85% of the world's Islamic population. A minority of Muslims, however, supported the candidacy of Ali ibn Abi Talib, the Prophet's cousin and son-in-law (Ali married Muhammad's daughter Fatima). This minority became known as *Shi'at Ali*, "the partisans of Ali," or simply the Shia.[2]

Ali ruled briefly as caliph but only after three other men from among the *Sahaba* (the Prophet's "Companions," who supported Muhammad in the dangerous early days of Islam) had been selected successively to rule. A number of the *Sahaba* had contested Ali's right to the caliphate. After his death in 661 Ali's supporters transferred their loyalty to his sons, first Hasan, and then, after Hasan's death, to the younger son Husain. Shias developed a theory of hereditary leadership based on family kinship linked to the prophet Muhammad, restricting the role of ruler to a line of Imams or spiritual leaders descended from Ali (revered as the first Imam) and Fatima.

Most Shias today throughout the world adhere to the Ithna-'Ashari ("Twelver") form of Shiism. Twelver Shiism is the officially recognized state-sponsored faith of the Islamic Republic of Iran. As the name implies, Twelver Shias acknowledge a succession of twelve Imams, beginning with Ali and ending with Muhammad al-Muntazar (the "awaited" or hidden Imam, who Twelvers say went into occultation in the ninth century and will return one day as the Mahdi—"the one rightly guided by God"—to purify the world and usher in Judgment Day). Shias believe these twelve Imams share with the prophet Muhammad and his daughter Fatima the quality of being *ma'sum* (sinless, infallible, and

2. For further information on early Islamic history and the rise of Shia Islam, see David Pinault, *The Shiites: Ritual and Popular Piety in a Muslim Community* (New York: St. Martin's Press, 1992), 4-26.

divinely protected against error). In Pakistan as throughout most of the Islamic world, Muslims use the term Shia to designate the Twelver form of Shiism. Other, numerically smaller, Shia denominations survive today —such as the Alawites (also called Nusairis) of Syria, and the Ismailis (also called Agha Khanis), who live in Pakistan's Northern Areas and in diaspora communities throughout the world—but for reasons having to do with politics and charges of doctrinal heterodoxy, many Muslims refuse to consider Alawites or Ismailis as Muslims at all. In this discussion I use the term Shia to refer to the dominant Twelver denomination.

Shiism evolved from a political orientation to a religious worldview in the aftermath of the battle of Karbala (AD 680). The events of Karbala are recounted annually during Shia rituals throughout the month of Muharram and can be summarized as follows. A tyrant named Yazid ibn Mu'awiya became caliph and tried to coerce an oath of allegiance from Ali's surviving son Husain. Rather than acknowledge an unjust ruler as caliph, Husain rode forth from Arabia with a small group of family members and warriors across the desert to Iraq, where he planned to lead Shia rebels in the city of Kufa in a revolt against Yazid.

Husain never reached Kufa. At a site in the Iraqi desert named Karbala (today the most important Shia pilgrimage shrine in the world), Yazid's soldiers intercepted and surrounded Husain's force. The enemy besieged Husain's camp for several days, inflicting torments of thirst on the Imam's family. They hoped to make Husain surrender and acknowledge Yazid's reign. Husain chose death instead. His battlefield martyrdom occurred on Ashura, the tenth day of Muharram (the focal point of Shia lamentation rituals annually, and a national holiday in Pakistan and India).

Although a defeat for Shia political hopes, the battle of Karbala is understood today as a spiritual victory. Shia theologians of the pre-modern era argued that Husain's battlefield death involved voluntary self-sacrifice, an act of martyrdom in exchange for which God granted Husain powers of intercession in paradise on behalf of sinful believers. Access to Husain's intercession is earned through annual rituals of commemoration during Muharram. In Pakistan (as in other Muslim regions where there are substantial Shia populations) Muharram rituals traditionally include some or all of the following components: (1) the *majlis* or lamentation gathering at shrines where preachers describe in detail the sufferings of the Karbala martyrs so as to elicit weeping and other signs of grief from the congregation; (2) public street processions, in which mourners cluster around a riderless horse called Zuljenah ("the winged one"), a stallion representing the steed once ridden at Karbala by Husain; (3) the performance of *matam*, a communal, ritualized, and very physical manifestation of grief for the Karbala martyrs, ranging from *hath ka matam* (repetitive breast-beating with the palm of the hand, done to the rhythm of chanted lamentation poems) to *zanjiri matam* (the phrase literally means *matam* involving chains, but the term is often used more generally to mean "bloody *matam*" or self-flagellation with razors, chains, and knives); (4) *tabarra*, public denunciation or disparagement of those *Sahaba*—especially the first three caliphs, Abu Bakr, Umar, and Uthman—who after Muhammad's death became Ali's rivals for power and blocked the Prophet's heirs and descendants from achieving the leadership that was theirs by hereditary birthright.[3] In some localities Shia leaders have recently curbed *tabarra* in the interest of sectarian reconciliation; but Pakistani Shias I interviewed asserted that the practice continues at many Muharram gatherings.

Sunni response to these rituals has often been very negative, especially with regard to *tabarra* (as it involves dishonoring the *Sahaba*, whom Sunnis revere) and *matam* (especially its bloodier manifestations, since self-flagellation violates Sunni notions of public decorum and ritual purity). To this day militant Sunni organizations in Pakistan focus precisely on such points of ritual in justifying anti-Shia violence.

Traditional Shia theology insists, however, that lamentation rituals—whether weeping or self-scourging—provide access to the intercession granted Husain by God. But there is also a sociological dimension to Muharram mourning. Shias I interviewed in Pakistan (and in the following point they echoed comments I had heard from Shias in India) emphasized the importance of performing their rituals in public, for the express purpose of asserting Shia communal presence and Shia solidarity.

It's hard to overstate the assertive quality of public Shia rituals in Sunni-majority Pakistan. Thousands of mourners march in procession through the streets and bring traffic to a halt for hours. Hundreds of participants beat their chests in unison, obeying the rhythm of lamentation poems blaring from loudspeakers mounted on trucks and rickshaws. Zealots scourge themselves with flails and leave paths of blood along the way.

The controversial and (from the Sunni perspective) repugnant quality of certain Shia rituals only reinforces the fact that Muharram practices can serve to mark out sectarian boundaries and maintain separate communal identities. As we will see, Iranian leaders have tried to rein in the practice of bloody *matam*; but in Pakistan such attempts have met considerable resistance.

---

3. David Pinault, *Horse of Karbala: Muslim Devotional Life in India* (New York: Palgrave, 2001), 11-27.

Sectarian violence in Pakistan:
The Political Background

Despite sporadic confrontations during Muharram, Shia–Sunni relations in Pakistan were relatively good during the nation's first thirty years of existence, from 1947 until the late 1970s. Founders of Pakistan such as Muhammad Ali Jinnah had envisioned their country as a homeland for Muslims but never attempted to impose Islamic law on its citizens. This facilitated sectarian relations among Muslims, as no one Muslim denomination was allowed to impose its interpretation of Islam on the state.

The situation changed in 1977 when General Zia ul-Haq seized power. To legitimize his authority and gain favor with prominent ulema (Muslim religious scholars), Zia in 1979 introduced an Islamization program to make Hanafi Sunni *fiqh* (Islamic jurisprudence) the law of the land and instituted the Hudood (Islamic penalties) Ordinances (legislation mandating public punishments such as scourging for various offenses). Zia's program entailed the universal imposition of aspects of Sunni *fiqh* (most notably the government's mandatory collection of *zakat* or "charity taxes") to which Pakistani Shias objected (Shias make such payments to charitable institutions rather than to the government).

To defend their communal identity in the face of Zia's program Shia ulema and other Shia leaders created the Tehrik-e Nifaz-e Fiqh-e Jafria (TNFJ, "the movement for the implementation of Shia law"). TNFJ spearheaded a movement that forced Zia to exempt Pakistani Shias from *zakat* payments to the government. Additionally, he agreed "not to impose the laws of any one *fiqh* on the followers of another *fiqh*." TNFJ remained focused on Pakistani domestic politics until Arif Husain al-Husaini became its leader in 1984. Trained at *madrasas* in Iran and a student of Ayatollah Ruhollah Khomeini, Husaini transformed TNFJ's orientation so as to align it with the goals of Khomeini's "Islamic revolution" and the foreign policy of the Iranian Islamic Republic. Khomeini emphasized *taqrib* ("rapprochement" between Sunnis and Shias) so as to downplay theological and ritual differences among Muslims and achieve tactical alliances with Sunni radical movements in the Arab Near East and elsewhere in the Islamic world. Khomeini's goal was to export the Iranian revolution via the theme of "unity among Muslims." This unity was to be achieved through a rhetoric of anti-imperialism that focused on the United States as the designated enemy of Islam.[4]

---

4. Afak Haydar, "The Politicization of the Shias and the Development of the Tehrik-e Nifaz-e Fiqh-e Jafaria in Pakistan," in Charles H. Kennedy, ed., *Pakistan: 1992* (Boulder, CO: Westview Press, 1993), 75-81; Pinault, *Horse of Karbala*, 165, 199.

After al-Husaini's murder in 1988, leadership of TNFJ passed to a cleric named Allama Seyyed Sajid Ali Naqvi. Although TNFJ changed its name to Tehrik-e Jafria Pakistan (TJP, "the Pakistan Shia movement"), Naqvi has remained the group's leader to the present day and has developed his predecessor's pro-Iranian ideology. (In recent years the TJP's name changed yet again, a point to which I'll return.)

Naqvi is known for a Khomeinist worldview that employs pan-Islamic and revolutionary themes. In a 1992 interview with the scholar Afak Haydar, Naqvi asserted that his organization "is not and does not want to be a sectarian group." Nevertheless the TJP has also worked to maintain its reputation as the primary defender of Pakistani Shias and has been implicated in clashes with Sunnis in various parts of Pakistan. In particular the TJP splinter group Sipah-e Muhammad ("the soldiers of Muhammad") has been notorious for violent assaults on Pakistani Sunnis. Both the TJP and Sipah-e Muhammad were banned in January 2002 as part of Musharraf's crackdown on sectarian groups, although (as will be seen) this hasn't kept Naqvi from exploiting recent international political events as a way of keeping his name in the headlines.[5]

One of the primary opponents of such Shia groups has been the SSP: Sipah-e Sahaba Pakistan ("the soldiers of the Prophet's Companions"). Although outlawed since 2002 (as will be discussed below), the SSP's ideology continues to influence sectarian politics to this day. Its roots go back to Deobandism. The latter is an Islamic reform movement that arose within India in 1867 as a response to British domination of the subcontinent. It advocated a renewal of the faith via a return to Islam in its earliest and purest form. This involved a program of traditionalist religious education, personal ethical rigor together with the strictest possible moral accountability, and the banning of popular religious rituals that Deobandis condemned as unislamic. Deobandi scholars condemned both Shia Islam and many practices linked to Sufism. In Pakistan Deobandi power has grown under the aegis of the JUI, the Jamiat-e Ulema-e Islam ("the association of religious scholars of Islam"). The JUI's influence is due in part to an extensive network of madrasas that has offered a fundamentalist interpretation of Islam to thousands of students, most notably the Taliban.[6]

5. Haydar, "The Politicization of the Shias," 85; Anwar H. Syed, "The Sunni–Shia Conflict in Pakistan," in Hafeez Malik, ed., *Pakistan: Founders' Aspirations and Today's Realities* (Oxford: Oxford University Press, 2001), 254.

6. Barbara Daly Metcalf, *Islamic Revival in British India: Deoband, 1860–1900* (Princeton: Princeton University Press, 1982); Ahmed Rashid, *Taliban: Militant Islam, Oil, and Fundamentalism in Central Asia* (New Haven: Yale University Press, 2000), 26, 89.

The SSP is described by Pakistani journalist Ahmed Rashid as an "extreme splinter faction of the JUI." The SSP's founder, Maulana Haq Nawaz Jhangvi, established it in 1985 in part to counter the economic power of Shia landlords who dominated much of the political landscape in his home district of Jhang in the Punjab. As the SSP's power grew beyond the Punjab its ideology evolved into a worldview that Jhangvi regarded as a comprehensive defense of Sunnism. This is reflected in the group's name: Sipah-e Sahaba, "the soldiers of the Prophet's Companions." The SSP regarded itself as the guardians of the reputation of the *Sahaba*, especially the first three caliphs, who (as noted above) are condemned by Shias via the practice of *tabarra* for having blocked Ali's path to the caliphate.[7]

The SSP pursued both theological and political confrontation with Pakistan's Shias. It agitated for "a purely Sunni state" in which Shias would be "declared a non-Muslim minority in Pakistan." In its propaganda the SSP tried to undercut the pan-Islamic appeal of the Iranian Republic, reminding Pakistani Sunni audiences of Khomeini's Shia background and drawing attention to those aspects of Shiism that could be relied on to offend Sunnis.[8]

The SSP's founder, Maulana Jhangvi, was murdered in 1990; Sunnis blamed Shia opponents for the killing. The SSP's militant wing, Lashkar-e Jhangvi ("the Jhangvi Army"), was named in honor of the slain founder. The SSP's subsequent leader (after the killing of Jhangvi's immediate successor), Maulana Muhammad A'zam Tariq, built a reputation for his skill in headline-generating confrontations (until he himself was murdered in 2003). In 1992, as a member of the National Assembly, Tariq attempted to introduce a bill labeled *Namoos-e Sahaba* ("the honor of the Prophet's Companions"). Its goal was to extend Ordinance 295, the current blasphemy law (which mandates death for anyone dishonoring the prophet Muhammad's name), so as to inflict capital punishment on individuals found guilty of insulting the Prophet's Companions— clearly an attempt to forbid the Shia practice of *tabarra*. As one Shia critic complained, "We look at this bill as an attempt to bar the Muharram ceremonies."[9]

7.   Rashid, *Taliban*, 92; Afak Haydar, "The Sipah-e-Sahaba Pakistan," in Malik, ed., *Pakistan*, 263-86.

8.   Aamer Ahmed Khan, "Sipah-e-Sahaba Pakistan," *The Herald* (Karachi) 25.6 (June 1994): 35; Muhammad Qasim Zaman, "Sectarianism in Pakistan: The Radicalization of Shii and Sunni Identities," *Modern Asian Studies* 32 (1998): 699-705.

9.   Aamer Ahmed Khan, "The Blasphemy Law: The Bigot's Charter?," *The Herald* (Karachi) 25.5 (May 1994): 44-46; Zaman, "Sectarianism in Pakistan," 702 n. 41.

The tragic part of all this is that in pre-Partition India (and in at least some parts of the subcontinent even today), Muharram was not only a Shia religious observance but also a *tamasha* (spectacle) and social event in which Hindus and Muslims often mingled companionably and in which some non-Shias participated to a greater or lesser extent.

Among the factors contributing to the politicizing of Pakistan's Muharram was the dislocation of Pakistani labor migrants in the 1970s and 1980s. Thousands of unskilled and semi-skilled workers from rural parts of the country migrated to the Persian Gulf states in search of jobs. They returned with their earnings not to their villages of origin but to Pakistan's urban centers, a movement involving over 10% of the country's population. These deracinated migrants no longer found so appealing the old regionally-based Islam I encountered at the Bari Imam shrine—the landscape-oriented faith of caves and saints' tombs and sacred trees. Deracinated Muslims, facing the challenges of modernity in unfamiliar city settings, were susceptible to evangelizing by missionaries of a new and universalist "urban, text-based Islam," an Islam all too ready to brand the traditional folk rituals of the countryside as Hindu-tainted and *kafir*. Scholar Muhammad Qasim Zaman comments, "The nerve centers of this 'new' Islam are not Sufi shrines but madrasas and sectarian organizations."[10]

Religious Apartheid and Its Implications for Pakistani Shias: The Case of the Ahmadiyya Community

Sectarian-minded Sunnis who later joined the SSP and targeted Shias got their start in the 1970s, as Zaman points out, by persecuting a minority population even more vulnerable than the Shias: Pakistan's Ahmadiyya community. Since its origin in British India, the Ahmadis have been condemned by fellow Muslims for denying the doctrine of *khatam-e nubuwwa* ("the seal of prophethood": the belief, shared by Shias and Sunnis, that Muhammad was the last prophet and there can be no other prophet after him). The Ahmadis ascribe the title of Muslim prophet to a nineteenth-century preacher in the Punjab, Mirza Ghulam Ahmad. In 1974 Sunni agitators succeeded in pressuring Pakistan's legislature into officially labeling the Ahmadis non-Muslim. Future SSP members also helped formulate legal provisions in 1984 that penalized any Ahmadis that might try to assert their faith publicly.[11]

10. Zaman, "Sectarianism in Pakistan," 715.
11. Avril A. Powell, "Ahmadiyya," in Richard C. Martin, ed., *Encyclopedia of Islam and the Muslim World* (New York: Macmillan, 2004), vol. 1, 30-32; Zaman, "Sectarianism in Pakistan," 691-92.

Adherents of the sect whom I interviewed in 2002 and 2005 described the systematic government-approved persecution they face. One Ahmadi I met was a minority-rights advocate who approached me at a reception after a lecture I gave in Islamabad. Fearful of being overheard in public discussing volatile topics, he sought me out later at the guesthouse where I stayed.

The first thing he said to me in our interview: "We Ahmadis consider ourselves good Muslims, as good as any Sunni or Shia. We observe the 5 Pillars, the same as they do." He acknowledged his sect differs from the others in considering Mirza Ghulam Ahmad a prophet. "But that shouldn't exclude us from Islam." As we talked he crossed the room to check no one was listening at the door.

"If you're an Ahmadi," he continued, "you're forbidden by law to call yourself Muslim. You can't call your mosque a mosque; you can't issue the *azan* [the Islamic call to prayer]; you can't say *al-salam 'alaykum* ["Peace be upon you," the salutation with which Muslims greet each other worldwide]." Ahmadis that are caught using this greeting, he said, are liable to prosecution under the blasphemy law. And in fact the *Human Rights Monitor* report published by Pakistan's Catholic Bishops Conference indicates that approximately 20% of the blasphemy cases recorded since 1987 have targeted Ahmadis.[12]

The restrictions imposed on Ahmadis include excruciatingly detailed prohibitions that are startling in their vindictive small-mindedness. According to my informants, Ahmadis are forbidden, for example, to have printed on their business cards the *basmala* (the Quranic phrase *Bismi Allah al-rahman al-rahim*, "In the name of Allah, the compassionate, the merciful"). Such prohibitions are designed to segregate the Ahmadis and stigmatize them as schismatic and heretical—a religious apartheid that is neither merciful nor compassionate.[13]

Once the SSP–Deobandi ideologues succeeded in excommunicating the Ahmadis, they set about trying to disenfranchise Pakistan's Shias. In 1986 a Karachi-based mufti, Wali Hassan Tonki, published a fatwa proclaiming that "the Shia are…outside the pale of Islam." Tonki justified his decree in part by referring to the Shia concept of the imamate, wherein the twelve Shia Imams, like the prophet Muhammad, are held to be not only sinless and infallible but also *mansus* (divinely designated to be leaders of the *ummah*). Therefore, reasoned Tonki, the Shias in effect regard their Imams as post-Muhammadan prophets. He explicitly

---

12. Mani, *Human Rights Monitor 2005*, 38-52.

13. For documentation concerning the arrest of Ahmadis for using the phrase *al-salam 'alaykum*, see Mani, *Human Rights Monitor 2005*, 45.

equated the Shias with the Ahmadis in their alleged disregard for the finality of Muhammad's prophethood; therefore, like the Ahmadis, the Shias, too, should be labeled non-Muslim. Another fatwa, this one issued by Jamia Ashrafia, a Deobandi madrasa in Lahore, declared Shias to be *kafirs*, arguing that Shia theology accords the first Imam, Ali, a rank equal to that of Muhammad.[14]

In December 2005 I visited the Jamia Ashrafia and interviewed Hafez As'ad Ubaid, a deputy administrator at the seminary who was also running for local political office in the city of Lahore. He boasted of the Ashrafia's size and importance (9,000 students, he said; biggest madrasa in the country) while denying his school's Deobandi curriculum espoused any kind of violence. With a politician's adroitness he distanced himself from the now-outlawed SSP but then disingenuously added that all Muslims should be able to consider themselves *sipah-e sahaba*, "since we should all think of ourselves as 'Soldiers of the Companions,' ready to uphold the honor of Muhammad and his *Sahaba*." He added that just because a Muslim loved Muhammad and his *Sahaba* didn't mean he belonged to the SSP. He topped all this off by adding he was glad to consider Sunnis and Shias alike to be Muslim.

Diplomatic double-talk, was the consensus among the friends who accompanied me after we left the madrasa. Nice of him to admit Shias are Muslim, laughed a Shia to whom I repeated the conversation. "But of course Ubaid is careful what he says. He and his family are into politics and are always aware they may need Shia votes in the next election."

"We Will Make a Pile of Corpses": Links Between Pakistani Militant Groups and the Taliban

During the 1990s, SSP leader Muhammad A'zam Tariq helped align his group with a pro-Taliban stance. This is not surprising, given the common Deobandi and anti-Shia ideological roots of both the Taliban and the SSP. According to journalist Ahmed Rashid, "Thousands of SSP members have fought alongside the Taliban," and SSP militants participated in the massacre of Iranian Shia diplomats in the Afghan city of Mazar-e Sharif in 1998.[15]

In 2001, less than three weeks after the September 11 terrorist attacks, the SSP's leader drew crowds in Pakistan by threatening vengeance against the U.S. if it dared to invade Taliban-controlled Afghanistan.

14. Khaled Ahmed, "Pakistani Madrassas and Apostatisation of the Shia," *Friday Times* (Lahore), December 16, 2005.

15. Rashid, *Taliban*, 74, 92.

"For the third Friday in a row," news sources reported on September 29, 2001, "pro-Taliban clerics in mosques across Pakistan orated against any U.S. attack on Afghanistan. At Islamabad's Red Mosque, about 3,000 people heard the leader of the Sipah-e-Sahaba Pakistan party, Azam [*sic*] Tariq, warn of suicide bombings in the city if Pakistan helped the U.S. go after bin Laden. 'If Americans attack Afghanistan, we will make a pile of corpses of the Americans by tying bombs to our bodies,' he warned."[16]

Immediately after the U.S.-led bombing campaign began on October 7, both the SSP and its ideological mentor the JUI became involved in further protest rallies. According to the London-based newspaper *The Guardian*,

> Maulana Atta-ur Rehman, the newly appointed leader of Jamiat Ulema-e Islam (JUI), one of the country's most extreme religious groups, told hundreds of supporters in Peshawar that it was their duty as Muslims to turn against the government. "We will have an open war against Jews, Christians, Israel, America, everyone," he shouted to the cheering crowd... "We condemn General Musharraf for supporting the Americans."

Police in Pakistan placed Maulana Fazlur Rehman, co-chief of the JUI, and SSP leader A'zam Tariq under house arrest. Both the SSP and its affiliate Lashkar-e Jhangvi were included in the government's ban on militant sectarian organizations in 2002.[17]

I mentioned above the network of madrasas run by the Deobandi-oriented JUI. Ahmed Rashid says of these schools and their instructors that "Saudi funds and scholarships brought them closer to ultraconservative Wahhabism." An analogous development is worth noting. In the 1990s Iran was reported to have provided funding and support for Shia groups such as TNFJ/TJP. Thus, as scholar Anwar Syed remarked in a study published in 2001, "Many Pakistani observers interpret the Shia–Sunni conflict as a 'proxy war' between the Saudi and Iranian governments waged on their [Pakistan's] soil." In recent years, however, the Islamic Republic of Iran—as we will see in a subsequent discussion—has sought to increase its influence among Sunnis worldwide by capitalizing on political conflicts where it feels Sunnis and Shias can unite in fighting common non-Muslim adversaries that may be labeled enemies of Islam.[18]

16. Mark McDonald and Juan Tamayo, "Taliban Unmoved by Pakistan Delegation," *San Jose Mercury News*, September 29, 2001.

17. Rory McCarthy, "Attack on Afghanistan: Hardline Clerics Call for National Revolt," *The Guardian* (London), October 10, 2001.

18. Ahmed Rashid, "The Taliban: Exporting Extremism," *Foreign Affairs* 78.6 (1999): 26; Syed, "The Sunni–Shia Conflict in Pakistan," 256.

Ritual Performance and Communal Identity: Muharram Observances and Sectarian Controversies in Lahore and Peshawar

My starting point for understanding Shia–Sunni relations in Pakistan was the city of Lahore, where I began studying Shia rituals during the Muharram season of March 2002. When I arrived, Shias and Sunnis alike were still discussing the ban imposed by President Musharraf in January 2002 on various sectarian groups, including A'zam Tariq's Sunni SSP and Allama Naqvi's Shia TJP.

Another development relevant to sectarian politics occurred several months later with the formation of the Muttahida Majlis-e Amal (also known as the MMA: "the United Action Forum"). A coalition of a half-dozen ideologically variegated religious parties, the MMA includes Deobandis, Barelvis, and Wahhabi sympathizers. They share in common opposition to Musharraf's policies. Despite the reputed anti-Shia bias of at least some of the MMA membership, Allama Naqvi decided to join this alliance. In the process Naqvi's own organization underwent a name change (the latest in a series of nomenclature shifts): his group became the Tehrik-e Islami Pakistan, "the Pakistan Islamic Movement." This denominationally flavorless label is apparently calculated to minimize sectarian friction within the MMA.

In October 2002 the MMA won elections in the NWFP and Baluchistan and began implementing aspects of Islamic law in both provinces. Lahore and the Punjab, however, escaped MMA domination. Lahori Shias I interviewed claimed that their city's freedom from the MMA's control makes it easier to celebrate Muharram without interference from Islamist politicians.

As in Shia communities throughout the world, Muharram in Lahore is characterized by the holding of *majalis*—lamentation gatherings in which *zakirs* (preachers) recall the suffering of Husain and the other Karbala martyrs. The *majalis* typically are held in the interior of *imambargahs* (Shia shrines) or in the courtyards of private homes. In Lahore nowadays each *majlis* tends to draw a congregation that is largely Shia. Of more universal appeal is a ritual that dominates many of the city's streets for several days during Muharram: the Zuljenah *jalus* or "Horse of Karbala" procession. As noted earlier, this is a public observance in which a riderless stallion is caparisoned to represent Zuljenah, the horse that carried Husain into battle at Karbala. Each stallion used in these processions is known as *shabih-e Zuljenah* ("the likeness of Zuljenah") and becomes a focus of popular devotion as it is led through the streets.

The greatest concentration of public Muharram observances in Lahore can be found in neighborhoods with substantial Shia populations, especially Islampura (also called Krishannagar) and parts of the Anderun Shahr (the walled "inner city" in the heart of Lahore, where numerous monuments date back to the Moghul era), particularly Mochi Darvaza and Heera Mandi. I found the densest clustering of Shia shrines in the Old City neighborhood of Mochi Darvaza. Here is located one of Lahore's best-known *imambargahs*, Nisar Haveli. This is the starting point for the city's most famous Muharram observance: the *bara Zuljenah jalus* ("the great Zuljenah procession"). This *jalus* lasts nearly twenty-four hours, from ten o'clock at night on the eve of Ashura until well after sunset the following day. It begins at Nisar Haveli and concludes at Karbala Gamay Shah, an important Shia devotional center located on the Lower Mall not far from the shrine of Data Ganj Bakhsh. Involving thousands of participants and onlookers, this procession traverses much of the Old City and nearby neighborhoods, halting along the way for prayers and lamentation rituals at dozens of Shia shrines.

Among the primary organizers of the Nisar Haveli-Karbala Gamay Shah procession is a prominent Lahori Shia family known as the Qizilbash. This family owns a half-dozen stallions that it makes available to local Shia communities for Zuljenah processions throughout the city. The horses are stabled at what is called the "Nawab Qizilbash palace" on Empress Road. In December 2002 I met Shia community leader Agha Reza Ali Qizilbash, who told me that his family obtains their stallions from the Pakistani army horse depot in Sargodha. His great-grandfather, he told me, established a *waqf* (charitable endowment) to cover the costs of stabling the animals as well as funding processions, *majalis*, and other Muharram activities.

Agha Qizilbash outlined for me his family history. Originally from Azerbaijan, the Qizilbash clan served the Safavid shahs of Iran as soldiers. A branch of the Qizilbash has been resident in Lahore since the 1800s. For over 150 years, Agha Qizilbash told me, his family has been sponsoring Zuljenah processions in Lahore. From Lahore, he asserted, the practice of holding Zuljenah parades spread all over India. He also pointed out that the Nisar Haveli *imambargah* that is so important for the Ashura *jalus* is the property of the Qizilbash family.

But the *bara jalus* sponsored by the Qizilbash clan is by no means the only such procession held in Lahore. The fifth to the tenth of Muharram is a time when dozens of Horse of Karbala processions take place throughout the city. The next biggest procession after the Nisar Haveli Ashura *jalus* is the Zuljenah parade held in Islampura that lasts throughout the day on the ninth of Muharram, drawing thousands of mourners and onlookers.

More typical, however, are the dozens of smaller-scale Zuljenah processions that are limited to individual neighborhoods throughout Lahore. Many such marches, each lasting only two or three hours, are held during the period from the fifth of Muharram to Ashura. To give an idea of the popularity of these neighborhood-based parades: in the course of a single afternoon, on the eighth of Muharram (March 23, 2002), I witnessed in quick succession four different Horse of Karbala processions, in Anarkali Bazaar, in the Heera Mandi quarter of the Walled City, in Islampura, and finally in the courtyard of the shrine of Gulistan-e Zehra.

In Lahore as in other South Asian cities, the Horse of Karbala processions are frequently linked with rituals involving petitionary prayer. The practice is illustrated in a Zuljenah *jalus* I witnessed on the eighth of Muharram, 2002, in the Heera Mandi quarter of the Walled City (Heera Mandi, the "Diamond Market," is a good place for watching Muharram rituals, in part because many of the *tava'if*—prostitutes—who populate this neighborhood are Shias. These women are lavish Muharram sponsors, I was told, and they pay for spectacular lamentation performances at this time of year as a way of demonstrating their piety).

On this particular afternoon I watched as a group of young men dressed in black tunics led a riderless stallion through the narrow streets. Outfitted splendidly, it wore a saddlecloth of black velvet threaded with gold brocade. From the saddle's pommel had been slung a sword and shield representing the weapons once wielded by the Imam Husain. Atop the saddle was fixed a gold *chhatri* (an ornamental parasol used to honor royalty—a custom borrowed from Hindu India). The animal's mane and ears had been carefully hennaed; from its bridle dangled silver pendants.

Activity swirled about the horse as the procession advanced. In front marched boys who sang *nauhajat* (Muharram lamentation poems), reciting the words from mimeographed sheets in their hands. A man passed out copies of the *nauha*-text to the crowd. Bystanders joined the marchers in *hath ka matam* (the most common type of Muharram lamentation gesture: rhythmic chest-beating with the palm of the hand, performed in time to the *nauha*-chant). Vendors kept pace with the horse, selling garlands of red carnations. Buyers draped the garlands over the saddle and *chhatri* and then pressed their hands to the horse's muzzle, its neck, flank, whatever part of its body they could reach in the throng. "*Savab ke lie*," came the explanation when I asked about this: to earn religious merit. Parents with young children in their arms stepped forward and offered ten-rupee notes to one of the *mujavirs* (custodians accompanying the horse). The *mujavirs* then halted Zuljenah while one child after another was passed beneath the horse's belly. "For the sake of the children's health and wellbeing," I was told.[19]

What I witnessed that afternoon seems to be one of the most typical forms of Muharram devotion in Lahore: a neighborhood procession. "Lahore is a city of shrines and pilgrimage places," as one resident told me. "That's why the Deobandis and other *tablighi* types don't have so much success here." (He was referring to puritan missionary-reformers who want to "purify" Islam of any practices that smack of paganism.) And Lahore in fact is crammed with shrines honoring assorted miracle-workers, holy women, Sufi saints, and martyred Imams. People go to such places to pray for intercession, healing, and blessing. The Zuljenah *jalus* is so popular because during Muharram a "likeness" (*shabih*) of the sacred goes out among the people. The shrine becomes mobile, transportable, accessible for every neighborhood and street corner. Wellbeing and the opportunity to earn religious merit come within the reach of all.

A neighborhood Zuljenah *jalus* is frequently sponsored by a local *matami guruh* ("lamentation association"). These are associations typically involving Shias who organize rituals in honor of the Karbala martyrs during Muharram. The Heera Mandi *jalus* described above was sponsored by a *matami guruh* called Anjuman-e Safinat Ahl al-Bayt ("the Association of the Ark of the Prophet's Household"). The procession's organizer, a man named Shahid Jafri, told me that this *anjuman* is headquartered in the Walled City neighborhood of Sayyid Mitha Bazaar, near the Lahori Gate. Sayyid Mitha had been the starting point for the afternoon's *jalus*, which traversed several neighborhoods within the Walled City.

Lahore has dozens of *matami guruhs*. Many of them draw their membership from the immediate locality in which they are based, and they confine their rituals to their own neighborhoods. The membership of other *matam* groups is determined by ethnicity or place of origin. I heard of a *guruh* whose members trace their ethnic origin to Iran; the members of other groups come from families that originate in specific parts of the Punjab.

While in Lahore I met several members of the Anjuman-e Imamia Lucknavi. This group's headquarters is in the "Mecca Colony" neighborhood of the city's Gulbarg district, but its members reside in various parts of Lahore. The men belonging to the Anjuman-e Imamia have in

---

19. For similar Zuljenah rituals in Ladakh (Jammu and Kashmir), see Pinault, *Horse of Karbala*, 109-80.

common a background as *muhajirs*: their families emigrated to Pakistan from the Indian city of Lucknow.

A member of this Lucknavi association, Nasir Husain Zaydi, took me to numerous Muharram observances in Lahore. On the eighth of Muharram, 2002, we attended a *majlis* followed by a Zuljenah procession at one of Lahore's largest Shia shrines, Gulistan-e Zehra. I estimated that there were over a thousand persons in attendance that night. Nasir's *anjuman* was present (seventy men, he said, nearly the whole membership), and they helped lead the crowd in *hath ka matam*. For Nasir, as for many Lucknavi *anjuman* members, this was very much a family affair. He performed *matam* in the company of his father and his ten-year-old son. (Public activities in such *matami guruhs*, as was the case with comparable groups I studied in Indian locales such as Hyderabad and Ladakh, are largely male occupations.)

Many Shias perform *matam* regardless of whether they belong formally to a *matam* group or not. What distinguishes the *matami guruhs* is their degree of organization and planning. Typically they arrange for several dozen members (or more) to lead a congregation in performing *matam* in unison. Sometimes they also provide a *nauha-khan* whose chant sets the cadence for the rhythmic chest-pounding of communal *hath ka matam*.

More controversial is a ritual practiced by many *matami guruhs* on the ninth and tenth of Muharram (the foremost holy days of the season): *zanjir zani* (also called *zanjiri matam*)—self-flagellation involving the use of cutting implements. Lahore's Zuljenah processions on the ninth and tenth of Muharram are occasions when hundreds of men will follow the lead of the *matami guruhs* in performing *zanjir zani*.

Elsewhere I have documented the justification for *zanjiri matam* offered by Shia mourners in India: the desire to honor the Karbala martyrs and demonstrate love for the Prophet's family; the hope of earning *shafa'ah* (intercession and forgiveness of sins in Paradise) by sharing vicariously in the martyrs' sufferings; and a sense of pride in being recognized publicly and communally as Shias.[20] In Lahore I encountered similar justifications.

And as in India, many Lahori Shias told me they were aware of a fatwa issued in 1994 by the "supreme spiritual guide" of the Islamic Republic of Iran, the Ayatollah Ali Khamenei. In this decree Khamenei declared "unlawful and forbidden" any act of *matam* performed in public involving the use of weapons to shed one's blood. The primary rationale offered by Khamenei in forbidding this practice was the harm that might

20. Pinault, *The Shiites*, 99-108.

befall the image of Shia Islam if outsiders saw Muharram mourners scourging themselves. "Propagandists of the Satan of Imperialism," claimed Khamenei, might point to bloody *matam* in order to "present both Islam and Shiism as an institution of superstition."[21]

Unstated by Khamenei in this decree is another concern: a desire on the part of Iran's leadership, dating back to the time of Ruhollah Khomeini, to achieve tactical alliances where possible with Sunni-oriented revolutionary groups in the Arab Middle East and elsewhere in the Islamic world. As noted above, this Khomeinist political orientation (which Khamenei has also pursued) is reflected in a theological policy of *taqrib*: minimizing doctrinal and ritual differences between the Sunni and Shia forms of Islam. Given the fact that the bloodier forms of *matam* have been a source of offense to Sunni polemicists for generations, it is not surprising that Khamenei and other members of Iran's clerical hierarchy have tried to discourage such practices by declaring their public performance "unlawful and forbidden."[22]

Khamenei's 1994 fatwa is certainly known to many Pakistani Shias today. Officers of the Anjuman-e Imamia Lucknavi and other Lahori *matami guruhs* took the initiative in mentioning the fatwa to me when I asked them whether self-flagellation was controversial in their nation. Local newspapers, they said, had covered the topic extensively when Khamenei first issued his decree. Not that this Iranian fatwa had had much effect in Pakistan, one Anjuman-e Imamia officer said to me: *zanjir zani* is as popular as ever in Lahore.

In my conversations with Pakistani Shias, not only in Lahore, but also in Peshawar and Islamabad, I detected considerable ambivalence concerning the implications of this fatwa emanating from the Islamic Republic of Iran. On the one hand, many Shias in Pakistan admire Iran and consider it the leader of the Shia community worldwide. I met a few Shias in Lahore who had made a pilgrimage to Iran to visit the tombs of the Imams at cities such as Mashhad. They were proud of their accomplishment. Several Shia *maulvis* (mullahs) I met in Lahore and Peshawar (especially those clerics who seemed influenced by Khomeinist ideology) claimed that numerous Pakistanis acknowledge Khamenei as their *marja'* (authoritative spiritual guide). They added that Pakistan's most prominent Shia leader, Allama Sajid Ali Naqvi, president of the TJP, is considered Khamenei's representative in Pakistan.

21. Seyyed 'Ali Khamenei, *'Ashura: bayyanat-e rehbar-e mu'azzam-e inqilab-e islami* (Qom: Daftar-e tablighat-e islami, 1994), 21-22.

22. Emmanuel Sivan, "Sunni Radicalism in the Middle East and the Iranian Revolution," *International Journal of Middle East Studies* 21 (1989): 1-30.

On the other hand, vague admiration for Iran as the leader of the world community of Shiism doesn't seem to translate into compliance with fatwas when it comes to on-the-ground realities in cities like Lahore. Part of the reason for this has to do with what scholar Nikki Keddie calls "Pakistan's virtual lack of the organized clerical structure which has been so important in modern Iranian Shi'ism."[23] Of the Shias I interviewed in 2002, many—especially the less-educated—seemed altogether unfamiliar even with the concept of the *marja'*.

This impression was confirmed in an interview I had in December 2002 with Khaled Ahmed, associate editor of Lahore's *Friday Times*. Khamenei, he asserted, doesn't wield much influence as a *marja'* among ordinary Shias in Pakistan. "Pakistani Shias tend to identify with individual favorite *zakirs* [preachers] in their home neighborhoods," he said, "rather than with a big leader such as Sajid Naqvi or Khamenei."

But there are other and even more compelling reasons why Khamenei's fatwa has found little acceptance in Pakistan. One reason was presented to me by Seyyed Muhammad Abbas, a senior vice president at a bank in Karachi. We met in March 2002 when I visited the Imambargah-e Gulistan-e Zehra in Lahore. He is one of the custodians there. Annually he takes time off from his bank job in Karachi to help with the rituals at Gulistan-e Zehra. Having heard of the intensity with which *zanjir zani* is performed at his shrine, I asked Seyyed Abbas about Khamenei's 1994 fatwa. He certainly knew about the decree but asserted that it hadn't discouraged traditional practice at Gulistan-e Zehra. "All's fair in love and war," he smiled, "and this [*zanjir zani*] is a matter of love. So people will continue to disregard the fatwa."

"This is a matter of love." With these words my informant echoed the opinion of numerous Shias I had interviewed in both Pakistan and India. They used similar language to justify Muharram flagellation. For them the bloodier forms of *matam* are a way of expressing their love for the Imam Husain and the other members of *Ahl al-Bayt* (the Prophet's family).

The issue resurfaced for me several months later, in December 2002, when I was invited to a reception at the University of Peshawar after my not-so-successful lecture on Shia–Sunni reconciliation. One corner of the reception was dominated by a dozen faculty members of the Shaykh Zayed Islamic Studies Center that I mentioned at the beginning of this chapter. As I noted earlier, the Zayed Center professors I met were Sunnis who openly voiced an anti-Shia bias.

23. Nikki R. Keddie, "Shi'ism and Change: Secularism and Myth," in L. Clarke, ed., *Shi'ite Heritage: Essays on Classical and Modern Traditions* (Binghamton, NY: Global Publications, 2001), 400.

Knowing of my interest in Muharram rituals, Qibla Ayaz (the Zayed Center's chairman) introduced me to a Shia who was talking in a very friendly way with several members of the center's faculty. This man, Seyyed Abd al-Husain Ra'is al-Sadat, is director of the Iranian Cultural Center in Peshawar. The conversation that followed showed me that Mr. Ra'is al-Sadat shares a certain amount of ideological ground with the *tabligh*-minded Sunnis of the Islamic Studies Center.

I discovered this because shortly after our introduction another man approached me, someone I'll call Dr. Akhtar. He is a Shia and a professor in the history department at the University of Peshawar. When Dr. Akhtar joined our conversation, several of the Zayed Center faculty were complaining about what they called the "ignorance" of Pakistan's Shia population. These "ignorant Shias," they said, persist in cutting themselves even though they've received a fatwa forbidding the practice from Khamenei, their own leader.

At this point Dr. Akhtar spoke up. He cited a precedent for *matam* from the life of the prophet Muhammad involving the battle of Uhud (AD 625), where the Prophet had been struck in the mouth by a rock and lost one of his teeth. One of the Prophet's followers was so overcome with sympathy when he saw this happen that he stooped and seized a stone and struck himself in the mouth so as to feel the Prophet's suffering. The Prophet had not condemned this man's action, implying that self-inflicted sympathetic pain is permissible. "It's a question of emotion," argued Dr. Akhtar. "Shias are overcome with emotion when they do *zanjiri matam*. The intensity of their feeling for Ahl al-Bayt earns them *savab* [religious merit] when they do this."

Courageous, I thought, to speak up like this before such a crowd. The Zayed Center professors all turned to Ra'is al-Sadat, obviously eager to hear what the Iranian Cultural Center's director would say in response to a fellow Shia. I guessed that he would side with the *tabligh*-crowd for the sake of furthering Khomeinist *taqrib*. I was right.

"Unfortunately," he began, "most Shias in this country lack education. That is why they disobey the instructions of Seyyed Khamenei." The Iranian Cultural Center's director went on to justify the 1994 fatwa by pointing out that all the *mazhabs* (denominations) of Islam, whether Sunni, Shia, etc., agree in forbidding any action that would cause harm to one's own body. "Except," he concluded, "for actions whereby one dies in a martyrdom operation while killing *kuffar* [unbelievers]."

When I returned to Lahore the following week I summarized this exchange during a conversation with Shia community leaders. One of them (a wealthy businessman who is most definitely not a member of any clerical hierarchy) reacted with considerable irritation. "Iranians.

They act as if the Quran had been revealed to them instead of to the Arabs. They have no business telling us what to do."

I found evidence of this disagreement within the Shia community on a number of occasions. During my trip to Peshawar in December 2002 I visited the Shahid 'Arif al-Husaini Madrasa, which is located in a part of Peshawar called Faisal Colony. The madrasa is named in honor of the Pakistani mullah who aligned his country's Shia TNFJ/TJP party with the pan-Islamic goals of Khomeini's revolution-for-export and the foreign policy of the Iranian Islamic Republic. Husaini was murdered by Sunni militants in 1988 (hence the title *shahid*, "martyr," in the Peshawar madrasa's name).[24]

The school's ideological orientation is apparent as one approaches. Its entrance archway presents flanking eight-foot-high wall portraits of Khomeini and the martyred Husaini, together with an Urdu translation of a statement attributed to Khomeini to the effect that he was stricken with grief when he heard of Husaini's murder.

After Husaini's death, leadership of the TJP passed to Allama Sajid Ali Naqvi. But it was not Naqvi that I was seeking out on this visit. The director of Peshawar's 'Arif al-Husaini academy is Allama Javad Hadi, a Pakistani cleric whom many individuals described to me as Naqvi's chief rival. This was a subject, however, that Allama Hadi seemed unwilling to discuss. Concerning Naqvi he said only that the two of them had once been in the TJP but that they had gone their separate ways in1997.

But Allama Hadi proved more than willing to enlighten me concerning *matam*. Escorting me to this meeting was a Shia I'd brought with me from Lahore. This young man was a *matami guruh* member and an enthusiastic practitioner of *zanjir zani* (he'd spoken with pride of the scars on his back, the product of self-scourging). I'll call this young man Rizvi. Rizvi introduced me to Allama Hadi by describing me as a scholar who was researching forms of Muharram mourning, including *zanjiri matam*.

This got Hadi's attention at once. With occasional assisting comments from the other madrasa faculty members who were present in the academy's guest-room, the director spent over an hour correcting what he feared were the erroneous impressions I'd accumulated concerning Muharram lamentation.

Muharram is simple, he argued. It has two purposes: to remember the Imam Husain, and to protest injustice. But over the centuries since the battle of Karbala, various people, to suit their own personal inclinations, have introduced innovations (*bid'a*) to the simple act of remembrance.

24. Haydar, "The Politicization of the Shias," 75-81.

These include *tazias* (cenotaphs of the Karbala martyrs that are carried in parades), Zuljenah processions, and so forth. Among the most extreme of these innovations, he said, is *zanjir zani*.

Shia mazhab 'aql ka mazhab aur mantiq ka mazhab hay: "The Shia denomination," he announced, "is the denomination of reason, of logic." People who are reasonable and educated, he said, will perform a simple, gentle *hath ka matam* while remembering Husain. "This," he explained, "is the only type of *matam* we do here during Muharram *majalis* at our madrasa." Only those who are uneducated, he added, get carried away and do *zanjir zani*.

At this point I asked Allama Hadi about the Shia doctrine of *shafa'ah* (intercession by the Imam Husain in exchange for *matam*). He replied forcefully that this is a part of the tradition that needs clarification. "If one does all five Pillars and fulfills all religious obligations and then in addition does the permissible form of *matam*, then one's *'azadari* [Muharram mourning] is *mustahabb* [meritorious, although not required by Islamic law] and one gains forgiveness of minor sins." He went on to emphasize that *'azadari* cannot gain one forgiveness of serious sin, nor does it excuse one from the five Pillars incumbent on all Muslims.

Up to this point my friend Rizvi had been listening quietly. But then he responded, and none too deferentially. "*Matam farz hay*": *matam* is a duty, he said. It is not simply *mustahabb* but rather an essential part of Shiism. If one wants to, he added, one can do simple *hath ka matam*. But whether one chooses *hath ka matam* or *zanjir zani*, both are genuine parts of Shiism. These things aren't optional, he insisted, and they're certainly not *bid'a*. They are a duty. He said all this so quickly and spoke with such emotion that I had trouble following his Urdu. Afterwards in our car I made him retrace his argument, which he was only too glad to do.

Allama Hadi and the other mullahs stared at him in silence as if hoping he would stop. But Rizvi wasn't done yet.

"*Rozah* [Ramadan fasting], *namaz* [prayer], hajj: all Muslims do these things," he continued. "Even the Wahhabis do these things. But without *matam*, *zanjir zani*, Zuljenah, the *tazias*, there'd be nothing left of Shiism. There'd be nothing to mark us as different from the Sunnis. There'd be nothing left of Shiism," he repeated. "We'd be left with only one *mazhab*."

Silence for an embarrassing moment, and then Allama Hadi turned to me blandly with some observation about Islamic doctrine as if my friend had never spoken. But the tension in the room lingered—a demonstration of the importance that Pakistani Shias assign to questions of Muharram ritual.

Stereotyped Notions of Shiism among Pakistani Sunnis

Everywhere I went in Pakistan, the Sunni Muslims I met were eager to hear what I was learning about Shia practices. In Peshawar and Islamabad I gave lectures on Muharram rituals and Sunni–Shia relations. In both cities the audience (to judge from their comments and questions) was made up largely of Sunnis. These lectures—and the dozens of conversations I had subsequently with individuals, in Peshawar, Islamabad, and Lahore—taught me several things.

First, many Sunnis are fascinated (even if they're also repelled) by Shia practices. This seemed to be true for both the Deobandi and Barelvi Sunnis I met (Deobandism, reformist in its ideology, condemns saint worship and other practices regarded as contaminations from Hinduism; the Barelvi denomination has a history of greater tolerance for Sufi-influenced rituals and other forms of South Asian folk Islam). Second, most of the Sunnis I interviewed were ignorant about Shiism and had little understanding of Shia doctrine and ritual. Third, these individuals displayed considerable antipathy and prejudice against the Shia form of Islam.

But many of these same Sunnis (in Lahore much more than in Peshawar) emphasized that they got along just fine with individual Shias, worked alongside Shias, and even had friends (or at least friendly acquaintances) who were Shias. "But the way I keep my friendship with Shia colleagues," explained one Lahori Sunni, "is that I avoid asking them questions about controversial issues."

I asked him for an example of a controversial issue. "If I say to my Shia colleagues, 'Why do you do this *zanjir zani*?,' I'm afraid they might get angry with me. It might mean the end of our dealings with each other." My informant then added that this was why he was so glad to be able to ask me about my Muharram research. "I can ask you questions I wouldn't dare ask my Shia colleagues. You're a foreigner; you're not Sunni or Shia. They won't get angry with you."

During my time in Pakistan from 2002 to 2005, I collected Sunni notions concerning Shia doctrine and practice. Of the sectarian stereotypes I encountered, the following six are among the most common:

First: Even if in public Shias behave well in their dealings with Sunnis, in private they curse (a practice called *tabarra*, as noted above) the caliphs Abu Bakr, Umar, and Uthman.

Second: Shias even today regard Sunnis as usurpers (this point is linked to the preceding).

Third: Shias want to dominate the whole world and impose their own *mazhab* on the Sunni majority. (When I probed further I found that my Sunni informants based this notion on their impressions of Khomeinist internationalism and Iran's attempts to influence Shia communities in Pakistan and elsewhere.)

Fourth: Shias believe, so several of my Lahori Sunni informants insisted, that Caliph Umar's manuscript of the Quran (which was subsequently copied and transmitted to Sunnis) is incomplete. Ten of its original forty *siparahs* (sections) were eaten up by a goat. This is why the Sunni version of the Quran has "only" thirty *siparahs* today. But the Quran manuscript given by the prophet Muhammad to Ali remains intact, so this fable goes, and thus Shias own the only Quran-version that is complete. (My Sunni informants were surprised when I told them that Shias nowadays claim they, too, recognize the same thirty *siparahs* and exactly the same Quran text as do Sunnis. I pointed out that Shia beliefs in the existence of divergent and incomplete Quran texts were characteristic of sects that had been rejected centuries ago as being guilty of *ghuluww*—doctrinal extremism—by mainstream Shia authorities.[25])

Worth noting in this context, however, is the persistence of a controversial account concerning Ayesha (Muhammad's youngest and favorite wife, a woman loathed by Shias for her hostility to Ali). According to this account, Ayesha left under her bed a scroll containing verses of the Quran. At the time of Muhammad's death, while Ayesha was outside overseeing his funeral, a goat wandered into her house and ate up the scroll. Arguments about this account circulate on the Internet. An anti-Shia posting on a Malaysian Islamic website mentions the story as an example of the heretical beliefs held by Shias and as proof of why Shias should be labeled *kafirs*.[26]

Fifth in the list of sectarian stereotypes: Shias engage in actions that render them *na-pak* (an Urdu translation of the Arabic word *najis*: "ritually impure"). In a December 2005 visit at the University of Peshawar's campus, Shia faculty members of the history department told me Sunnis in the NWFP learn their bigoted stereotypes from mullahs in the local mosques: "The *maulvis* tell their congregations: 'Don't eat with Shias. They spit in their food. Don't eat their meat. Shias don't do *halal dhibh* [butchering of animals in the ritually correct manner].'" One Shia historian told me what happened when a Shia student prayed on campus in a university-run Sunni mosque. "After the student left, the Sunnis

25. Moojan Momen, *An Introduction to Shii Islam* (New Haven: Yale University Press, 1985), 74-78, 172-73.

26. Haq Char Yar, "Is Shia Kafir? Decide Yourself," www.darulkautsar.com.

washed down the place where he'd prayed. That's because Shias are regarded as *na-pak*." Sunnis to whom I mentioned this issue, on the other hand, referred with very evident distaste to the Shia practice of self-flagellation. "Cutting themselves and calling that *'ibadat* [worship]: that's what makes Shias *najis*," was how one Sunni cleric put it. (And in fact, according to Islamic law, spurting blood normally invalidates one's prayer until one ritually purifies oneself.[27])

In the NWFP, Sunni notions of Shias as unclean go so far as to lead Sunnis occasionally to compare Shias' behavior with that of animals considered in Islamic law impure. An historian named Salman Bangash gave me an example. "I was chatting one day with colleagues. A Sunni who didn't know my background said, 'Beware of Shias. They'll attack you and bite you in the face like a dog. Just like a dog.' A friend who was there interrupted to say, 'Then you'd better watch out. Salman's a Shia.'" The bigoted Sunni, said Salman, simply couldn't believe that someone as well-mannered and soft-spoken and educated as he could be a Shia. "It didn't fit his picture."

Sixth among the sectarian stereotypes harbored by Sunnis: During Muharram Shias drink milk that has been blessed by having *shabih-e Zuljenah* ("the likeness of Zuljenah," the Horse of Karbala parade-stallion) take a few sips from it first.

A number of Sunnis described for me versions of this Zuljenah custom as practiced by Shias in Lahore. Various kinds of *tabarruk* (food distributed as a "blessing" during Muharram processions) are sampled by Zuljenah before being distributed to the crowds along the parade route. A Sunni woman living in Islampura told me that during one Muharram season she saw a Zuljenah horse being led to the house of her Shia neighbors. It advanced to the threshold of the open doorway, its mouth touched the bread laid before it, and then the family snatched the food away for themselves. In exchange for this blessing, she said, the family gave the horse's attendant a cash donation. Her evaluation: *jhuta khana khana thik nehin hay* ("It's not good to eat 'used'/ 'second-hand' food"). Witnessing this, she told me, confirmed her impression of Shias as ignorant and not as careful as they should be in matters of health and hygiene.

I brought up this topic with some of the Shias I knew best in the Anjuman-e Imamia Lucknavi. They confirmed that in fact the practice exists of having the *shabih-e Zuljenah* bless food by consuming a small portion of it. But they clearly were embarrassed when I mentioned this. "Only uneducated people do this," they said defensively.

---

27. Pinault, *Horse of Karbala*, 29-37.

But Pakistani Sunnis have their own Muharram customs involving food, especially with regard to the preparation of what is known as the *sabil*. This is a refreshment stand from which water, tea, etc. is offered to passers-by to commemorate the thirst suffered in the desert by the Karbala martyrs.

When I asked Sunnis in Lahore whether they did anything else to mark the occasion, I heard divergent opinions. Several young men said that on Ashura they watch the big Zuljenah procession *tamasha deikhne ke lie* ("in order to see the spectacle"), especially, they said, the spectacularly bloody *zanjir zani*. Other individuals told me they stayed away for fear of trouble. One woman said to me: "If they [the Shias] found out I'm Sunni, they might cause me problems."

Concerning Lahori Sunni participation in Muharram, the most controversial topic I raised had to do with the question of whether Sunnis perform *matam*. Shias I interviewed in Lahore emphasized that *matam* is primarily a Shia practice. One Shia with whom I spoke, however, said that he had heard of Sunnis occasionally doing *zanjiri matam* in order to fulfill religious vows in exchange for divine favors. "They'll do the *zanjir zani*," he said, "alongside the *matami guruhs*."

When I repeated this to my driver, a Sunni Pashtun from the NWFP, he was emphatic in denying that Sunnis ever do *matam*. As for vows, he said, when Sunnis in Lahore undertake any actions connected with such matters they simply go to Data Darbar (the shrine of the Sufi master Hujwiri, also known as Data Ganj Bakhsh). And the Data Darbar, he reminded me, is not a Shia place.

One of my Sunni informants, a woman from Islampura, told me that the only Sunnis she had ever heard of doing *matam* would be those who are paid to do so by Shia *jalus*-organizers. In her own neighborhood she had seen impoverished-looking Sunni men and boys bringing up the rear of Ashura processions, wearing black tunics and performing *hath ka matam*. But these are only gypsies (*khanah bi-dosh*), she said, and Shia organizers hire such participants merely to enlarge the size of the parade. During such processions, she added, gypsy women and girls work the crowds along the route, begging for rupees and collecting free *tabarruk*-food.

One of my Urdu tutors in Lahore told me that in Multan Sunnis perform *hath ka matam*. But he regarded this as exceptional. In general both the Shias and the Sunnis I encountered in Pakistan seemed to agree with the opinion voiced by the Muslims I met in India: *matam* is something that Shias do. The reason has to do with the fact that this ritual is useful for demarcating and preserving Shia identity as a distinctive minority community in relation to the Sunni majority.[28]

Professor Anees Ahmad of Islamabad's International Islamic University told me in a March 2002 interview that in his view the gap between Sunnis and Shias in Pakistan is widening. This is partly because of clerics who have come under "Salafi influence"—a reformist ideology linked to Saudi Wahhabism. Such Salafi-minded *maulvis*, Professor Ahmad said, have been telling their congregations that even looking at the Shias' *jalus* is *haram* (forbidden). Another informant in Islamabad told me he had heard of a local *maulvi* who was claiming that Sunnis should abandon old Ashura customs such as the *sabil* and preparing food for charity. To counter such polarization, Professor Ahmad told me, he has taken the students in his courses to visit the madrasas of various denominations—Deobandi, Barelvi, Ahl-e hadith, Shia. For most of his students, such visits are their first exposure to a sect other than their own. Unfortunately, he added, he is the only professor he knows of to offer such an experience.

"Despots and Caesars of the Pagan Past": Muharram Politics in the Urdu Press

Given the sectarian misunderstandings described above, and Sunni antipathy to various aspects of Shia belief and ritual, one might well wonder how Sunnis and Shias reacted to the ban on militant sectarian groups imposed by President Musharraf beginning in January 2002. In fact many Sunnis I met in Lahore voiced support for what they called the goals of the outlawed SSP, namely "guarding the honor" of the *Sahaba*. My informants expressed resentment at the Shia custom of *tabarra*. Nevertheless, among the Barelvi Sunnis and Shias I met, I found near-unanimity in their rejection of sectarian violence. Sunnis and Shias alike supported Musharraf's campaign against sectarian organizations.

Pakistan's newspapers, which enjoy considerable freedom of expression, reflected a range of political views in 2002 with regard to the commemoration of Karbala. Musharraf's Muharram speech characterized the season as a month of "dignity and respect." He combined an appeal for religious tolerance and national unity with the statement that "we should never become a source of suffering for human beings of any

---

28. For *matam* in Multan and Sunni participation in *matam*, see Richard K. Wolf, "Embodiment and Ambivalence: Emotion in South Asian Muharram Drumming," *Yearbook for Traditional Music* 32 (2000): 96.

race or religion." Many of the newspaper editorials discussing the 2002 Muharram season used the occasion to deplore the Sunni–Shia violence that occurs at this time of year. At the same time such essays voiced support for the government's ban on militant sectarian groups. The Lahore-based paper *Ruznama-ye Avaz* stated,

> This year, too, members of every denomination have honored Husain on Ashura… But unfortunately sectarian bigots from certain regions in our country have polluted the realm of religious harmony, and in some places during Ashura violence has occurred and troubling acts of terrorism have become manifest. All of this conflicts with reverence for Ashura, and right-minded Muslims of all denominations should feel distress in their hearts in response to these bloody events.

The editorial warns that sectarian discord is fomented in order to weaken the nation of Pakistan.[29]

This theme recurred in many editorials. The newspaper *Khabarain* complained, "Sectarian elements…commit acts of terror against the safety of our dear nation." An essay published by *Ruznama-ye Pakistan* criticized the tendency among many Pakistani ulema to inflict *takfir* (denunciation of someone as a *kafir*) on those who disagree with their own religious stance. The result: "the killing of Muslims by Muslims. This easily does the work of the enemies of the nation."

While walking about Lahore's Old City neighborhoods I saw an Urdu-language poster entitled "Muharram 1423/2002: An Appeal for Shia–Sunni Unity." It was displayed on a wall beside the Nisar Haveli shrine. "The best way to demonstrate one's belief in the unique sacrifice of Imam Husain," it announced, "is to preserve the realm of peace, affection, and love during the sacred month of Muharram." The text refers to the activities of *Pakistan ke dushman* ("Pakistan's enemies"): "Throughout the country they light the fire of discord, riots, and the bigotry of sectarianism."

Common to the texts cited above, which implicitly or explicitly support the government's policy on sectarianism, are the following three points. They avoid references to controversial and potentially divisive ritual practices; they argue for the universal values of sacrifice and generosity enshrined in Husain's death (points on which all Muslims can agree); and they emphasize national unity, while identifying sectarian militants as "enemies of Pakistan."

---

29. "President Calls for Promoting Tolerance," *Dawn* (Pakistan), March 16, 2002. The Muharram essay in *Ruznama-ye Avaz*, like those appearing in other Urdu-language newspapers cited further on in my article, appeared in the Ashura (March 25, 2002) issue.

Most of the newspaper articles and posters I saw endorsed such themes. There were, however, exceptions. Two essays published in the Ashura (March 25, 2002) edition of *Ruznama-ye Din* merit attention. The first is an opinion piece entitled *Shahadat 'uzma ka paigham* ("The Message of the Great Martyrdom"). It proclaims that "the real message of Ashura" is the need for the continual "revival of jihad" as embodied in Husain's resistance to the reign of the tyrant Yazid. This article claims that "Yazid was the first person who, in order to carry out the contemptible scheme of making people forsake jihad, increased within the Muslim government the showy monuments and the lifestyle of the despots and Caesars of the pagan past." Yazid is said to have "wanted to wrench the swords and lances from the hands of Muslims and instill in them a fondness for peacocks and music"—the latter items being symbolic of the frivolous pleasures of palatial self-indulgence. Yazid's purpose? To create "an abundance of the things of the good life, so as to make the Muslim community accustomed to bodily ease and thereby create 'harmless' Muslims." The anonymous author of this essay then updates his sketch of Yazid: "For centuries, governments and personalities responsible for despotic and imperialistic schemes have tried to estrange members of the Islamic world from any acquaintance with the spirit of jihad."

Without ever referring overtly to Pakistan, this article conveys profound hostility to the policies that Musharraf initiated after the September 11 terrorist attacks. The essay follows the longstanding tradition (once used to great effect in Iran under Shah Reza Pahlevi) of the politicized Muharram sermon, in which the preacher implicitly equates the reigning government of the day with that of the villainous Yazid. This essay goes further, offering a veiled critique of westernization ("lifestyle of the...Caesars"), a condemnation of materialism ("peacocks and music"), and, I would argue, an unspoken nostalgia for the puritan austerity of Afghanistan's Taliban regime.

This editorial concludes by reminding readers that "the desert plains of Karbala were watered not with the salty flow of tears but with the blood from noble veins." Here, it seems, is an oblique criticism of the most common form of Muharram ritual: weeping in honor of the Karbala martyrs. This article offers a very different interpretation of Muharram: the real commemoration of Husain's death involves engaging in jihad in the most physical and lethal sense.

The same issue of *Ruznama-ye Din* published an opinion piece by Allama Sajid Naqvi, the Shia cleric who heads the Tehrik-e Jafria Pakistan. The essay identified his affiliation as Qa'id-e Millet-e Jafria Pakistan, "Chief of the Shia Community of Pakistan." The latter title was one of the more recent designations for the TJP (the name-change was necessitated by the ban imposed on Naqvi's TJP as part of the government's January 2002 campaign against sectarian groups). Like the editorial described above, Naqvi's essay used the Karbala story to condemn Pakistan's present government. He was selective in his retelling of the tale, emphasizing not the martyrs' sufferings (a standard theme of Muharram sermons) but instead Husain's defiance of the tyrant. "Yazid's goal," we are told, "was to reintroduce the days of paganism in place of Islam." Naqvi then connected the past with the present. What the Karbala martyrs accomplished was to "cause the word '*Husainiyat*' [the principles of Husain's life and martyrdom] to be inscribed on the palace walls of each epoch's Yazid."

Although a religious authority and a prominent Shia cleric, Naqvi made no reference in this essay to Muharram rituals or controversial practices such as *zanjiri matam* or *tabarra*. Instead he emphasized *inqilab-e Husaini*, "Husain's revolution," a phrase popularized with the fall of the Shah and the establishing of the Islamic Republic of Iran. Naqvi remains consistently Khomeinist in his orientation, avoiding Shia–Sunni polemics and instead attempting to rally opposition to the present government of Pakistan wherever he can.

Conclusion:
Tactical Alliances with Traditional Enemies—
Shia Participation in the MMA

As mentioned above, Allama Naqvi's political party underwent various name-changes in 2002. The conspicuously Shia nomenclature of Tehrik-e Jafria and Millet-e Jafria gave way to the title Tehrik-e Islami. The non-denominational tone of the new name was apparently intended to reduce sectarian tensions after Naqvi joined the Muttahida Majlis-e Amal (MMA).

The MMA gained attention worldwide in October 2002 when it won provincial elections in Baluchistan and the NWFP. In December 2002 and January 2003 journalists based in Peshawar reported on the various decrees issued by the new MMA provincial government. These included a ban on cinema billboards that were regarded as purveyors of "obscenity," a "campaign to close down all 'pornographic' and unlicensed movie theaters," a ban on music in public transit vehicles, and a crackdown on "revellers" at celebrations involving alcohol and "female dancers." Press reports early in 2003 indicated that religious authorities in the Dir district of the NWFP, emboldened by the MMA's electoral success, had imposed *nizam-e salaat* (a "regime of prayer") in their region of the North-West Frontier. Under this new regulation, volunteers see to it that local businesses shut down for thirty minutes at the start of each *azan* or call to prayer. Observers have begun to speak of the "Talibanization" of those provinces of Pakistan now ruled by the MMA.[30]

The conservative religious parties comprising the MMA include the Jamiat-e Ulema-e Islam (JUI), many of whose members are Deobandis with longstanding pro-Taliban sympathies. Among the JUI's ideological offshoots, as noted above, is the now-outlawed Sunni SSP, which built a fearsome reputation for killing Shias in Pakistan and helping the Taliban kill Shias in Afghanistan.[31]

Nevertheless this history did not prevent Allama Naqvi, currently Pakistan's most prominent Shia leader, from joining the MMA. The alliance can be seen as tactical. Naqvi shares with other MMA leaders an orientation that opposes the administration of President Musharraf, especially in terms of cooperating with the foreign policy of the US. The MMA thus offers Naqvi a broader platform from which to pursue his Khomeinist internationalist anti-Americanism.

The MMA's success has generated a very mixed response within Pakistan. An article that appeared in the December 2002 issue of the Karachi-based *Herald* defended the religious alliance and praised the MMA's electoral victory as "an omen of good cheer" insofar as it had led to "the refurbished image of fundamentalism transformed into democratic moderation." And Qazi Hussain Ahmad, head of the Jamaat-e Islami (one of the most powerful parties constituting the MMA), in an interview shortly after the October 2002 victory, claimed that the MMA deserved a large share of the credit for diminishing "the menace of sectarianism" in recent months. He also noted with pride an event that was covered extensively by the Pakistani media: the coming together of MMA leaders to lead public prayer. "We have read our prayers *ba-jamaat* [all together] in Karachi, before everyone," he enthused, "all of us together, Shia and Sunni."[32]

Many of the Pakistanis I interviewed in December 2002, however, in Lahore, Islamabad, and Peshawar alike, were much more cynical. "Only

30. "Cinemas Reel As MMA Cracks the Whip," *Daily Times* (Lahore), December 20, 2002; Juliette Terzieff, "Pakistani Religious Bloc Exerts Pressure on Province," *San Francisco Chronicle*, January 14, 2003.

31. Rashid, *Taliban*, 74, 92.

32. Akbar Naqvi, "The Politics of Maslehat," *Herald* (Karachi) 33.12 (December 2002): 61-62; Sairah Irshad Khan, "Election Special," *Newsline* (Karachi) 14.5 (November 2002): 42.

a photo op" is how several informants responded to pictures of the MMA leaders together in prayer. Such pictures inspired considerable irreverence. "Look at the TV," one Sunni informant joked to me, "and see all those beards gathered together, and then you'll realize what MMA stands for: *Maulvis, Maulvis,* and More *Maulvis.*"

The Shias I interviewed concerning the MMA tended to focus on the event that affected them most directly: Allama Naqvi's alliance with the likes of the JUI. Among the various Shias I interviewed—*matami guruh* members and Shia community organizers in Lahore, professors and lecturers at the University of Peshawar—most registered their surprise and disappointment (and, in some cases, anger) at Naqvi's adherence to the MMA. One Lahori Shia I interviewed—a businessman and distinguished community leader—in reply to the topic of Naqvi and the MMA, proceeded to recount for me the history of anti-Shia violence in the Punjab. He told me of an incident in which SSP militants threw acid at a Zuljenah stallion. "Mughulpura locality, Lahore, 1986," he said grimly. "Be sure you write that down." He then showed me photos of Shia shrines in Lahore that had been destroyed in riots the same year. "Now you can understand," he concluded, "why so many Shias don't care for Allama Naqvi any more. He joined the MMA, joined forces with the Sunnis who have always hated us." A Hazara Shia in Peshawar responded to my question about Naqvi and the MMA by recalling Taliban violence against the Hazaras of Bamiyan. He recited with bitterness examples of SSP rhetoric: "Kill a Shia, go to Paradise."

Yet there is another side to this issue. Many of the same Shias who voiced annoyance with Naqvi conceded that his political maneuverings may have secured some gains for the Pakistani Shia community. Shia faculty members at the University of Peshawar identified for me three positive aspects of Naqvi's alliance with the MMA. First, if Naqvi hadn't joined, Shias in the NWFP would not have had the chance to be part of the political decision-making process in the wake of the MMA's electoral victory in the North-West Frontier (although one cynic immediately asserted that Naqvi's party is by far the weakest member of the MMA: "He's a junior member, that's all. So we don't have any real power in any case"). Second, the much-publicized Shia–Sunni alliance apparently contributed to a decrease in sectarian violence in 2002 (although my Shia informants also gave credit for this improvement to Musharraf's ban on sectarian extremist groups). And third, the pictures of Shia and Sunni leaders together at prayer have helped the status generally of the Shia community in Pakistan. In the words of one Shia informant at the University of Peshawar: "When the common people see Allama Naqvi doing *namaz* [prayer] with Fazlur Rehman [head of the JUI] and with other Deobandis and Ahl-e Hadith, then the ordinary people will find it more difficult to label Shias *kuffar*." In response to this comment, another Shia lecturer at the University of Peshawar stated, "We are struggling for our survival. The case of the Ahmadis is threatening us. We're always afraid that what the Sunnis did to them, the Sunnis might do to us." (As noted above, in 1974 legislation was passed in Pakistan stripping members of the Ahmadiyya sect of their status as Muslims.)

One of the Shia professors at the University of Peshawar summarized Shia responses in the NWFP to Allama Naqvi's alliance with the MMA: "We recognize its practical value. But we aren't happy with it."

When I returned to Peshawar in December 2005, the MMA still ruled the NWFP and Naqvi was still a member of this Islamist coalition. Shias I talked to then were more disillusioned with him than ever. They admired his political survival skills but considered him a headline-grabber and opportunist who'd done little to help local Shias. "The MMA keeps saying, 'Sunnis and Shias are brothers,'" complained a Shia lecturer in the University of Peshawar's history department, "but it does nothing to help us."

He gave me an example. On the university's campus, he said, there are over fifteen Sunni mosques but not one place of prayer for Shias. "We used to be allowed to pray on the lawn of a house belonging to a Shia professor here on campus," he said, "but we were barred from doing that any more." So in February 2005 a group of Shia students approached a senior provincial minister in the MMA government and asked him, in the name of Sunni–Shia harmony, for help in establishing a mosque on campus where Shias could pray. He refused.

The Shias went away feeling insulted. "The MMA minister implied we'd turn any mosque into an *imambargah* [Shia lamentation hall]," said my informant, "and do *matam* and create sectarian tensions and proselytize."

What would happen, I asked, if a Shia student simply walked into a Sunni mosque on campus and joined Sunnis for Friday prayers? "They'd see us with our hands at our sides," came the reply. (Sunnis fold their arms across their waists while Shias differ in letting their arms dangle by their sides at a certain moment in their ritual prayers.) "Or they'd see us using the *sajda-gah*." (This is a disk, said to be made of dust from Karbala, which many Shias place on the floor before them in prayer. Each time they do the prostration, their heads touch the *sajda-gah* as a mark of humility and devotion.) "They'd see these differences," he said, "and know we're Shia. If only one of us were there at a time, we'd feel very uncomfortable. If there were a number of us, the whole prayer service would be disrupted."

Did Naqvi, I asked, intervene in this issue to help the Shias?

"Naqvi?" frowned my informant. "He did nothing."

Many questions are still unanswered concerning the future of Sunni–Shia political alliances. It remains to be seen whether Allama Naqvi can find any real areas of cooperation with other MMA members beyond a generalized anti-Musharraf and anti-American rhetoric. Naqvi's position in the MMA and his subservience to Iran's Khomeinist program may be advantageous and attention-getting nationally and internationally. Less certain, however, is their appeal locally. Pakistani Shias have traditionally shown considerable independence in matters of *zanjiri matam* and other points of ritual. It seems likely that at the popular level, local Shia communities throughout Pakistan will continue to find ways to insist on both their distinctiveness and their separate identity, regardless of the alliances forged in their name by politicians who claim to be their leaders.

5

SPURTING BLOOD AND ATTEMPTS
TO REGULATE RITUAL:
PAKISTANI SHIAS AND IRAN'S BID FOR LEADERSHIP
OF GLOBAL ISLAM

Avoiding Slander and Dishonor:
A View from the Iranian Cultural Center
on Self-Flagellation Rituals

I had the opportunity to update my impression of Iran's dealings with
Pakistan's Shias in a visit to the Iranian Cultural Center in Lahore in
December 2005. I was accompanied on this visit by my friend Nasir
Zaydi, a devout Shia who's also an officer in Anjuman-e Lucknavi, a
matam-association that sponsors numerous public lamentation rituals
during Muharram.

From the street all one sees of the center is a high metal gate and a
blank concrete wall. Strangers wanting to visit have to plead for entrance
via an intercom voice box set in the wall by the gate. Not very inviting,
but an understandable precaution: in 1990 Iran's consul-general was
murdered in Lahore, and in January 1997 a mob of Sunni militants
attacked Lahore's Iranian Cultural Center, ransacking it and setting it on
fire. The militant group Sipah-e Sahaba was implicated in both acts of
violence.[1]

Once inside the gate we had to present ourselves at the security booth
—which also doubles as a bookstore. While Nasir worked on talking the
guards into letting us visit, I browsed the titles on display. Persian-
language dictionaries. A book entitled *Imam Khomeini and the Islamic*

---

1. U.S. Department of State, "Country Reports on Human Rights Practices 2001:
Pakistan," March 4, 2002 (www.fas.org/terrorism/at/docs/HR%20report/Pakistan.
htm); Regional Information Base on Terrorism, "Millat-e Islamia Pakistan
(Previously Known as Sipah-e Sahaba Pakistan)" (www.ribt.org); *The New York
Times*, "Angry at Attack, Pakistanis Set Iran Center Afire," January 20, 1997.

Revolution, beside a poster celebrating the centenary of Khomeini's birth. But there were also publications on more general topics. A book called *What Is Islam?* An English-language children's magazine published in Teheran by the "Islamic Thought Foundation," featuring articles such as "Hijab: Multicultural Voice for Muslim Women: We are More Precious Than Diamonds and Pearls," and "Ramadan: Starting Point for Becoming a Better Person." I also spotted another Teheran-published magazine, this one in Arabic, called *al-Wahdah* ("Unity"), offering essays denouncing Israel and presenting discussions of "American Sponsorship for Dominating the Islamic World." All in all, an interesting introduction to how the center packages its presentation of Iran and Islam to the Muslims of Lahore.

A twenty-minute wait, and then a guard escorted us to the center's main building, a structure separated from the gate by a wide lawn and a driveway at least a hundred yards long—obviously a precaution against car-bombs or the like that might be detonated on the street.

Another twenty-minute wait, this time in a waiting room featuring a TV that played a video of muppet-like puppets shrilling at each other in Farsi.

We were rescued from the muppets by a young bearded man named Zaheer ul-Hasan, a Pakistani employee at the center. With him was the center's director, an Iranian who never gave us his name and who spoke only in Persian and only to Zaheer. The latter translated his boss's comments into Urdu for our benefit.

The director wasn't friendly. I hadn't expected him to be. The translator shuttled between us with nervous smiles.

I asked the director his opinion about the legitimacy of the various forms of *matam* that are popular during Muharram among Pakistan's Shias. He had plenty to say about this.

Matam itself, he said through his interpreter, is permissible as a sign of grief for the Karbala Martyrs, but only as long as it's not taken to extremes. But the director presented a lengthy indictment of popular practices that are *haram* (forbidden). As each forbidden ritual was identified, Zaheer preceded the comment with the phrase *Irani ulema ke mutabiq aur Irani maulvion ke mutabiq* ("according to Iranian religious scholars and Iranian mullahs"). My friend Nasir frowned each time this phrase was pronounced and at various points looked ready to interrupt. But for the moment he kept silent.

The following practices, said the Iranian director, are forbidden: taking off one's shirt to do *matam*; *shamsheer zani* (gashing one's forehead with a knife); *zanjiri matam* (self-scourging with a flail to which are attached blades and chains); and, in general, cutting oneself so as to shed one's blood. Before we left, the director presented us with copies of an Urdu-language text that had been published in the Iranian city of Qom: *Istifta'at ke jawabat* ("Replies to Requests for Fatwas"), authored by Iran's supreme cleric, Seyyed Ali Khamenei. A brief English caption on the back cover described the author as "The Grand Marja' [spiritual guide] of Shiism and the Grand Leader of the Muslim *Ummah*"—a claim to Islamic hegemony that is intriguing in light of the discussion to follow.

Back out on the street and in our car once more, Nasir and I leafed through Khamenei's text. It offered a lengthy section on "mourning practices." Over the years I've collected various kinds of Shia publications in Pakistan and India; but this was the most detailed exposition on *matam* I'd ever seen distributed by Iranian sources to Shias in the subcontinent.

A half-dozen fatwas, in question-and-answer format, bore directly on the topic of bloody *matam*. Question 359 asks, "What is the ruling on striking oneself with chains to which blades are attached?" Khamenei's reply: "If the act of striking oneself with the aforementioned chains takes place where people can see it, or if the act contributes to the dishonoring of the [Shia] *mazhab* ["sect" or "denomination"], or if it causes bodily harm, then it is not permissible."[2]

Question 369 notes that "during lamentation gatherings in honor of the Imams, some people claw and tear in grief at their faces so much that they draw blood." The Grand Leader's ruling: "There is no legal merit in these practices." He then reiterates the criteria mentioned earlier: "If such practices cause bodily harm or insult the sect in the eyes of onlookers, then they are not permissible."[3]

So too with Question 378:

> On Ashura various practices take place, for example, striking oneself on the head with a sword, and walking on fire, which cause spiritual and bodily harm. Moreover, these things make the Twelver denomination [*mazhab-e ithna-'ashari*] look ugly to the ulema of various other denominations and their followers, as well as to the general population of the rest of the world. Sometimes these practices even bring dishonor to our sect. What is your estimable view of this?[4]

2. Seyyed 'Ali Khamenei, *Istifta'at ke jawabat hissa-ye davvom: mu'amalat* (Qom: Nur mataf, 2002), 191.

3. Khamenei, *Istifta'at ke jawabat*, 195.

4. Khamenei, *Istifta'at ke jawabat*, 198.

Khamenei's estimable view (unsurprising, given how the question was phrased): such practices are *haram*. His fatwa recapitulates what most displeases him about exuberant and bloody forms of Muharram lamentation: "These things frequently bring about slander and dishonor for the sect of *Ahl-e Bayt* [the family of the prophet]."[5]

The fatwa in reply to Question 379 takes his disapprobation even further: "Is *shamsheer zani* [cutting one's forehead with a knife] permissible when done in private, or does your fatwa apply to all circumstances in general?" Khamenei's reply: "*Shamsheer zani*, as it is commonly called, cannot be considered a display of sadness or sorrow. It did not exist in the time of the Imams or their successors... Nowadays this practice brings dishonor and shame to the sect. Therefore this practice is not permissible under any circumstances."[6]

So this collection of fatwas (published in 2002) goes beyond Khamenei's well-known 1994 decree in which he forbade bloody *matam* performed in public. The text I was given in Lahore extends the range of prohibitions even further, to include clawing one's face, walking on fire, and performing self-mortification in private and away from the eyes of onlookers. But common to the 1994 and 2002 fatwas alike is a concern with public relations: how Shiism might appear to Sunni clerics, to the clerics' followers, and to the world in general. All this is consistent with the Khomeinist policy of *taqrib*: reducing Sunni–Shia differences for the sake of political cooperation.

One might question the necessity of a ban on self-scourging that is done in private: after all, how would hidden actions trigger "slander and dishonor"? But one could view Khamenei's fatwa on this point as an exercise in imposing spiritual discipline and displaying total control over the lives of believers. It's as if he let himself be inspired by Pakistani ideologue Abu'l 'Ala Mawdudi's writings on "the Islamic State": "In such a state no one can regard any field of his affairs as personal and private."[7] Mawdudi and Khamenei, totalitarian Sunni and stringent Shia, have found something on which they can agree: a vision of the Muslim future, with believers boxed in an Islamist panopticon, policed by fatwas, under the unwinking gaze of Allah's lieutenants.

One more fatwa from the text given me by the Iranian Cultural Center is worth quoting here—a reply to Question 374: "If someone dies while

5. Khamenei, *Istifta'at ke jawabat*, 198.
6. Khamenei, *Istifta'at ke jawabat*, 198.
7. Abu'l 'Ala Mawdudi, "Political Theory of Islam," in John Donohue and John Esposito, eds., *Islam in Transition: Muslim Perspectives* (2d ed.; New York: Oxford University Press, 2007), 266.

mourning the Imams by performing *qameh zani* [bloody matam], should this be considered an act of suicide?" An important question, this, given Islam's prohibition against killing oneself.

Khamenei's answer: "If this is not the primary cause of death, then it's not suicide. But if a person's life is put at risk through this action and death comes about through *qameh zani*, then the ruling is that this is suicide."[8]

The issue is by no means hypothetical. In 1991—at the request of Shia community leaders in Hyderabad, India—I found myself serving as a first-aid volunteer at a medical tent set up outside the Hazrat Abbas Shrine to treat flagellants who had seriously injured themselves in mourning the Karbala Martyrs. I helped bandage dozens of badly bleeding worshippers. Several had to be rushed to hospitals in ambulances. Physicians I met that day told me stories of Shias who had died performing *matam*.

Traditional Muharram lamentation is extravagant in its forms of expression; worshippers pride themselves on becoming so caught up in mourning that they disregard their personal well-being and safety. This attitude is reflected in the lyrics of some of the *nauhajat* (lamentation poems) that mourners chant as a rhythmic accompaniment while striking themselves in the collective act of *matam*:

> We must live for the sake of Husain;
> We must die for the sake of Husain.
> This body might survive; it might cease to be;
> Yet *matam* in honor of the one wronged must be performed.
>
> …
>
> If fate were to grant us this happiness,
> We must give away this life of ours as a sacrifice.
> Either with tears, or with heart's blood,
> We must dampen our tunics with weeping.
>
> …
>
> Even if streaks of blood now flow from our breasts,
> May our hands never cease:
> Let this *matam* continue.[9]

Another motif of ecstatic self-abnegation appears in a poem chanted by a Hyderabadi *matam*-group called Anjuman-e Parwaneh-ye Shabbir ("the Association of the Moths of Husain"):

> Praise, O give praise, to the beloved splendor of Husain,
> We are his lovers, the moths of Husain.

8.   Khamenei, *Istifta'at ke jawabat*, 197.

9.   'Ali Javid Maqsud, *Yeh matam kayse ruk ja'ay: nauhe* (Hyderabad, India: Maktab-e Turabia, n.d.), 8-9. For a translation and discussion of the entire poem, see David Pinault, *Horse of Karbala*, 40-41.

We are his lovers, who offer our lives for him...
No one has ever seen or heard of
Such lamentation for any sultan.
Never before has there been such *matam*
For one who announced the word of the Quran.
For thirteen hundred years there has been wondrous *matam*.
Praise, o give praise, to the beloved splendor of Husain.
We are his lovers, the moths of Husain.
...

You, too, join these moths and say:
Praise, o give praise, to the beloved splendor of Husain;
We are his lovers, the moths of Husain.[10]

This poem borrows imagery from the Sufi mystical tradition. Just as the moth risks self-destruction, so strongly is it attracted to the candle-flame, so too the true lover of Allah flings aside worldly considerations in pursuit of union with the divine light. Shia mourners who call themselves "moths of Husain" modify this Sufi motif by describing their "wondrous *matam*" as proof of their self-abnegating love for the Imam.

But Khamenei's fatwas evince little patience with this kind of Islam. The decrees issued by the "Grand Leader of the Muslim *Ummah*" reflect a mentality that is rational, pragmatic, and calculating, one that is geared to a larger political goal: subsuming regional forms of Shia practice into a trans-national Shiism that is denominationally flavorless and capable of being packaged as the champion and defender of global Islam.

My friend Nasir would have none of this. He said he was tired of clerical authorities telling ordinary Shias what they may or may not do to mourn Husain. He demonstrated his annoyance via a story that plays with Quranic motifs:

After Joseph's brothers throw him down a well, they go to their father, Hazrat Ya'qoub (the Quranic Jacob), and they tell him Joseph has been eaten by hyenas.[11] Anguished with grief, Ya'qoub then summons all the local hyenas. They emerge from the desert and gather around him.

They deny they ate Joseph; but Ya'qoub persists in his accusation. Then the hyenas swear an oath: "If we lied to you about eating Joseph,

---

10. Allamah Najm Effendi, "Parwaneh-ye Shabbir," in Mir Ahmed 'Ali, ed., *Karbala-wale: nauhajat-e anjuman-e parwaneh-ye shabbir* (Hyderabad, India: Maktab-e Turabia, 1989), 9. For a translation and discussion of the entire poem, see Pinault, *Horse of Karbala*, 38-39.

11. The version of this tale that appears in Islamic scripture (Quran 12.17) mentions a wolf, but I certainly didn't want to interrupt a good story with quibbles over details.

let our punishment be that in the fifteenth century [hijri, that is, the twenty-first century AD] we have to come back to life as *maulvis*."

Hyena-mullahs: a nice way of summarizing one Pakistani Shia's response to fatwas that try to limit his preferred way of mourning the Imams.

Pakistani Shias, Iran, and the Question of Global Leadership of Islam

Even if the Ayatollah Khamenei's fatwas haven't been altogether successful in Pakistan, they have had a more favorable reception among Shia leaders in Lebanon, where the practice of spectacularly gory forms of *matam* has long been widespread. Scholar Lara Deeb reports, "[F]ollowing the lead of Iran, Shii clerics issued fatwas condemning the practice as un-Islamic, and Hizbullah banned it outright in the mid-1990s." Hezbollah's ban makes sense, given how extensively this group has been supported and funded by Iran. But Deeb notes that despite such fatwas in Lebanon, "The practice persists."[12]

The complexity of Iran's relations with Shia populations worldwide is reflected in the career of Munawwar Abbas Alvi, former president of the Sipah-e Muhammad Pakistan ("the Soldiers of Muhammad" or SMP). Banned by President Pervez Musharraf since January 2002, the SMP once had a fearsome reputation as the most violent Shia extremist group in Pakistan. A splinter faction of the Tehrik-e Jafria and the Imamia Students Organization, the SMP prided itself on defending the country's Shias by killing Sunni militant leaders. Journalists I met in Islamabad and Lahore described how the Islamic Republic of Iran once funded the SMP as part of Iran's "proxy war" against Saudi Wahhabi influence in Pakistan.[13]

Jailed from 1997 to 2001 for his SMP activities, Alvi has turned over a new leaf—or at least he's assumed a new role. Now a supporter of Musharraf, Alvi is currently a leading member of a government-sponsored "Interreligious Peace Council" that is responsible for conciliatory "sectarian dialogue" among the country's Muslims.

I interviewed Alvi on two occasions in Lahore in December 2005. His is a presence that's hard to miss. Bulky and barrel-chested, he's blessed

12. Lara Deeb, "Living Ashura in Lebanon: Mourning Transformed to Sacrifice," *Comparative Studies of South Asia, Africa and the Middle East* 25.1 (2005): 128 n. 31.

13. Aamer Ahmed Khan, "Sipah-e Mohammed," *The Herald* (Karachi) 25.6 (June 1994), 37; Haydar, "The Politicization of the Shias," 75-85; Syed, "The Sunni–Shia Conflict in Pakistan," 254-56.

with a voice that's operatic in the self-dramatizing way it swoops from growl to roar to shriek. Anyone measuring the worth of a man by how much space he takes up in a room would have to say this guy is very important indeed.

One night I trailed Alvi as he and his entourage made their way on foot, slowly and majestically, through the crowded alleys of a Shia neighborhood called Bibi Pak Daman. Individuals hailed him or approached to ask favors or just show their respect. He may not be the SMP boss anymore, but he still has what it takes to make followers fawn.

Alvi gave me his version of the SMP's history: "Sipah-e Muhammad was founded in order to create unity among Muslims. But immediately thereafter Muhammad A'zam Tariq [head of the Sunni SSP] insulted the Imam Mahdi [the twelfth Shia Imam] and said Shias are *kafirs*. Then the Shia *naujavanan* [youngbloods/youths] rose up to defend the honor of Shiism." The Karachi-based magazine *The Herald* reported in 1994 that the SMP pressured Pakistan's Shia clerics to issue a death sentence against Tariq; and the SMP described the Sunni leader as "the worst Rushdie."[14] (Salman Rushdie, ever since writing *The Satanic Verses*, has provided disgruntled Pakistanis with the gold standard by which apostates and bad Muslims can be judged.)

In our conversation Alvi asserted that the SMP had never done anything worse than engage in "self-defense" and had always been motivated by "a wish to unite Shias and Sunnis." He was affable enough until I asked him about Iranian financial support for the SMP in the 1990s. At that he turned angry ("Things get exciting here," I noted in my journal at the time) and denied the SMP had ever taken money from Iran. The Islamic Republic, he said, had never supported Shia militarism in Pakistan and had never funded conflict between Sunnis and Shias. He followed this with a speech blaming America and India for the country's sectarian troubles and concluded by saying America would be wise to open dialogue with Iran.

In short, Alvi presented the SMP's history in a way that's consistent with Iran's own recent policy of downplaying sectarian differences in Islam. But with regard to at least one point Alvi showed himself to be very much a traditional Pakistani Shia. He told me that in 1992 he'd been suffering from heart disease but during Muharram he'd insisted on doing *zanjir zani* (self-scourging with chains and blades) anyway. The result: "I experienced a *mu'jizat* [miracle] through Husain: I was cured of my heart trouble. This was *shafa'at-e Imam-e Husain ki vajah se* [on account of the intercession of Imam Husain]." Alvi told me he's aware of

14. Khan, "Sipah-e Mohammed," 37.

Khamenei's various fatwas against bloody *matam* but said as far as he was concerned the ayatollah's decrees applied only to Iranians.

Another Pakistani Shia whose life reflects the shifts and contrarieties in the evolution of Iran's global politics is a Pashtun called Syed Mujavir (the name is a pseudonym). An intellectual and scholar from the North-West Frontier Province, Mujavir is an impressive figure, tall, trim, bearded and elegant in a tailored suit. I met him in December 2005 while interviewing educated Shia professionals in Peshawar.

In our interview Mujavir reminisced about his life. He'd spent time in Iran and as a young man had participated in the 1987 Meccan Hajj "demonstrations" that led to a riot and the deaths of over 400 persons. Although he refrained from specifying the details of his role, his voice as he referred to his own participation was filled with enthusiasm and pride. Some months later, when I emailed Mujavir a request for more information about the Hajj riots, this is what he wrote me:

> About 1987, please note that there was almost nothing sectarian about it. It was [a] stunningly well-organized demonstration and although Iranians were in overwhelming majority in that demonstration, there were US citizens, and if you see the pictures you will know that many nationalities and sects including the Saudis even participated in it. Basically it was [an] anti-super-power demo.[15]

He added that the superpowers being denounced by the demonstrators were the USA and the Soviet Union. He concluded by exclaiming, "The huge demo was not sectarian at all!" Thus Mujavir in his email memoir minimized the notion of there being a Shia or exclusively Iranian dimension to the riots.

News reports from the time offer a fuller picture. Even before the 1987 flashpoint, there had been disturbances; in 1986 Iranian pilgrims had tried to smuggle into Saudi Arabia 330 pounds of plastic explosives. At the onset of the 1987 Hajj season the Ayatollah Khomeini had made speeches for the purpose of politicizing the pilgrimage. According to *New York Times* reports from that period, Khomeini broadcasted radio messages to the 155,000 Iranian pilgrims encamped in Mecca, in which he "urged the pilgrims to carry out a 'disavowal of the pagans,' over the Gulf war, calling for a 'unity rally' to seek 'deliverance from infidels.' He urged Moslems, 'Break America's teeth in its mouth.'"[16]

15. Email communication of August 16, 2006.
16. John Kifner, "400 Die as Iranian Marchers Battle Saudi Police in Mecca," *The New York Times*, August 2, 1987; Elaine Sciolino, "Mecca Tragedy: Chain of Events Begins to Emerge," *The New York Times*, September 6, 1987.

Thousands of Iranians obeyed the ayatollah's orders, filling the streets outside Mecca's Grand Mosque after Friday prayers on July 31, 1987. Many of them were armed with knives and sticks. Carrying giant portraits of Khomeini and a banner proclaiming "Victory is made by waves of martyrs!," they repeated chants calling for death to America, the USSR, and Israel. A *New York Times* reporter noted that "it appeared likely that Shiites from Lebanon and Pakistan may have joined the Iranians in the demonstration."[17]

The demonstration degenerated into a riot when the marchers clashed with a cordon of Saudi policemen. Witnesses reported demonstrators overturning cars and setting them on fire. In five hours of street fighting, dozens of Saudis and hundreds of Iranians died—knifed, stoned, shot, and trampled underfoot.

Iran immediately blamed the Saudi government. Speaker of the Iranian parliament Hashemi Rafsanjani told crowds assembled in Teheran, "We...oblige ourselves to avenge these martyrs by uprooting Saudi rulers from the region... To take revenge for the sacred bloodshed is to free the holy shrines from the mischievous and wicked Wahhabi."[18]

Teheran's adversaries offered a different interpretation. "Saudi officials," according to *The New York Times*, "said Iranians who had been arrested admitted there had been a plot to seize the Grand Mosque and to force the many thousands inside to swear fealty to Ayatollah Ruhollah Khomeini, the Iranian leader, as leader of the world's 850 million Moslems."[19]

In other words, despite their clashing ideologies Saudi Arabia and Iran could agree on one thing: Khomeini's government was using the Hajj riot to contest the Wahhabi Sunnis' right to custodianship of the most universal of global Islam's symbols: the pilgrimage to Mecca.

In our conversation, Mujavir asserted that Shia–Sunni relations in Pakistan are much better today than they were at the height of Saudi–Iranian rivalry in the 1980s, when the Saudis funded Pakistani dictator Zia ul-Haq and Khomeini backed militant activities among Pakistani Shias.

To close our interview Mujavir characterized himself as an internationalist. "Nationalism is a stupid idea," he said, "the stupidest idea possible." When I asked him what he proposed as an alternative vision of

17. Kifner, "400 Die"; Robert D. McFadden, "Death in Mecca: In a Time of Prayer, Tensions Explode and Yield Violence," *The New York Times*, August 3, 1987.

18. John Kifner, "Iranian Officials Urge 'Uprooting' of Saudi Royalty," *The New York Times*, August 3, 1987.

19. "Saudi King Vows Strong Defense of Homeland and Holy Sites," *The New York Times*, August 6, 1987.

collective identity, he singled out the Iranian Revolution as a model. He emphasized what he called its international quality and Iran's future as the vanguard of a global Islamic movement. "Its success," he concluded, "is inevitable."

One can see this "international quality" at work in a development noted by Lahore's *Daily Times*. At the height of the Hezbollah–Israel war in the summer of 2006, the Pakistani government announced it had "banned Pakistani Shias from visiting Iran after local and U.S. intelligence sources expressed fear that they might sneak into southern Lebanon to join the Hezbollah fight against Israel." The report added that "Interior Ministry sources said that the government had received intelligence reports indicating that groups within Pakistan sympathetic to Hezbollah were trying to secretly send Shias to fight Israel."[20]

This development can be set alongside another, more recent, one, from 2007: in Palestine, members of Fatah have taken to taunting their rivals in Hamas by calling them "Shia"—a derogatory reminder of the support given Hamas by the present Iranian regime.

Fatah's taunt illuminates a fear present among both Sunni militants and Arab governments in countries such as Egypt and Saudi Arabia: that Teheran will use its support for Hamas and Hezbollah to expand its influence throughout the Arab Middle East. Teheran's Sunni adversaries are currently doing their best to remind Middle Eastern Muslims that the Iranians are Shia, Persian, and non-Arab: that is, alien. Saudis refer to Iranians as "Safavids" (a sixteenth-century Iranian dynasty that once fought the Sunni Ottomans) and "*Rawafid*" ("rejectionists," that is, those who reject the authority of the *Sahaba*, including the first three Sunni caliphs. *Rawafid* is an old derogatory term for Shias, one that is calculated to remind the Arab masses of Shia doctrines that are especially offensive to Sunnis).[21]

These insults help explain the thinking behind the destruction of the Shia shrine of Samarra by Iraqi Sunni militants in 2006, as well as the killings of Shias sponsored by al-Qaeda terrorist Abu Musab al-Zarqawi: this kind of violence heightens sectarian awareness, increases Shia-Sunni violence, and consequently lessens the likelihood of Iran gaining more acceptance among the region's Sunnis.

Teheran for its part realizes that to increase its influence in the Sunni Middle East it must minimize sectarian conflict. Scholar Vali Nasr comments,

20. "Shias' Travel to Iran Banned," *Daily Times* (Lahore), July 30, 2006 (www.dailytimes.com.pk).

21. "Shias and Sunnis: The Widening Gulf," *The Economist*, February 1, 2007 (www.economist.com).

> When Abu Musab Zarqawi gave his famous declaration that you should kill Shiites anywhere, anyhow, any time, a deputy commander of Iran's Revolutionary Guard…gave a very rare interview, saying there is no such thing as Abu Musab Zarqawi; these are Zionist creations designed to confuse the Muslims and sow discord among them. The line was very clearly being laid that you don't want to engage the sectarian issue; you want to bypass it.[22]

And the way Iran's leadership does this is by blaming sectarian tensions on the entities most universally reviled in the Muslim world: Zionism; Israel; America.

Hence the tactics employed by Iranian president Mahmoud Ahmadinejad, who is very Khomeinist in his efforts to replace Saudi Arabia with Iran as leader of global Islam. His embracing of the Palestinian issue and his support for Hamas; his threats to wipe Israel off the map; his dismissal of the Jewish Holocaust as a myth—these are not the actions of a lunatic, as some might claim, but the deliberate policy of a politician who is counting on hatred of Israel as a way of uniting Sunnis and Shias.

One can see this strategy at work in recent events in Pakistan. In July 2006 a prominent Shia cleric named Allama Hassan Turabi was killed by a suicide bomber. A pan-Islamist in outlook, Turabi was known for his outspoken support for Hamas and Hezbollah and his hostility to Israel. He was killed just after leading a protest rally in Karachi directed against Israel and the USA. Turabi convened the rally in conjunction with the MMA, a group I described earlier—a coalition of Sunni and Shia Islamists who share enmity towards Musharraf's government and who capitalize on international issues to strengthen their own position at home.

The consensus among Pakistanis I asked about Turabi's murder was that it was the work of Sunni extremists, possibly involving the outlawed Sipah-e Sahaba.[23] Not so, claimed Shia leaders interviewed by *The New York Times*: "Everyone knows who is responsible. There is no Shiite–Sunni strife. These are American agents."[24]

This accusation was repeated at Turabi's funeral. An article about the funeral published by IRNA (the Islamic Republic News Agency, Iran's official news outlet) focused on a speech given at the burial service by

22.   Vali Nasr, "The Revival of Shia Islam," speech presented to the Pew Forum on Religion and Public Life, July 24, 2006 (http://pewforum.org/events/index.php?EventID=120).

23.   Khaled Ahmed of Lahore's *DailyTimes* wrote this about how Turabi died: "When he [Turabi] reached home, a man trained in Afghanistan through a jihadi madrassa (Sipah Sahaba?) killed him by embracing him and then blowing himself up." Personal email communication, August 17, 2006.

24.   Salman Masood, "A Top Shiite Leader in Pakistan Dies in a Suicide Bombing," *The New York Times*, July 15, 2006.

Allama Sajid Ali Naqvi. I discussed him earlier: Pakistan's highest-profile Shia cleric and a member of the MMA, Naqvi is head of Tehrik-e Islami Pakistan, also known as Islami Tehrik ("the Islamic Movement," formerly Tehrik-e Jafria Pakistan). IRNA's report on the funeral mentioned that participants chanted slogans against the U.S. and Israel. It also gave highlights from Naqvi's funeral speech: "Sajid Ali Naqvi said the [Pakistani] government has failed to control terrorist elements... Allama Sajid Naqvi said mosques and religious leaders are not safe and the rulers have lost the right to rule. He asked the people to be calm and frustrate [the] designs of those who are trying to pitch Muslims against each other."[25] Anti-Americanism and anti-Zionism; denunciations of the local national government and calls for pan-Islamic unity: all this conforms to the Khomeinist agenda of Ahmadinejad's government. No wonder Iran's official news agency gave Naqvi's role such coverage.

Relevant here are comments made by *Daily Times* editor Khaled Ahmed in an interview I had with him in Lahore in December 2005: "Naqvi still takes orders from Iran. Iran feeds him anti-Americanism and tells Naqvi to blame America for everything that happens. If Iraqi Sunnis kill Shias in Najaf and Karbala, Iran tells Shia leaders in Pakistan like Naqvi, 'Blame America,' and so they do."

Iran's news agency also featured Naqvi in its coverage of Pakistan's reaction to Pope Benedict's Regensburg speech in September 2006. IRNA's article began by announcing that the Islamist MMA was about to "observe a countrywide protest day...to express the outrage of Pakistani Muslims against the disgusting remarks of Pope Benedict XVI against Islam." It noted that Naqvi was among those Muslim clerics who "have appealed to the nation to come out on the streets to voice their peaceful protest against the anti-Islam campaign by the West."[26]

Iran's agenda in Pakistan is clear: minimize sectarian differences—both ritual and political—among Muslims in the name of a united *ummah* led by Iran, while identifying America and Israel as enemies whom all Muslims can abhor.

Can anything hinder this movement? At the very least it's too soon to say that Pakistan's Shias are ready to surrender their religious autonomy for Ahmadinejad's sake. Forms of local resistance can be seen at work if one knows where to look. Hyena-mullah jokes and bloody *matam* are ways of reasserting traditional regional Islam in defiance of the trend towards a globalized and militant form of the faith.

25. "Thousands Attend Slain Pakistani Religious Leader Funeral," *Islamic Republic News Agency*, July 15, 2006 (www2.irna.com/en/news/view).

26. "MMA to Hold Protest Rally Against Pope's Remarks on Friday," *Islamic Republic News Agency*, September 20, 2006 (www.irna.com/en/news/view).

RAW MEAT SKYWARD:
PARIAH-KITE RITUALS IN LAHORE

Pariah Kites: The Poetry of Initial Encounters

I'd glimpsed them up in the sky now and again, without any attentiveness on my part, on every trip I'd made to the subcontinent. But as for really seeing them, really noting them: I remember the first time clearly.

Thursday, the sixth of Muharram, March 21, 2002. Mid-afternoon, and I was returning from Shahdara, a town north of Lahore on the other side of the Ravi River. I'd visited Shahdara's Shia shrines in the company of my friend Nasir Husain Zaydi.

We were stuck in an oven-box of a little car, crawling under a hot sun in backed-up traffic on the Ravi Bridge. Glare headachingly bright. Exhaust fumes; hard to breathe. No air conditioning in our car.

Nasir apologized and said best to keep the windows rolled up to keep out the smog. He was telling me something about blood rituals and self-flagellation. The heat made it hard to concentrate on what he was saying.

In front of us, haltered oxen stood squeezed in the back of a Datsun pickup. One ox blinked and shook its head. A message, I thought. Help. I'm a prisoner. We're all prisoners. Nasir was saying something about the Iranian Islamic Revolution and the revival of Shia pride.

For my own revival I rolled down the window and looked out. And then I saw them.

Birds, dozens of them. Big, too. Circling far above, gliding along the thermals over the river. Carving elegant curves through the air, free of the traffic-crawl below.

One bird suddenly dipped a wing and rode the airdrafts down in a swift dive. One moment it was hundreds of feet above us. The next, it was gliding level with the bridge, keeping pace with our car. It was just beyond the bridge railing, no more than twelve feet from where I sat.

Big wings, was my first impression, close enough so I could distinguish the feathering. A sharply curved beak in a head that turned from side to side. As the head turned I could see its eyes. The gaze fell briefly on me, then flicked away to the river below.

I felt—and so strong was the impression I made sure to write it down later—the presence of an alien intelligence. Cold assessment, and a sentience as remote and hard as stone. And yet it was a feeling of contact, of kinship, of shared perception as we both stared out over the water. I thought of California poet Robinson Jeffers's poem *Rock and Hawk*: "Bright power...fierce consciousness...the falcon's realist eyes."[1]

I pointed out the bird gliding beside us to Nasir. Almost as big as an eagle, I said.

Nothing so noble, was his opinion. "Just a *cheel*." These birds were pariah kites. Scavengers and thieves, he explained. "Always picking at garbage heaps." He shrugged.

The bird dipped out of sight. But as our car inched along the bridge I stared up at the *cheels* overhead. Philosopher Jerry Gill defines reality as "the intersecting of symbiotic dimensions," and I'd just had an experience of intersection that made me want to learn more about the dimension inhabited by Lahore's pariah kites.[2]

Of Warlords, Trash, and the Philosopher's Stone: Pariah-Kite Legends from Old India

After the encounter on the Ravi Bridge, I began to watch for the presence of these birds. On early morning walks in Lahore's Cantonment district, when the streets were still largely empty, I'd look up and see I had company: the first kites of the day. Easy to spot: forked tail, five-foot wingspan, and a drawn-out piercing cry that echoed along the sky.

Midday, when summer air-currents offer hot gusts and lift-off glide-waves to tempt all things with wings, is when these birds are most easily seen. Many a time, on foot among the crowds in the Old City quarter, where the alleys are so narrow one feels walled in among flesh and sweat and heat, I'd turn my gaze briefly skyward. With luck I'd see a *cheel*, framed by the rooftops overhead, soaring about at its ease.

"Looking for refuse," as one shopkeeper told me. "And if they see you outside carrying a bit of food, they might just come down and snap the bit right out of your hand."

1. Robinson Jeffers, *Selected Poems* (New York: Vintage Books, 1965), 56.
2. Jerry H. Gill, *Mediated Transcendence: A Postmodern Reflection* (Macon, GA: Mercer University Press, 1989), 154.

"Everywhere parasitic on man," is how the *Collins' Birds of India* handbook unflatteringly describes the *cheel* in its eating habits.[3] Still, a noble sight, to see a hundred of them riding a thermal air-spout at noon, in a slow helix up in the sky.

Twilight, and they settle into treetops beside wastefields, sharing the habitat with crows, sparrows and ruby-headed parakeets. Rudyard Kipling's verse comes to mind: "Now Chil the kite brings home the night, that Mang the bat sets free."[4]

The writer's father, John Lockwood Kipling, was a keen observer of the subcontinent's animal life. His book *Beast and Man in India* (1891) reflects the pleasure he took in studying the behavior of the region's pariah kites. He claimed that the bird's Hindustani/Urdu name, *cheel/chil* (plural: *cheelayn*), was derived from "its shrill thin scream." Readers of his book can glimpse one of the things Lockwood Kipling did for amusement when he wanted a break from his duties in the museum's galleries: "Those who delight in the flight of birds, which surely is one of the most fascinating things in life, may find less interesting diversions than throwing fragments of food from a high roof when a fleet of swift pirates soon assembles."[5]

A gifted amateur naturalist, Lockwood Kipling was good at describing how *cheels* attack a swarm of winged white ants as the termites rise up into the sky:

> The birds assemble in great numbers for this dainty feast, the kite with the rest. One would think this wide-gaping bird would sail round in the insect cloud open-mouthed, whale-fashion. But he uses his claws even for this minute game, and the action of carrying them to his beak as he flies produces a series of most graceful curtseying undulations.[6]

The subcontinent has its share of stories about pariah kites. I came upon one such tale in a visit to Jodhpur's Meherangarh Fort in the Indian province of Rajasthan. On the fortress wall is a shrine to Chamunda (one of the manifestations of the warrior-goddess Durga). A doorkeeper pointed to the *cheels* gliding above the ramparts and told me they were sacred to Chamunda.

He said centuries ago the goddess showed herself to one of the city's Rajput rulers at a time when Jodhpur was threatened with invasion by Muslim warlords. "I will help you fight off the Muslims," she promised.

3. Martin Woodcock, *Collins' Birds of India* (London: Harper Collins, 1980), 32.
4. Rudyard Kipling, *The Jungle Books* (London: Penguin, 1987), 35.
5. John Lockwood Kipling, *Beast and Man in India* (London: Macmillan & Co., 1891), 34.
6. Kipling, *Beast and Man in India*, 34.

She gave him a sword and then assured triumph for the Hindus by taking the shape of thousands of *cheels* that clawed at the faces of the invaders.

In Lahore, in the library of the Berkeley Urdu Language Program, I came upon a book that listed a number of South Asian folk traditions concerning pariah kites. This was S. W. Fallon's *New Hindustani–English Dictionary* (not so new now, since it was published in Benares in 1879). Under the heading *Chil/Cheel*, this dictionary lists several vivid expressions and proverbs. "*Do pahar ki chil*: A noonday kite (a child who won't keep inside the house)." "*Chil ki tarah mandlala*: To haunt, hang about, or hover like a kite." "*Chil ke ghar men paras hota hai*: The philosopher's stone is in the kite's nest."[7]

Lockwood Kipling—who seems to have been well acquainted with Fallon's *Dictionary*—comments as follows on this last expression: "The *paras* or philosopher's stone is said in a proverb to be in the kite's nest, a dark saying based on the kite's trick of sometimes carrying off gold ornaments, or on the Muhammadan women's superstition that young kites cannot see until there is gold in the nest."[8]

The most interesting of all the Hindustani *cheel*-phrases collected in Fallon's *Dictionary* is: "*Kali chil, mangal ka roz*!: A pice [a small coin] to let the kite go on Tuesday!" Here is Lockwood Kipling's comment on the saying: "A Delhi street-cry raised by ragged fowlers is—'Free the kite on Tuesday.'… The practice in the Delhi region is for a mother to pay a pice to the fowler, who swings the kite round over her child's head and lets it go. This ceremony is thought most lucky on a Tuesday or Saturday."[9]

In fact in Lahore's Anarkali Bazaar and Old City quarter I myself have seen men walking about with wicker baskets filled with chirping sparrows. For a few rupees these birdmen will set a sparrow free. Onlookers told me this was an act of charity that earned the donor *savab*—religious merit.

"Free the kite on Tuesday": reading these nineteenth-century texts made me wonder if twenty-first-century Lahore retains any religious rituals involving the *cheels* I enjoyed watching so much. The answer, I found, is yes—and the rituals are curiouser, more interesting, and more controversial than anything I read about in Fallon's *Dictionary*.

---

7. S. W. Fallon, *A New Hindustani–English Dictionary* (Benares: Medical Hall Press, 1879), 570.

8. Kipling, *Beast and Man in India*, 35.

9. Fallon, *A New Hindustani–English Dictionary*, 570; Kipling, *Beast and Man in India*, 35.

Mind the Claws:
Or, the Hazards of Tossing Raw Meat from a Bridge

As I mentioned earlier, pariah kites first came to my attention during the 2002 Muharram season. But at that time I was too taken up with documenting Shia rituals to give the kites their due.

My chance to focus on them came a couple of visits later, in March 2004. An early-morning walk in my Cantonment neighborhood gave me another close look at one of these birds. A *cheel*, perched on a nearby rooftop, rose up, circled directly over my head at a height of no more than fifteen feet, and then settled onto the topmost branch of the closest tree.

I stopped and stared. In the morning light its head seemed a pale gold, its body deep brown, its V-shaped tail barred with dark stripes. A good two feet tall it stood: big. It eyed me, wheeled away, and then flew off east into the emergent sun.

I enthused about this sighting when my driver Imtiyaz Yusuf came by later that morning. He responded to my enthusiasm with a suggestion: why not head over to the Ravi Bridge to see the *cheel-gosht ka sadqah*?

I had to ask him to explain what this meant. *Sadqah*, I knew already, is an Urdu term (derived from Arabic) used to designate acts of charity. (Fallon defines it as "alms dedicated to pious purposes; propitiatory offerings to avert sickness"[10]). But the term *cheel-gosht* puzzled me. Literally it means "kite-meat"; so *cheel-gosht ka sadqah* must mean something like "kite-meat alms." But the term's precise meaning eluded me.

Imtiyaz rephrased the term for me. Think of the *sadqah*, he said, as *cheelon ke lie gosht*: alms that involve meat intended as an offering to the kites. The practice, he said, takes place at the Ravi Bridge every day. Although one can catch the show at almost any hour, the morning is the best time to go. That's when the birds are good and hungry.

This I had to see. We drove past familiar landmarks. Mall Road past the museum and Kim's Gun and Anarkali Bazaar; then Circular Road around the Old City, with a glimpse of the domes of the Badshahi Mosque before heading up Ravi Road to the bridge.

The southwestern foot of the bridge offers a parking turnoff. We got out of the car and paused below the bridge by the shore.

But not for long. The river—with its fouled sluggish water and exposed mudbanks and profligate trash in abundance—exudes a sewage-drainage stink that catches you like a clenched hand to the throat. We hurried up the stairs to the top of the bridge.

---

10. Fallon, *A New Hindustani–English Dictionary*, 830.

Lots of traffic up here—noise and exhaust-haze—but a stiff breeze blew and kept away the worst of the stench from below. We stood by the railing on the bridge footpath and took in the view. Below, black water-buffaloes, submerged to their eyes, cooling off in mid-river. Along the shore, dozens of tents and huts: an encampment of some kind (more on this later). And up above, plenty of *cheels*, hovering over the bridge.

We didn't have long to contemplate the view. Boys and men—some as young as ten, others in their fifties and sixties—converged on us. Each gripped plastic bags in both hands. *Cheel-gosht, cheel-gosht*, cried two of the boys.

Imtiyaz looked up at the sky, then at me. "So," he said. "Do you want to feed the kites?"

I said okay. The boys shook their bags at me and hurried forward at a run. I wondered what I was letting myself in for.

The process seemed simple. Each bag contained chunks of raw bloody meat. Bits of goat, one of the boys said. Also mutton and beef. (I learned later there is a slaughterhouse across the river in Shahdara that sells these scraps cheap.)

Each bag, explained my driver, costs five rupees (about ten cents). All I had to do was pay one of the *cheel-gosht* vendors and be sure to touch the bag before he offered it to the kites. Part of the ritual, he said. The vendor would take care of the rest.

Sounded easy enough. I handed a five-rupee note to one of the kite-meat boys. He thrust a bag at me. As soon as I touched it, he stepped to the railing and shook the bag out over the river. Morsels dropped to the water. But several pieces of meat, sticky with blood and goo, adhered to the plastic. Impatient, the boy flung the whole bag over the railing as well.

It never touched the water. A rush of *cheels* hurtled by us. One bird caught the bag in midair. Others swooped after the scattered meat. I saw one kite dive in a fast slicing arc, skim the water and then climb away fast with a bit of raw flesh in its talons.

I wasn't the only customer. Again and again, motorists stopped on the bridge, rolled down their car-windows, and waved money at the vendors. Many of the cars looked expensive—a late-model Toyota, a BMW, a Pajero SUV. This *cheel-gosht* business apparently wasn't the sole domain of the poor. Quite a few drivers were well-dressed, in business outfits. Professionals, many of them seemed, commuters on their way to work.

And they were in a hurry. A vendor would take the outthrust rupees and the client would touch the *cheel-gosht* bag. Most drivers then sped off without even waiting to watch the offering take place. Sometimes the vendor flung the whole bag carelessly over the railing without bothering to shake out the contents.

Me, I wanted more of a show. I also didn't like the idea of the birds ingesting plastic to get at their food. I bought another dime-bag and told the boy this time to take out the meat and throw it to the *cheels* one bit at a time. I told him to throw each piece up high.

So you can have a real spectacle?, he said.

I said yes that was the idea.

He grinned and stood beside me and waved the bag above his head to get the birds' attention.

We got more attention than we'd planned for. A sudden whir and snap and the bag was gone: a kite had passed neatly between us and snatched the thing. Gave us both a fright—but worth it, just to see that flash of claws. A reminder: these creatures are raptors after all.

The boy shrieked and laughed and shrugged. I gave him five more rupees for another bag. This time we took turns taking streaming gobs of meat and flinging them up in the air. A messy business: my shirt was soon spattered with blood.

But I got the spectacle I'd wanted. Kites filled the sky overhead and caught each piece on the fly. Not once did any birds collide. And the delicacy of the catch was impressive. A kite would wing after its food and in mid-air grab the meat in its talons. Then, poised above us, it would stoop forward, its head curving down to its toes to transfer the meal to its beak. Lockwood Kipling had pegged it right: the kite's method of in-flight dining truly "produces a series of most graceful curtseying undulations."

"Hurl It Far from Yourself": The Logic of Pariah-Kite Rituals

After my initial pariah-kite encounters, I returned to the Ravi Bridge a number of times and interviewed both *cheel-gosht* vendors and their clients. They offered me various rationales to explain the thinking that underlies the meat-offering ritual.

First of all, as one vendor—a man in his late fifties—explained, *Yeh cheelayn Allah ke makhluq hayn*: "These kites are God's creatures." As is the case with other birds, one can earn *savab* (religious merit) for feeding them.

The vendor asked if I'd been to the Wazir Khan Mosque in Lahore's Old City. I said yes. Every time I'd been there, I'd bought a handful of birdseed from a merchant who squats by a grain sack near the entrance. Pigeons flock to the mosque's courtyard to eat the food scattered by worshippers. "And every time you do that," said my informant, "you get *savab* for feeding Allah's creatures."

But the *cheel gosht ka sadqah*—and this is a point many interviewees insisted on—generally involves more than just a generalized pious wish to earn merit. Typically, I was told, donors may be motivated to give by various *pareshaniyan* ("troubles," "worries," "problems") involving health, work, or family.

One of the vendors—a middle-aged man who lived in the squatters' camp by the bridge—put it this way. "If you have a problem, come out to the bridge and buy some meat. Be sure to touch the bag it's in." It's even better, he suggested, if the vendor presses the meat-bag to the customer's forehead and whirls the bag seven times around the troubled person's head. "Then you make sure the bag is flung up into the air. The *cheel* eats the meat and at the same time eats up your problem." He pantomimed the ritual with great whirlings of his arm as he talked.

Another informant explained the kind of *du'a* (personal petitionary prayer) that should accompany the offering of meat to the *cheels*: "If you have troubles that you want to make leave, then you should throw meat to the kites. And as the kites fly away with the food, you should ask God that in a similar way your troubles, too, will depart."

Muhammad Razzaq, field director of the Berkeley Urdu Language Program in Lahore, told me of another kind of *sadqah*: "If you have troubles, place meat overnight by your bed. Then early in the morning, before sunrise, while other people are still asleep, get up, touch the meat, take it outside, and hurl it far away from yourself, where some animal or bird will eat it."

In other words, it's not essential that a pariah kite be the specific agent for removing the trouble-laden food. This point is illustrated by something I witnessed while out walking along Canal Road in a neighborhood of Lahore called Shadman Colony. Here there's a wide median strip, grassy, beside a water source (the canal), with a number of trees and lots of crows.

A man and several boys paraded about the strip, holding up bags of raw meat for passers-by to see. Motorists pulled over, just as they do on the Ravi Bridge. The man in charge followed a slightly more elaborate procedure than the ones I witnessed on the bridge (possibly, I suspect, because there were fewer customers and less of a rushed and crowded atmosphere here in the relatively quiet locality of Shadman).

He passed the meat-bag in a circle seven times around the client's head, pressing the bag to the individual's forehead on each pass. Then he turned and opened the bag and scattered its contents across the grass. The crows dropped from the trees and made short work of the meat.

Between customers I asked the vendor about his work. He enumerated the anxieties people bring to this ritual: worries about a child's health; wanting to protect a new car or new motorbike and guarantee somehow it would never involve its owner in an accident.

Is it good work, this bird-meat business?, I asked. He smiled and nodded at the boys and said it provided a fulltime income for himself and his sons.

Extrapolating from the crows in Shadman and the kites on the bridge, one can say the essential element of this ritual is simple. Touch the meat; transfer the trouble; make sure the food—and by analogy the trouble—gets carried off by some creature.

Ancient logic, ancient ritual—as old as the Hebrew scriptures, where the Israelite high priest lays hands on a scapegoat to transfer the people's sins to the goat before it's driven into the wastelands as an offering to the desert-devil Azazel.[11]

Kite, crow, demon: all can be relied on to gobble up offerings. The troubles that taint the meat never seem to spoil the taste.

Pariah Kites and the Art of Survival in Lahore

The Ravi Bridge is a good place to watch pariah kites. But it also gives you a view of the dozens of makeshift huts and stained burlap tents that line both sides of the river.

One morning in December 2005 at the Urdu Center I told my friend Muhammad Razzaq I planned to return to the Ravi and interview the riverbank squatters. "You'll want company," he decided.

I had plenty that day—not only Imtiyaz the driver and my guide Reza, but also Muhammad Razzaq and Mushtaq, the Urdu Center's cook, who said he was in the mood for an outing.

Not much of an outing, I wanted to say at first as the five of us stood on the bridge. Stench below, smog above, car horns blaring, the pavement beneath our feet quivering from the weight of endless freight trucks. But the guys with me leaned over the railing and laughed and shouted to each other as if they were on holiday.

And why not? We had a bit of sky and a view downriver and a hundred big-winged birds to watch. This was Lahore's wild outdoors.

Once we'd had enough of throwing meat to the *cheels* we made our way down a litter-strewn sand-slope to the huts and tents on the riverbank by the northern end of the bridge.

---

11. Leviticus 16.6-28; Walter Burkert, *Creation of the Sacred: Tracks of Biology in Early Religions* (Cambridge, MA: Harvard University Press, 1996), 53-55.

No one came forward. For a minute or so we stood about uncertainly near the edge of the encampment. My guys seemed as hesitant as I as to how to proceed. Imtiyaz said this was the first time he'd seen the settlement up close. Muhammad turned to me and said, "We don't want to just wander about and walk in on any women unannounced."

Not many individuals in sight at first. Two men lounged on charpoys. They wore bright-colored vests—one green, one scarlet—over impressively filthy tunics. Both men were bearded and dirty. A man with a sack of fruit stood by their rope-beds. He looked as if he was trying to sell them some, and they looked as if they were trying to cadge food for free.

One man turned on his bed and gave us an indifferent gaze. His eyes were watery-red and unfocused.

"Malangs," said Imtiyaz by way of explanation.

Outlaw Sufis, in other words: a species known for its mad dancers and hashish-smokers. Neither malang made any effort to rise or greet us. Imtiyaz said they'd probably had their fair share of dope the night before.

But someone else came forward to welcome us. A man in his fifties, rail-thin, his skin burnt dark from years in the sun. A long white mustache, carefully groomed; a length of faded blue cloth twisted turban-style atop his head; and a woolen shawl carefully wrapped about his chest: these gave him a statesman's air. Clinging to the tail of his shawl were two children, one of them a very pretty girl with gold-stud earrings.

The man greeted us warmly and walked about with us while water-buffaloes nearby browsed on dusty grass and clumps of sedge. Like most of the people I encountered in this city, he spoke Punjabi as his first language. So I asked my questions in Urdu and Muhammad translated them into Punjabi. The man was chatty and animated and glad to talk with us.

He was from Sheikhupura, he said—a town some thirty-five miles north of Lahore. He'd come here with his family three or four years ago in search of work. He did in fact find a job—using a cart and donkey to haul things about in the city. But he couldn't find anyplace he could afford to live in Lahore, so he and his family had chosen to camp out here by the river.

It wasn't so bad here, he said. Almost all the people living as squatters on this north shore of the Ravi were also from his town of Sheikhupura. So he and his family didn't feel alone.

As our Sheikhupura host spoke, other individuals came forward, men, boys, a few young girls. In this and subsequent conversations I was able to piece together details about the lives of the squatters who survive on the banks of the Ravi.

Some individuals were beggars, getting by on charity (like the malangs I'd spotted). Others were day-laborers or vendors who sold types of food—fruit, bread, and so on.

But at least a dozen of the Ravi squatters I met told me they made their fulltime living selling *cheel-gosht* on the bridge to motorists. One man told me he was also from Sheikhupura and spent most of his nights camped out by the bridge. He showed me the plastic meat-bags he was selling. They contained bits of cow-kidneys and livers, he said. Like the other men I met he said he got the scraps from the nearby slaughterhouse in Shahdara. The thirty-five miles between his home-town and Lahore made it impossible for him to go home often. So he lived here on the riverbank for a week or more at a time, then returned to Sheikhupura for a few days before coming back to Lahore.

Lahore draws unskilled labor from a number of towns. Another kite-meat vendor I met told me he's from Gujranwala (about forty-two miles north of Lahore). He'd been living here on the shore of the Ravi by the bridge for almost twenty years. Once a month he went home to give money to his wife and family.

From these talks I acquired a sense of the riverbank by the Ravi Bridge—despite its polluted wasteland appearance—as a valued perch for the survival-minded from throughout the Punjab. For those who earn their rupees selling *cheel-gosht*, a number of factors conveniently converge at this location: a slaughterhouse; a traffic bottleneck on the bridge and a ceaseless stream of potential clients; unclaimed real estate for the squatting; and—for company—squadrons of magnificent birds with limitless appetites for all the merit-yielding alms they can get. One could do worse.

But survival and pariah kite-meat weren't the only topics I learned about from the squatters. On that day in December 2005 when I met the white-mustached gentleman from Sheikhupura who welcomed us so courteously, a pedestrian on the bridge spotted me and my friends and hurried down the slope to join us by the water.

Turns out he was a peddler, quick to spot a knot of potential customers. He carried a covered basket and a portable stand made of bamboo. In no time he'd set up the stand and placed the basket on top and showed us what he had for sale: bread and biscuits and fresh chicken patties.

Friendly and easy to talk to, this individual, like itinerant salesmen anywhere you care to name. He heard me asking questions about religious life and *cheel-gosht* rituals. At this he got excited and broke into our talk to say he'd seen something here by the bridge that was stranger than any kite-meat charity.

Strange always gets my attention. I asked what he'd seen.

It was part of his job, he said, to go back and forth along this bridge all day. He sold to motorists, donkey-cart drivers, squatters under the bridge, anyone with a few rupees to spend. He did this all day and stayed on the bridge until his stock was exhausted—until nine, ten, sometimes eleven pm.

Sometimes, he said, when he finished late and he finally headed home for the night, he'd see solitary men seated in isolated spots on the riverbank, doing *wird* (religious chanting). He never disturbed them because he knew they were undertaking a *chillah*—the forty-day ritual that—if it doesn't end in something disastrous—gives a person mastery over an assortment of jinns.

This seemed to me an appropriate place for such disciplines, for the Ravi has its own history as a nexus of illuminationist encounters. While meditating on the shore of the river, Mulla Shah (a seventeenth-century resident of Lahore and a Sufi mentor of Prince Dara Shikoh) experienced a vision in which "a man emerged out of the water"—a man who proved to be al-Khidr. Revered as a guide for spiritual wayfarers, al-Khidr is a legendary figure believed to have gained immortality by drinking from the "Spring of Life." He approached the Sufi on the riverbank, spoke briefly with him, and then vanished.[12]

My *cheel-gosht* informants on the Ravi Bridge had a lot to say about mystical disciplines and the *chillah*. But this takes us into the realm of the demonic—a topic I'll save for the next chapter.

Conclusion: Rituals for the Road

Back in my room at night in the Cantonment, and I was packing my bag for next morning. Muhammad and Reza and Imtiyaz and I had organized a car-trip to Peshawar, and we were planning an early start.

A knock at my door. Ranee the housekeeper asked whether I'd like to join Fatima Sahiba in the parlor for tea.

I said sure. I liked my landlady's company, and Fatima liked asking me about the things I saw each day in this city of hers that she loved.

She often disapproved of the individuals I consorted with, but she liked my stories anyway. She said they involved people she'd never normally talk to—Shia flagellants, parrot fortune-tellers, and so on.

Today's experiences were no exception. She listened avidly as I told her about the Ravi Bridge and my conversations with the kite-meat men

---

12. Bikrama Jit Hasrat, *Dara Shikoh: Life and Works* (2d ed.; Delhi: Munshiram Manoharlal, 1982), 93-94.

and their lives on the riverbank. And as soon as I finished, she put down her teacup and said, "You know these types of people are not good Muslims."

My landlady enjoyed a good argument in the evening. To keep the discussion going I said that as far as I could tell, all these people I spoke to regarded themselves as proper Muslims.

She admitted she herself years ago used to give money for food to be fed to the *cheels*. But she stopped when her *maulvi* told her this custom is "against Islam." Her local mullah, she said, explained that the practice came from Hinduism. " 'And if it comes from Hinduism,' my *maulvi* says, 'we must eliminate it'."

She said her mullah reminded her the goal is to purify Islam. So instead of feeding *cheels* and continuing a corrupt Hindu practice, her mullah advised her, she should donate her money to the mosque, and he would see to it that the money would be used to feed the poor instead of feeding some birds.

Ranee the housekeeper poured us more tea. Before I went off to bed Fatima Sahiba told me to remember: all this kite-meat business wasn't the right form of Islam.

I said I'd be sure to keep it in mind.

Which made me smile the next morning when my guys came to get me and we left the city by way of the Ravi Bridge. Razzaq had us stop by the river and clapped his hands and announced, "Time for *sadqah*." He waved over a *cheel-gosht* boy from the crowd on the bridge.

I recognized the kid from one of my interviews. He lived in Shahdara, just across the Ravi. Unlike the riverbank squatters from Sheikhupura and Gujranwala, he walked back and forth every day between his home and the bridge.

First Muhammad ordered up four bags of meat, one for each person in our car. We each in turn touched a bag. As my bag was presented to me, Muhammad suggested I might want to pray for a safe trip. Imtiyaz seconded the idea. This was the way to start things right, he said, with an offering to keep us all unharmed.

I got out of our little Hyundai to watch as the boy flung the flesh out over the water. The kites overhead spotted their meal fast. The nearest raptor gave me a good show. Abruptly it closed its wings and folded them tightly against its chest and then pitched headlong in a rocking side-to-side high-dive. Its claws hooked a meat-gob before the morsel could touch the water.

Muhammad wasn't quite done yet with the *sadqah*. For an extra ten rupees he bought two more *gosht*-bags and motioned to the Hyundai.

The boy walked all the way around our car, lifting the bags shoulder-high and twirling them dramatically as he completed his circle. Then he pitched this meat, too, at the kites.

Muhammad explained these two bags were intended to enhance the likelihood that the car itself would come through the trip all right—no accidents or mechanical mishaps. Lots of people, he said, do a *cheel ka sadqah* at the beginning of a trip to ensure a safe journey. For Lahoris heading north, the Ravi Bridge—the last stop before leaving the city—is a good place to do a kite-offering.

"So," said Muhammad with a big smile as we all squeezed back into the Hyundai and drove across the bridge, "this way—God willing—we'll have no worries on our trip."

Did it work?

We made it all the way to Islamabad and Peshawar, through the Punjab to the North-West Frontier Province, and then safely back to Lahore again.

And our car didn't break down once.

7

JINNS AND SORCERY IN LAHORE:
TEXTUAL SOURCES AND PERSONAL EXPERIENCES

Introduction: What Buzzes in the Brain

Tell friends you've been interviewing Lahori sorcerers, and you're likely to be asked: have you had any creepy moments in such dealings? Any encounters that have spooked you?

Well, one or two. Most of my interviews have been pleasant, even prosaic. But then there's the time Mustafa was telling me how he used his tame jinn to facilitate his travel arrangements:

Mustafa and I are sitting facing each other across a small worktable. He tells me he employs his jinn to help others but sometimes the jinn does favors for him as well. For example: at one time Mustafa was having trouble getting a visa from the Indian Embassy to visit his family in Delhi. His solution: he dispatched his jinn to the consulate. It then "went into the brains of the embassy people" and somehow induced them to grant the visa.

A disturbing image hits me: jinns buzzing around in people's heads.

Mustafa has guessed what I'm thinking. No sooner does he mention his jinn than he leans suddenly across the table and taps my hand and jabs a finger at my face and says, "Yes, like that—it can go straight to your brain."

I flinch and back away. A reflex—I can't help it: like dodging the threat of a fly up one's nose. An instinctive reaction, I tell myself.

Yet I feel embarrassed. I look again at Mustafa. He's watching me, with a slow sly smile on his face.

Another creepy moment: hearing about the night Mustafa's son (who also practices sorcery) found out his house was besieged by angry jinns—swarms of them—and learning from him what form they took, by the thousands, when the young man made them show themselves, and how the whole family had to fight them for possession of the house.

But to savor a story like this, one should start at the beginning. In my case, the beginning had to do with outdoor advertising, newspaper ads, and Urdu lessons with a jinn-master.

"If You Are Afflicted With Any Kind of Trouble At All": *Marketing Strategies for Sorcerers*

The research project that brought me to Lahore to begin with involved Shia ritual. But Lahore is so rich in the visual stimulants it offers that it's hard to stay focused for long on exclusively one topic.

Among the stimulants I noticed one day while traversing Anarkali Bazaar was a big placard on which were painted a black hand and a text in Urdu. I was riding in a car with my research assistant Reza. We passed the sign before I could read it all; but I caught the words "palmist" and "astrologer."

Interesting. More intriguing, however, and puzzling to me were other words I glimpsed on the sign: *jadoo-shekan* ("magic-breaking") and *'amil* ("practitioner").

I turned to Reza for an explanation. I knew *jadoo* refers to magic of the dark or illicit kind, but what was entailed in "breaking" *jadoo*? And what kind of practices, I asked, is an *'amil*/practitioner engaged in?

Reza hesitated. He looked uncomfortable. When he spoke he chose a dismissive tone. Such people only want money, he said. *'Amils* generally aren't good Muslims, their practices are unislamic, and their spells often don't work. Only uneducated people, he said, waste their rupees consulting *'amils* and asking them for healings and the miraculous resolution of difficult family circumstances. *'Amils*, he concluded, were charlatans, experts in exploiting the ignorant. The whole business, he implied, wasn't worth my time.

His vehemence surprised me at first. After all, he himself—a very active member of Lahore's Twelver Shia community—had often told me stories of healings and miraculous resolutions to problems.

But Reza's stories were linked to Shia shrines and Shia rituals. The whole realm of the *'amil* apparently represented a rival enterprise—one that competed with the spiritual leaders to whom Reza owed allegiance (though in fact the realms of the *'amil* and of Shia devotion overlap at many points).

Yet there was another factor as well. Katherine Pratt Ewing, who did extensive research among Sufi masters in Lahore, notes a frequent phenomenon in interactions between Pakistani Muslims and foreign ethnographers. Many Pakistanis, eager to identify themselves with the rationalism and scientific empiricism associated with modernity, are quick to disown aspects of popular Islamic practice they consider irrational in their dealings with academic representatives of the modern West. Ewing found herself in this bearer-of-modernity role in her dealings with Sufis; and I experienced this, too, in my talks with Muslims such as Reza. But as Ewing also astutely notes, people are segmented in their identities. We may pride ourselves on consistency in our views, and we may present ourselves as rational empiricists in public dealings with outsiders. But in our private lives we might very well fall back on traditional worldviews and traditional rituals for dealing with the large and messy patches of our lives that resist resolution by rational discursive analysis. This was as true for my assistant Reza as a Shia as it is for me as a Catholic.[1]

Nevertheless Reza wouldn't tell me anything else about *'amils*. For that I had to turn to my Urdu tutor Qamar Jalil, who suggested I look in the advertising pages of local Lahori newspapers.

This was good advice. Here's an example of what I found—the March 21, 2004 issue of the "Sunday Magazine" supplement to the Urdu-language newspaper *Khabarein*. Jostling for attention amid blurbs for facial creams, hair oil, male potency lotions, and breast-enlargement schemes, numerous advertisements trumpeted the claims of rival *'amils*.

One practitioner, based in the Punjabi town of Faisalabad, bore the titles of "professor" and "hajji" (veteran of the pilgrimage—Hajj—to Mecca), thereby insisting simultaneously on both his scientific-scholarly and orthodox-devotional qualifications. (This advertisement also featured a photo of the *'amil*: frowning, bearded, and wearing a prayer cap, the man seemed a very picture of foursquare Islamic sobriety.) The ad described him as *Shahanshah-e jinnat*: "the supreme shah of the jinns," and it followed this with a promise that was headlined in black and yellow: *Jo chahoge mil ja'ayga*: "You will get what you want." How could a claim like this fail to draw readers?

Another ad featured the "internationally renowned Professor Baba Nihal Shah" ("Baba"—literally "father," "grandfather," or "old man"—is a word commonly used as an honorific in addressing *'amils* and other men thought to have holy powers).

Baba Nihal's claims encompass the whole world of domestic worries. "If you are afflicted with any kind of trouble at all"—here the ad enumerates treachery in business dealings, marital problems, unemployment, mental anxiety, alcoholism, and "enmity in your home"; in short: "if you consider yourself desperate as to your own fate and have lost courage"—

---

1. Katherine Pratt Ewing, *Arguing Sainthood: Modernity, Psychoanalysis, and Islam* (Durham: Duke University Press, 1997), 103-27.

then, counsels the ad, "At the first opportunity take the time to arrange a meeting with Baba Nihal Shah, and God willing, all your desires and hopes will be fulfilled. If you've already wasted time and money going to 'practitioners' (*'amilon*), astrologers, and conjurers, then do not despair: there is no problem Baba Nihal Shah can't solve." The ad goes on to describe him as *jinnat ke be taj badshah*: "the uncrowned king of the jinns."

Under a supplementary headline—"He breaks the power of black magic (*kala jadoo*), satanic spirits, and demons"—the same ad also features what purports to be a testimonial from "a mother in Lahore."

The mother in question tells a sad story of how her cherished son's behavior mysteriously changed for the worse shortly after he got married. "He would come home late at night. He would quarrel with his wife over the slightest things. It reached the point that seeing his wife's face did not please him; instead he loathed the sight of her." (Bear in mind it's not uncommon for newlywed Pakistanis to move in with the husband's parents, thereby affording the mother a ringside perch for observing the progress of the son's marriage.)

The woman's daughter-in-law was miserable; her son wept tears of blood. Distraught, the mother sent for "various *'amils*, astrologers, and prestigious purveyors of medicines." All for nought: "Lots of rupees were wasted in this process."

Salvation came only when this Lahori mother happened upon an ad for Nihal Shah's services. "One day I glanced at the newspaper. I saw Shah Sahib's name. Without thinking I knew I had to go to him. I told him the whole story."

Nihal Shah told the mother her son would be healed within three days. "As soon as I heard what Shah Sahib said, tranquility came to my heart." And this *'amil* was as good as his word. "In this way Allah made manifest a miracle: on the third day, my son came home, and although my eyes couldn't believe it, it was true: now my son has been restored to happiness." She concludes with praise for Nihal Shah: "From the depths of my heart I am grateful to Shah Sahib."

As advertising, this can't be beat. It presents a domestic situation with which many readers can identify. Interesting to note, too, is how open-ended this testimonial is. Never explained is precisely what or who was afflicting the woman's son. But the headline preceding the testimonial, with its assertion that Nihal Shah "breaks the power of black magic," implies that demonic forces of some kind had been at work. Thus readers who know of quarreling newlyweds are implicitly encouraged to be on the lookout for the malefic influence of satanic magic—and by extension such readers are also encouraged to give Baba Nihal Shah a call.

Jinns in the Quran and Medieval Islamic Storytelling

Many Pakistani spirit-beliefs can be traced back to ancient pre-Islamic Arabia, where jinns were revered and feared as nature demons. Trees, pools, caves, and abandoned ruins might each constitute the residence of a jinn. But it was especially the desert regions—the uninhabited wastelands—that formed the realms of these beings. As with the god Pan of Greek antiquity, the Arab jinns were linked with the feelings of awe and unease that unpeopled nature inspires in solitary human wayfarers. Unpredictable and morally capricious, the beings that inhabited such regions might well choose to lash out at any humans that ventured into their territory.

But these spirit forces were not always—or at least not entirely—harmful. According to pagan Arab belief, they could choose to initiate relations with individual humans (in which case the individual was said to be *majnun*, possessed by a jinn).

But the Quran doesn't deny the jinns' existence. Far from it. Instead it circumscribes their power in accordance with the Islamic concept of *tawhid*: the monotheistic assertion of Allah's oneness. Jinns, like humans, are said to have been created by Allah. Jinns are made of fire, humans of clay; one race is invisible, the other visible. Although they normally have much longer lifespans than humans (I met persons in Lahore who claimed they'd had encounters with jinns that knew the prophet Muhammad fourteen centuries ago), nevertheless they are mortal. Jinns die and—so I was frequently told in Lahore—some get killed by sorcerers.

From a theological point of view, the most important trait jinns share with us is that they are volitional. Jinns, like humans, are capable of moral choices. Chapter 72 of the Quran depicts a company of jinns gathering around Muhammad—at a time when humans rejected God's word—and listening awe-struck to the revelation.

This means that there are Muslim and non-Muslim jinns, just as there are Muslim and non-Muslim people—a point (as we will see) of considerable importance for the popular religious imagination in Pakistan today.

The Quran also implies that jinns share human appetites. Among the pleasures reserved for believers in paradise are virginal houris, "whom neither man nor jinn has yet deflowered." Another appetite shared with humans is the desire to gain power by learning divine secrets. The Quran depicts jinns confessing the following behavior: "And we probed and searched heaven, but we found it filled with fierce guards and blazing comet-fires. We used to perch in heaven's vicinity, attempting to listen." Medieval Arab folk traditions describe heaven's angels casting fireballs at prying jinns and hurling them down from the sky. This is worth know-ing, because, as we will see, the use of jinns as spies to ferret out secrets is popular among Lahori sorcerers today.[2]

Among the jinns mentioned in the Quran are the *shayatin* or "satans" (*shayatin* is the plural of *shaitan*; the Quran characterizes Satan as one of the jinns). These *shaitans* are "infidels" or non-Muslim and hence are immoral in their behavior and rebellious against God's authority.[3]

The Quran counters this rebelliousness via the figure of King Solomon. Allah is said to have given this prophet mastery of both the wind ("which storms violently in its blowing") and the *shaitans* (who are described as "bound up in chains").[4] In describing the extent of Solomon's power, Islamic scripture repeatedly groups together the wind and the *shaitans* (both of which are elemental, invisible, and unruly). These Quranic verses thereby implicitly confirm the pagan understanding of the jinns as part of the undomesticated natural forces of the earth.

Solomon is said to have coerced some jinns into service as divers (Quranic commentary describes these *shaitans* as retrieving pearls for Solomon from the ocean depths). Other jinns were conscripted into enormous armies, where they joined the ranks of armed men under the prophet's command. These human-genie legions of clay and fire were created to invade neighboring kingdoms of unbelievers that resisted the message of Islam. Thus the jinns were linked to the early history of Muslim jihad.[5]

But it is not only in the Quran that one hears of jinns' enlistment in the wars of humans. Consider the military campaigns of India's seventeenth-century Moghul emperors. As noted in a previous chapter, Shah Jahan sent his favorite son, Dara Shikoh, on an expedition against the Afghan fortresses of Kandahar (also known as Qandhar). Chroniclers of the time report that when he set out from Lahore, Prince Dara included in his army various specialists in spiritual warfare, including "a number of pious ulamas [Muslim religious scholars] and Hindu magicians as a supple-ment to his war-like equipments." The following detail is of particular interest: "A Hindu *sannayasi* [renunciant/ascetic] was employed by the prince to work a miracle in the expedition; and a Haji, a master of forty genii, who claimed to be a great magician and hypnotist, was entrusted to secure the reduction of Qandhar by prayers and magic." But Kandahar

2. Quran 55.74, 72.8-9; E. W. Lane, *Manners and Customs of the Modern Egyptians* (London: J. M. Dent & Sons, 1908), 230.
   3. Quran 18.50; Lane, *Manners and Customs*, 228.
   4. Quran 21.81-82, 34.12-13, 38.36-38.
   5. Quran 21.82, 34.12-13, 38.36-38; Abdullah Yusuf Ali, *The Meaning of the Holy Quran* (Beltsville, MD: Amana, 1989), 812 n. 2738.

defied all such tactics. Dara Shikoh lacked the martial skills as well as the perfect mastery of the jinn-world possessed by King Solomon.[6]

A medieval Arabic source, al-Qazwini's thirteenth-century *'Aja'ib al-makhluqat* ("The Wonders of Created Beings"), described the race of jinns in ways that are reflected in Muslim folk beliefs of the subcontinent today. The following passage is from a chapter in Qazwini's text called "Wondrous Stories Concerning the Jinns." God has just granted Solomon dominion over the jinns, and Gabriel summons them all to manifest themselves so that the prophet-king can inspect them:

> Then the jinns and *shaitans* emerged, from the deserts, mountains, and hills, from the dried river-beds, waterless wastelands, and thickets. They said, "We are here, at your command!" The angels herded them along, the way a shepherd herds his goats, until all the jinns were assembled, in a packed crowd...before Solomon.
>
> He gazed at their features, at the marvels of their varied shapes. There were white jinns and black, yellow jinns and fair-skinned and piebald. The forms some took resembled horses; others, mules and lions. Some had elephant-trunks; others, tails, and hooves, and horns.
>
> Then Solomon prostrated himself before Allah most exalted and said, "O God, give me strength and the ability to inspire awe. For I cannot bear to look at them."
>
> Then Gabriel came to him and said, "Allah has given you power over them, so get up and rise from your place."
>
> Then he rose...and he asked them about their religions and their tribes and their dwellings and their food and drink.[7]

A nicely imagined scene, three aspects of which are worth noting here. First, so dreadful are these creatures to look at that even Solomon feels weak-kneed. This is Qazwini's way of asserting a basic point of Islamic doctrine: any power an individual human might acquire in controlling jinns comes about only *bi-idhni Allah*, "with God's permission." Second, although their elemental essence is fire, jinns can mimic creatures of clay by taking on the shape of animals when they are summoned to present themselves. Third, jinns can belong to any one of a number of "religions and tribes"—a bit of data that will be important in the sectarian landscape of present-day Pakistan.

In popular Islamic literature of the pre-modern era, the concept of the jinn offered a way to understand non-Muslim faiths. In the *Arabian Nights* story called "The City of Brass," a rebellious jinn known as

6. Bikrama Jit Hasrat, *Dara Shikuh: Life and Works* (2d ed.; Delhi: Munshiram Manoharlal, 1982), 41.

7. Zakariyya ibn Muhammad al-Qazwini, *'Aja'ib al-makhluqat wa-ghara'ib al-mawjudat* (Cairo: Mustafa al-Babi al-Halabi, 1966), 215-16.

Dahish ibn al-A'mash inhabits a red carnelian idol. Dahish speaks through its mouth and issues commands to the pagans that worship it. When the prophet Solomon hears of the idol, he calls on the pagans to smash this symbol of false religion. But Dahish urges them to resist, animating the statue so that it seems to be reciting seductively bellicose poetry. War ensues; the prophet's hordes triumph; paganism is brought low.[8]

Dahish's idol is reminiscent of one of the most notorious historical artifacts of the pre-Islamic era: a statue of the god Hubal, made of red agate in the form of a man. The medieval Muslim scholar Ibn al-Kalbi tells us in his *Book of Idols* that the pagan Arabs used to offer sacrifices to Hubal and consult it as an oracle.[9]

The *Arabian Nights* story may be interpreted as a Muslim attempt at using Islamic cosmology and Islamic conceptual categories to understand otherwise incomprehensible pagan ritual. In the Muslim worldview, jinns are real; they are known for seductive speech (after all, the worst of them—Satan—is denounced in the Quran as *alladhi yuwaswis fi sudur al-nass*, "the one who whispers temptingly into the hearts of human-kind"); and they have a reputation for intruding themselves into human affairs. So what is to prevent them from animating a statue and speaking through its lips and making it seem alluringly alive? Small wonder, then, if pagans bow down before it.[10]

An analogous explanatory model can be seen at work in the writings of an author from a different religious tradition: Justin Martyr, the second-century Christian Church father. Rather than deny the existence of the gods of the Greco-Roman pantheon, he conceded they were real. But he equated them with the offspring of the biblical "sons of God," who in chapter 6 of Genesis are said to have mated with human women. Justin described these hybrid offspring as *daimones* (demons). Among the ancient Greeks and Romans, the term was favorable, denoting minor gods that were benevolent to our race. But for early Christians, *daimones* were demonic: the children of the "sons of God" and earthly females were foul devils, and their leader, Zeus-Jupiter, was known to the Christians as Satan.[11]

---

8. 'Abd al-Rahman al-Safati al-Sharqawi, ed., *Alf laylah wa-layla* (Cairo: Bulaq, 1835), vol. 2, 37-52.

9. William H. McNeill and Marilyn Robinson Waldman, *The Islamic World* (Chicago: University of Chicago Press, 1973), 10-11.

10. Quran 6.112, 114.5.

11. Adela Yarbro Collins, "Satan's Throne: Revelations from Revelation," *Biblical Archaeology Review* 32.3 (May 2006): 26-39.

Thus medieval Muslim storytellers and early Christian authors found a way to fit paganism into monotheistic cosmology, by matching polytheistic belief with references in biblical and Quranic scripture (sons of God and satanic jinns). Thereby the object of pagan worship was acknowledged as something real and powerful. But it was construed as evil rather than good, and subordinate to the one true God.

But in at least some parts of the Islamic world, the jinns' linkage with pre-Islamic paganism is not always understood as negative. Edward William Lane, an Englishman resident in Cairo in the early nineteenth century, was a close observer of Egyptian Muslim religious beliefs. Among his numerous reports on the genii (jinns), one in particular is relevant here:

> Some of the people of Cairo say that a party of genii, in the forms and garb of ordinary mortals, used to hold a midnight "*sook*" (or market) during the first ten days of Muharram, in a street called Es-Saleebeh, in the southern part of the metropolis, before an ancient sarcophagus, which was called "el-Hod el-Marsoud" (or "the Enchanted Trough")... It was removed by the French during their occupation of Egypt, and is now in the British Museum. Since its removal, the *sook* of the genii, it is said, has been discontinued.[12]

But the goods offered for sale by these jinns, so Lane's Egyptian informants insisted, were beneficial rather than harmful: "Whoever happened to pass through the street where they were assembled, and bought anything of them, whether dates or other fruit, cakes, bread, &c., immediately after found his purchase converted into gold."[13]

This anecdote, which occurs in the context of a discussion of Egyptian Muslim beliefs about benevolent jinns, implies a positive assessment of Egypt's pharaonic legacy: in some unexplained way, the "enchanted sarcophagus" provided a gathering point for jinns that distributed largesse to passers-by. Once this physical link with the pagan past disappeared, so too did the handouts of gold.

I mention Lane's report because Pakistan, like Egypt, is a Muslim country where numerous artifacts survive from the country's pre-Islamic heritage. In contemporary Pakistan, both Muslim folk belief and Urdu pulp fiction (as we will see) invoke the jinns frequently, as a way of commenting on the still-thriving presence of Hinduism across the border in neighboring India, and as a way of confronting the lingering—and disturbing—physical legacy of the Hindu gods in Muslim Lahore.

12. Lane, *Manners and Customs*, 433.
13. Lane, *Manners and Customs*, 433.

Sorcery in Lahore: Initial Encounters

One of my first meetings with a "spiritual practitioner" in Lahore came about when I happened across a multicolored leaflet, illustrated with images of a lamp, a zodiacal chart, and a palmist's hand (within which was inscribed a skull and crossbones), advertising the services of an individual named Pirzada Hafeez Shah (Pirzada is an honorific title, indicating someone is the descendant of a Sufi master).

The Urdu text caught my attention right away with this headline: "Why shouldn't wishes come true? Fate can be changed through the influence of prayer. A message of healing for those who are suffering and in despair."

The leaflet specified the kinds of problems Hafeez Shah was ready to handle: "Every type of situation—for example, the influence of evil satanic amulets, travel abroad, failure in love, lucky lottery numbers, problems with relatives, friendship, enmity, fights at home, failure in business—all these things are resolved by means of *nuri 'ilm* [literally, 'luminous knowledge' or white magic] and are accomplished with the utmost secrecy."

"Success," the leaflet promised, "will be achieved in twenty-four hours."

After a build-up like that I was eager to meet this man. I phoned the number printed on the sheet and spoke with an assistant. I told him who I was and said something about my research interests and asked if I might interview Hafeez Shah. I was instructed to come the following afternoon and was given an address in Lahore's Gulberg quarter.

I showed up the next day with my driver and two Pakistani friends. We knew we'd found the right place when we saw a sun-blistered placard: Hafeez Shah. *Khavvateen ke lie purdah*: "Private space for ladies."

"Women," commented one of my friends, "provide most of the business for *'amils*." Children's health, husband's job, quarrels with the relatives, oppression by a bullying mother-in-law with whom one has to share a house: "Women," as he summed it up, "have it a lot worse in life. The *'amil* provides some relief."

From the outside the site didn't look overly impressive. Hafeez Shah's office was one of many crowding the second floor of a badly weathered cinderblock storefront strip. Beneath his office was a bakery. The stairs were littered with bread crusts, corn cobs, and plastic bags. Knots of snarled truck traffic belched fumes in our faces.

Upstairs was better. We went through a glass-fronted entranceway and found ourselves in a tiny but neatly arranged reception area. A deferential assistant behind a counter had us sit while he made a phone call.

Shelves behind the counter displayed enormous Quran-texts bound in green leather. The walls were covered in tilework that depicted flower vases alternating with scriptural verses.

The assistant put down his phone. He looked embarrassed. He said Hafeez Sahib wasn't in. He'd had to go somewhere on urgent religious business. Could we come back tomorrow?

My friends saw the disappointment on my face and jumped from their seats. Perhaps Mister Hafeez doesn't realize it, they said, but this is a big professor doctor Sahib, come all the way from California, USA, to interview people like Mister Hafeez. The professor wants to meet with the *'amil* today, not tomorrow.

The assistant said he could do nothing.

My friends said he should phone his boss again and ask him to rush over here.

My friends' voices got louder. The assistant's voice got louder, too.

Finally my guys wore down the receptionist. He sighed and picked up the phone again and dialed. A minute's worth of pleading whispers, and then he stepped around the counter to a door at the back of the office. He opened the door and ushered us in.

Within this inner room—to my surprise, and that of my friends—sat the man I'd been trying to meet: Pirzada Hafeez Shah. Beside him on a couch lounged a young man. The two were watching TV.

My guys and I traded glances. All this time our sorcerer hadn't been away on urgent religious business but instead was at his ease in his sanctum. Later my friends speculated that Hafeez Shah had instructed his receptionist to make us wait and re-book our appointment just so he could give the appearance of having a busy schedule.

Mister Hafeez was young, in his late twenties, pudgy and bearded. He wore a baggy *shalwar-qameez* (trousers and tunic) and a brocaded vest. I got things off to an awkward start through a careless choice of words: I asked him to tell me about his practice of *jadoo* (magic).

That made him sit up. He was an *'amil ruhani* ("spiritual practitioner"), he said, and *'amils* don't do *jadoo. Jadoo* is something only magicians—*jadoogars*—do, those who dabble in *kala 'ilm* ("black knowledge"), *kala jadoo* ("black magic").

In that case, I asked, how would you describe your own work?

'Amils like himself, he said, are those who *break* the spells cast by *jadoogars.* "We counter black knowledge with luminous knowledge."

And this in fact proved to be the answer I got in every talk I had with a practitioner of sorcery. They themselves didn't do *jadoo*, they said; magic was something perpetrated by others. My informants insisted that what they themselves did was to negate the malicious effect of charms and amulets created by workers in *jadoo*. In short, magic was wrong and casting spells to harm others was wrong.

But defending oneself and one's clients against magic was perfectly moral, they argued. After all, I was frequently told, the last two chapters of the Quran are amuletic and are meant to serve as a defense against the black *jadoo* associated with satanic whisperings. With the Quran as a precedent, no one, they said, could object to defensive sorcery.

Hafeez Shah evaded my subsequent questions. He shied away from talk about jinns, his fee scale, and the specific types of talismans he created. "I never ask for money," he said. He insisted everything he did was undertaken *fi sabil Allah*, "in the path of God," out of selfless religious duty. In other words, he earned so much divine merit in his job that he'd never accept anything except purely voluntary donations. (My friends' caustic comment on this, once we'd left the office: "Yeah. That's what they all say.")

But Hafeez Shah did have some information he was eager to share. Black *jadoo*, he said, is often triggered by *hasad* and *chashm-e bad*: envy and the evil eye. One must beware the eye of envious neighbors. And when I asked him about his job qualifications, whether he'd had to go through a special course of study to be qualified as a sorcerer, he said only two things were needed: a thorough knowledge of the Quran, and steadfast *yaqeen* (certainty and absolute conviction in one's faith).

To illustrate for me the importance of *yaqeen*, abruptly he asked whether I knew the shape of the letter *alif*. I said yes: it's the first letter of the Arabic (and Urdu) alphabet; its shape is a simple vertical stroke like the upright blade of a dagger.

"Then perhaps you will understand this," he said. "One *alif* from the Quran, just one, recited with *yaqeen*, is enough to slice a rock in two." As he said this he extended his index finger and slashed it down through the air like a knife halving a grapefruit.

Impressive.

He waved his *alif*-finger at me. "That's what you need for breaking spells," he said. "Quran recitation, done with *yaqeen*."

He smiled. He looked pleased with his flourish.

On the way out I saw the reception room now held customers. Several women, all veiled. They sat huddled together talking but stopped as we passed through the room.

They looked worried, all of them. Worried, but hopeful, maybe, too.

With any luck, I thought as my friends and I retreated down the stairs, they've come equipped with *yaqeen*: enough to help Mister Hafeez slice in two any problems they might have.

"This is the time they are abroad in the air":
Warnings to Children about Jinns

Luckily for me, other sorcerers I met in Lahore were more communicative than the dagger-*alif*-wielding Hafeez Shah. Particularly helpful to me were a father and son, both of whom engaged to some extent in *nuri 'ilm* practices. I met them through a woman I'll call Nabeela, a young Urdu-language instructor at BULPIP (the Lahore headquarters of the University of California's "Berkeley Urdu Language Program in Pakistan").

Knowing of my interest in folk religion, Nabeela one day mentioned during our tutoring session something she knew would get my attention. A friend of hers at Punjab University, who had been enduring intense emotional distress, suddenly announced one day she'd figured out what was the source of her troubles. She'd become *majnun*.

"I told her this was *fazool bat* [nonsense]," recalled my instructor. Nabeela told me she'd suggested to her friend that she take a harder look at the dynamics of her own life before blaming her troubles on the interference of jinns.

I asked whether her friend took her advice.

She said no. I asked whether she'd been able to offer her friend any other help.

"Yes, I did." She said she'd encouraged her friend to keep repeating *Surat al-Fatihah, Ayat al-Kursi,* and *Surat al-Nas* (all of these are Quran-passages believed to be efficacious against jinns).

I reminded Nabeela she'd said this *majnun* business was *fazool bat.*

She looked uncomfortable. She said yes she knew that, and yes she and her friend were both university-educated, but all the same it was just as well to be on the safe side.

This illustrates a point I noticed repeatedly in my visits to Pakistan. It is unsurprising to find belief in jinns widespread among all social classes of Muslims—after all, jinns are referred to repeatedly in Islam's scripture. What surprised me, however, was to find anxiety about the active intrusive presence of malevolent spirit-forces among both the educated and uneducated, the higher- and lower-income groups alike.

I found this to be the case also among Muslim students I've taught in California, at Santa Clara University. Several of my Pakistani Muslim students—all of them female, all from prosperous families—volunteered information on the jinn-lore to which they'd been exposed since childhood.

An example is Jameela, a young woman from Karachi's Clifton locality—a fashionable and well-to-do neighborhood. This is what she had to say:

> We couldn't have a dog when I was little, because there's a *hadith* [a statement attributed to the prophet Muhammad] that says: "No angel will enter a house where there's a dog or a picture," and if no angels are there, a jinn can get in.
>
> When I was a little girl my mother always told me, "Never stand in a doorway during *maghrib azan* [the evening call to prayer, at sunset]: this is the time when *churails* [ghosts of women who died in pregnancy or childbirth] and jinns are abroad in the air. They might take you."
>
> Mother also said, "Never wear perfume if you go out at *maghrib*; never go out with your hair wet or loose or uncovered. Jinns are much more attracted to women than to men, so be careful not to do anything to attract them."
>
> If we were outside playing, Mother would always call us in as soon as she heard the *maghrib azan*. It was like a warning bell, this *azan*.
>
> My mother wouldn't let us sit under trees as it got near sunset. Jinns will drop down on us from the treetops, she said. They perch in trees.

Jameela laughed as she recalled her mother's talk, but it struck me as a nervous laugh. She said even now she remembered the warning whenever she heard the *maghrib azan*.

Easy enough, of course, to psychologize all this and discuss it as a parental ploy to keep attractive young daughters indoors. But as Jameela spoke, a vision came to me, of winged spirits swarming through the evening air and then roosting on some tree-branch like a flock of restless crows to eye stray children below. Yes, I could imagine how a memory like that might arouse unease.

Later, I was to hear a sorcerer assign a religious denominational identity to treetop-perching jinns; but I'll save this explanation for below, when I discuss sectarianism in the spirit-world.

The Thing on the Wall: The Use of Children to Contact the Spirit-World— and What Happens When the Contact Goes Bad

Now back to my Urdu tutor Nabeela. Perceiving my interest in the jinn-realm, she suggested I seek out a gentleman living in Lahore who, she said, was known for a fact to use a *ma'sum beta* to establish contact with jinns.

Beta is the Urdu for child or boy; *ma'sum* means innocent, sinless, or pure. *Ma'sum beta* refers to a child that is not yet sexually active.

I asked Nabeela exactly how "pure children" were used to establish such contact. She said I should ask the man myself.

I did. In fact I hired him as one of my Urdu tutors. I'll call this man Mustafa Akhtar.

Mustafa was in his late fifties, from a *muhajir* background (which meant that his family had emigrated from India—from Delhi, in his case—to Pakistan in 1947, at the time of Partition and the creation of the national Muslim homeland). Conservative and pious in his worldview, he favored a carefully trimmed beard and a neatly shaved upper lip—a grooming style he referred to as *sunnah* (conforming to the example offered by the lifestyle and personal habits of the prophet Muhammad).

And yes, he said without hesitation when I raised the question, he did make use of a *ma'sum beta* when he wished to summon a jinn. Or more specifically, a *ma'sum beti*: a girl. His daughter, to be precise. She was nine years old, he said.

But before we reached that point in our Urdu conversations, Mustafa told me something first of how he'd initially chanced to have direct experience of genies.

He'd had a neighbor, he said, who was an *'amil*, a practitioner of the good kind of sorcery, he said: *nuri 'ilm*. This sorcerer controlled so many dozens of jinns that he offered to make Mustafa a gift of one. Without giving the matter much thought, Mustafa accepted.

The jinn the *'amil* chose for him was Muslim—hence, said Mustafa, benevolent and obedient. But this was a jinn that took its Islam seriously. It was strictly orthodox in its observance of prayer and the like, and it expected the same of its humans (as Mustafa was to learn later). Its name: Suleiman (Arabic for Solomon, a good name for a good Muslim jinn).

Mustafa lacked the skill—so he told me—to summon his jinn unaided; nor could he make the creature render itself visible to him. He couldn't do these things because he'd never undergone a *chillah* (the "forty-day retreat," about which I was to learn more in subsequent visits). But with the help of his daughter—his *ma'sum beti*—he could summon Suleiman whenever he needed.

Here's how it worked:

> I have my daughter sit down [he said] and close her eyes. Then I recite *Ya Nur* ("O Light," one of Allah's "beautiful names") eleven times. Then *Ayat al-Kursi* (the "throne verse," Quran 2.255), once. Then I breathe on my daughter, to transfer to her the power of these words to protect her body against the jinns.

> Then I ask her: Can you see anything? Yes, she'll say. She can see the jinn, even though I, her father, cannot. Then I'll explain to her the job for which the jinn has been summoned.

I asked Mustafa about the jobs the jinns are made to do. "Black *jadoo*" practitioners, he said, use genies for harmful, even murderous, designs against neighbors and rivals (and the way to summon "satanic" jinns for such purposes, he said, entails invocation-rituals that include blasphemous acts such as tearing a page of the Quran).

But *'amils* that do *nuri 'ilm* use their jinns benevolently, for chores ranging from finding lost objects around the house to medical diagnoses. He gave me an example of how he'd used Suleiman not so long ago. Mustafa had had no contact for some time with his relatives back in Delhi, and he wanted to know how they were. He commissioned Suleiman to check up on them. To do this, said Mustafa, the jinn went to India in the company of Mustafa's daughter's *hamzad*. (Literally meaning "twin" or "born together," *hamzad* has a special significance in the context of sorcery: "a jinn, or familiar spirit, said to be produced at the moment of the birth of every child, and to accompany him through life."[14])

His daughter's *hamzad*, he said, had readier access to knowledge of family matters—such as the location of his relatives' home in Delhi—than would an "outsider" jinn such as Suleiman. Together the two spirits shot off to India's capital, where the girl's *hamzad* found the house and pointed it out to Suleiman. Then Suleiman listened in on the relatives' doings, and the pair returned to Lahore in a flash. Suleiman reported his findings to the girl, who conveyed all the information to her father.

"All of us," Mustafa told me, "have a *hamzad*. You do; I do. On our own we can't access or make use of our 'twin,' but jinns can do this for us."

Fascinating, this anecdote, in part because of the way it suggests how the spirit-world can be marshaled to compensate for difficulties in cross-border contacts between families that are cut off from each other because of the sporadically hostile quality of international relations between Pakistan and India.

In another conversation Mustafa explained that sometimes he would have his daughter stare into a mirror, and the jinn would suddenly show itself in the glass. At other times, the jinn would even use the girl's thumbnail as a view-screen in which it would display itself to her.

---

14. John T. Platts, *A Dictionary of Urdu, Classical Hindi and English* (Oxford: Clarendon Press, 1884), 1234.

Wouldn't the sight of a jinn, I asked, frighten a little girl? (At that moment I was thinking: it would be enough to frighten *me*, for sure.)

No, no, said Mustafa, with a smile that suggested: Everything stays firmly under control. *Yeh jinn insani shakl leta hay*: "This jinn takes on a human shape," so as not to frighten the child. According to his daughter, Suleiman most typically appeared in the form of a man in his fifties, handsome and bearded. "Much like you," I said. He took this as a compliment. I left it at that.

The invocation-ritual described by Mustafa apparently has a long lineage. The *Leyden Papyrus*, a Greco-Egyptian magical text of the third century AD, features numerous spells for conjuring forth a variety of gods. As with Mustafa's use of a *ma'sum beta*, many of the spells stipulate that the magician "bring a pure child" to the invocation site. Other spells in the papyrus make clear what type of purity is involved: "You take a boy, pure, before he has gone with a woman"; "You take a clean bright lamp…you make the boy stand before it, he being pure and not having gone with a woman."[15]

The logic underlying the use of children for divination is explored in a Latin text of the second century AD, Apuleius's *Apology*. Apuleius, a neo-Platonic philosopher who wrote about the Egyptian Isis-cult, composed the *Apology* to defend himself in court against a charge of harming individuals through the practice of sorcery. In the following passage he declares his own beliefs about divinatory practices:

> I believe in Plato's assertion that there exist certain divine powers that are positioned, in nature and in place, midway between gods and humans. It is these intermediary powers that govern all gifts of divination and the miracles wrought by mages. I also think it possible for the human soul, especially the simple soul of a child [*animum humanum praesertim puerilem et simplicem*]—whether via the chanting of verses or the incantatory effect of inhaling certain scents—to be lulled asleep. Then for a little while, it forgets its present surroundings and is detached from all memory of its body. Thereupon it returns to its true nature, which is immortal and divine. While it is in this kind of sleep, it may foretell things of the future.[16]

Two points are worth noting here. First is that the "intermediary powers" he describes bear at least some resemblance to the jinns. Second—and much more interesting—is what Apuleius says about the divinatory

---

15. F. L. Griffith and Herbert Thompson, eds., *The Leyden Papyrus: An Egyptian Magical Book* (New York: Dover, 1974), 77, 35, 159.

16. Paul Vallette, ed., *Apulée: Apologie* (Paris: Société d'édition "Les Belles Lettres," 1924), 52-53.

potential of the *animum humanum praesertim puerilem et simplicem*: "the human soul, especially the simple soul of a child." Implicit in this Latin text, I think, as in the Egyptian *Leyden Papyrus*, and in the Pakistani use of the *ma'sum beta*, is the assumption that the pre-sexual self, because it is not yet fully entangled in the social world of adult relations, is *simplex* and *ma'sum*: simple and pure. Hence it offers a clearer mirror for catching a glimpse of the divine, of the realms that are not subject to the limitations of bodies of flesh.

The *Leyden Papyrus* offers what I consider another point of comparison with the jinn-summonings I learned about in Lahore. The "pure" child to be used as a medium in the Egyptian ritual is positioned by the sorcerer so that the child's face is directly over a bowl filled with water or oil—a reflective surface meant to function, I believe, like the mirror used in Lahori ritual.

The Egyptian magician then chants, "Open to me the earth, open to me the Underworld, open to me the abyss," while invoking various deities: "a rearing uraeus [cobra]", "the lion-ram," "Balkam the dread one of heaven," "the almighty four-faced demon," etc. Other spells may invoke the spirits of persons who have been drowned or murdered. Meanwhile the child is expected to be ready for the appearance of Anubis (the jackal-god of the Egyptian underworld). When Anubis appears, the child is to say, "Go forth, bring in the gods."[17]

Naturally the papyrus has nothing to say about what all this must have been like as an emotional experience for the "pure child" who was used as a medium—with one's face inches above a lamp-lit basin, in which one is to be on the lookout for jackal-gods, four-faced demons, and drowned and murdered men. But one does get a hint of the dangers involved: the magician calls on any benevolent god that might be present, saying, "Do thou protect this boy whose face is bent down."[18]

Which brings us back to Mustafa and his daughter. At first when I asked whether it was frightening for the girl to find herself used as a medium, he said no, not at all. As mentioned above, Suleiman the jinn, being well-intentioned, appeared to her in an *insani shakl*, "human shape," reassuringly like that of her own father.

17. Griffith and Thompson, *The Leyden Papyrus*, 21.

18. Griffith and Thompson, *The Leyden Papyrus*, 25. The use of children for divination in the setting of the Subcontinent has its own history in fiction of the British colonial era. See Wilkie Collins's *The Moonstone* (1868), Rudyard Kipling's *Kim* (1901), and Talbot Mundy's *Om: The Secret of Ahbor Valley* (1924). All these novels refer to boys being made to gaze into ink-pools for the purpose of clairvoyant contemplation.

But in a subsequent session Mustafa told me of an incident that was much more disturbing. One night, he said, he used his daughter to summon Suleiman and then had her command the spirit to go to the house of another *'amil*. He said he wanted Suleiman to "learn what he could" of the other *'amil*'s household (which I took to mean that Suleiman was supposed to snoop about—like one of the Quran's heaven-probing jinns —and spy out the man's professional secrets).

Although Mustafa didn't explain the identity of this sorcerer in any detail, the latter was apparently a rival—and, as Mustafa found out, a much more skilled "practitioner" than he.

Suleiman was abjectly unable to enter the other sorcerer's house at all: the rival had "*lakhs* [hundreds of thousands] of demons at his command."

Unfortunately the matter didn't end there. By way of retaliation, the other sorcerer sent one of his own jinns to terrify Mustafa's household.

Mustafa's family was sitting quietly at home when his daughter looked up and suddenly screamed. She said she'd just seen *eik bahut unchi chiz* ("a very tall thing") of indeterminate shape, outlined on the wall. No reassuring human figure this time; just a huge thing on the wall.

It had to have been an *'ifrit*, said Mustafa: a species of jinn known for its violence and malice.

The girl, I thought, was the one who ended up paying the price for her father's dabbling. Having been trained to catch mirror-glimmerings of "luminous" jinns, it was unsurprising that eventually she would also happen upon glimpses of the manifestations of sorcery's darker side as well.

On the Dangers of Dancing in Mixed Company

Mustafa's daughter was not the only member of his family to get caught up in sorcery. His son Tariq—a man in his late twenties when I first met him—became involved as well, to the extent that—unlike his father—he became a professional specialist in *nuri 'ilm*, with a diploma to prove it.

Tariq's interest arose when his father's "gift" jinn Suleiman started getting out of control.

Was there an incident, I asked Mustafa, that triggered this loss of control?

Apparently there was. Suleiman, he reminded me, was not only a Muslim but a piously observant and orthodox jinn. It became angry when the family attended a wedding and Tariq indulged himself in a considerable amount of dancing.

I asked whether dancing was really all that bad.

It wasn't just the dancing, explained Mustafa. It was also the fact that it was in mixed company. Dancing, and the presence of men and women together: that was enough to disrupt Mustafa's relationship with the jinn.

Thereafter Tariq began to experience petty harassment: money stolen, a pair of his lace-up shoes mysteriously tangled and left dangling from a coat-rack—troubling behavior, which the family knew had to be the work of the jinn. Finally Suleiman ceased responding to any attempts at invocation by Mustafa.

But this wasn't the end of the family's dealings with the jinn-realm. Tariq apprenticed himself to a Sufi named Ustad Muhammad Aman Allah, a member of the Chhisti and Qadiri *tariqas* (Sufi orders), who was also a master sorcerer. Mustafa assured me his son was far more proficient as a jinn-tamer than he was, and soon I arranged to hire Tariq as an Urdu conversation-partner as well.

The young man wasn't the easiest tutor to get on with—he seemed suspicious when I explained I was an academic researcher and I admitted I'm a non-Muslim and a Christian. He eyed me warily as I did my constant note-scribbling, and at times he was clearly reluctant to share key bits of information with an outsider and unbeliever. And I made things worse by showing enthusiastic interest in Shia self-flagellation, parrot fortune-telling, and other practices that are condemned as heretical by many Muslims. Nonetheless I learned a lot from him. I met with Tariq repeatedly in the course of several trips to Pakistan, and over time I heard plenty of strange stories.

He warmed to me a bit (or at least became less unfriendly) the day his father told me Tariq had just recently finished his studies with his mentor and had been awarded an *ijazah* (a permit to undertake practice on his own). I asked Tariq whether he had a diploma he could show me. The young man was happy to oblige.

He pointed with pride to the key sentences in the certificate:

> Together with permission to practice, Tariq Akhtar is given this testimonial of accomplishment as a spiritual practitioner and healer of bodily conditions. Through the grace and favor of Allah most exalted, he is enabled to undertake treatment for dealing with jinns, magic [*jadoo*], and bodily illnesses.

This same mentor had also written a booklet called *Chehel kaf ki qalami* ("Manuscript of the Forty K's"). Tariq had a copy, and he let me glance at it briefly.

It begins by urging the neophyte to read the following saying of the prophet Muhammad: "Any one of you who can help his brother should certainly do so." First the text is given in its original Arabic. Thereafter follows a translation in Urdu—but a translation that adds information concerning the type of help to be offered: "Any one of you who can help his brother (in the form of breathing upon him in prayer or through the use of talismans) should certainly do so." ("Breathing in prayer" upon someone—*dam* is the Urdu term used here—is a very popular practice. The practitioner holds his hands to his face while praying and then breathes upon the beneficiary, pointing his hands at the other person or touching the patient; the efficacy of the prayer is thus transferred via the breath.)

Citing a prophetic *hadith* at the very beginning of this book is, of course, a way of emphasizing the orthodox quality of the practices contained therein.

I asked about the "forty k's" (*chehel kaf*) mentioned in the booklet's title. He explained this was "an Arabic prayer in the classical style of the holy Quran," to be chanted by the *'amil* before beginning the treatment of clients. He explained that the Arabic letter *kaf* appears in the prayer exactly forty times (an auspicious number).

He recited the prayer for me, and he did so in a staccato hurried murmur that was all but incomprehensible (I caught bits of it—*kafaka rabbuka kam yakfika*, "Your Lord has protected you; how often does he protect you." Also something-something *kaukab al-falak*, "the star of the celestial sphere"; but that was all).

Nonetheless the burst of rapid-fire *kaf*s was impressive, and I told him so. That made him happy. He said the text should be recited fast but with no slip-of-the-tongue mispronunciations: quite a challenge.

Few clients, I imagine, could ever understand what he was saying; but intelligibility wasn't the point. The point was to take classical Arabic phrasing and turn it into something incantatory and, quite literally, spell-binding.

Throne-Verse and Safety Ring: Precautionary Measures for the Forty-Day Retreat

But it was the *chillah*—the forty-day retreat—that I particularly wanted to hear about. I wasn't sure how much Tariq would be willing to share with me on this topic. But he, unlike his father, had completed the *chillah*, and he was proud to tell me stories of his experiences. He sketched for me the regimen one must undergo:

> First you seek permission from your *murshid* [guide/spiritual director]. He will stipulate a particular *surah* [Quran chapter] for you to recite and indicate how many times a night you must repeat it during each of the

forty nights of the retreat. You must complete all the stipulated recitations for all forty nights without interruption in order for the *chillah* to be effective and for the goal of jinn-mastery to be attained.

A book by the nineteenth-century Indian Muslim author Ja'far Sharif, the *Qanun-i-Islam*, describes what would-be jinn-masters did to achieve the necessary state of spiritual focus: "They go to a house or place outside the town, or to a mountain, cave, or well, or some place where water is at hand. The noise of a town distracts the attention, and in this work the mind must be concentrated and the thoughts must not wander."[19]

The way Tariq put it is that *chillah*-disciples may seek out *viran jaghayn*, "deserted places," such as the banks of Lahore's Ravi River by night. But it is also possible, he said, to do the retreat right in one's own room in the city—"provided you can be left alone for forty nights."

He also emphasized the need for "purity": abstention from sexual relations and from eating meat. These things, too, constitute distractions.

Each night, he said, you begin by reciting *Ayat al-Kursi*, the Quranic "throne-verse," so named because it refers to God's throne, which is said to "extend over the heavens and the earth"; it also asserts that neither drowsiness nor sleep can overtake Allah. Thus the verse emphasizes both God's vigilance and wide-ranging power—traits that pious Muslims believe can be invoked for one's own protection. Hence *Ayat al-Kursi* is one of the most frequently recited Quran verses for purposes of talismanic self-defense.

Having begun by reciting this verse, said Tariq, you then sit and with your finger make the motion of drawing a circle around yourself, to demonstrate to any beings that are watching that this has become a protected area. *'Ifrits*, *shaitans*, jinns of any kind cannot enter this circle. This, he said, is your "safety ring."

Excursus:
A Note on Magic Circles, from Pariah-Kite Bridge

On one of my visits to Lahore's Ravi Bridge in December 2005, I had the opportunity to learn more about the art of summoning jinns.

It was a sunny morning, traffic on the bridge was heavy, and the men and boys who make a living selling *cheel-gosht* (meat for pariah kites) to passing motorists were doing brisk business. I inquired whether other rituals besides kite-meat offerings take place here along the river. Several vendors said they'd occasionally observed a *chillah* occurring on the riverbank at night.

19. Ja'far Sharif. *Islam in India or the Qanun-i-Islam* (London: Curzon Press, 1972), 220.

One detail in particular from our conversation is immediately relevant in this context. A sixty-year-old man from the Punjabi town of Gujranwala, who told me he'd been working as a vendor along the river for many years, said he'd heard that for the *chillah* to be successful, the would-be "practitioner" needs to draw a protective circle around himself. One should use either an iron rod or a knife containing iron to draw the circle. The rod or knife is then stuck upright in the ground in the circle's center.

This is necessary for protection, the man from Gujranwala emphasized. *Buri taqatayn* (malevolent powers) will try to assail you, try to do you harm, in order to keep you from controlling them and to keep you from becoming an *'amil.*

I asked about the significance of iron. No consensus here. *Loha lohay ko katta hay*, one man said, quoting a proverb: "Iron cuts iron." So maybe, he reasoned, the iron rod and knife indicate that one is summoning *buri taqatayn* to fight off other *buri taqatayn.* But he admitted this was speculation.

Pertinent to this question is a remark by Edward Lane on nineteenth-century Egyptian magical practices. He describes a defense against the *zoba'ah* (desert whirlwind): "A charm is usually uttered by the Egyptians to avert the *zoba'ah*, when it seems to be approaching them: some of them exclaim, "Iron, thou unlucky!"—as ginn are supposed to have a great dread of that metal." Ja'far Sharif also notes the use of iron in Indian rituals "to scare evil spirits."[20]

But again, why iron rather than some other substance? A scholar of Tibetan Buddhism named Thomas Marcotty offers a useful historical perspective. In an exhaustive study of Tibetan "dagger priests," who use iron-bladed knives to repel demons, Marcotty traces the origin of such rituals to ancient Mesopotamia:

> Sumerian daggers...served for the so-called soil consecration. This means they were driven into the ground as a kind of border marking to indicate to everybody, mainly the roaming demons, that the thus marked and bordered area was inhabited by man and thus out of bounds to demons...
>
> To this desire of denying access to demons may have been added a more practical purpose. Anyone who [has] struck a tent on a camping site will now know what this is about: ritual daggers resemble the pegs by the aid of which nomads used to tie their tents to the ground from times immemorial. Such pegs should best be made of iron so that the tent dwellers may be in a better position to drive them also into stony soil.[21]

20. Lane, *Manners and Customs*, 229-30; Sharif, *Islam in India*, 23, 93 n. 3.

21. Thomas Marcotty, *Dagger Blessing: The Tibetan Phurpa Cult* (Delhi: B. R. Publishing, 1987), 12.

The Shape That Things May Take:
On Asking for a Glimpse of Jinns

"And thus out of bounds to demons": a reassuring thought, as one constructs one's magic circle.

But now back to Tariq Akhtar, and his ritual for undertaking and surviving the *chillah*:

> After you've drawn the ring around yourself [he said], you recite the Throne-Verse yet again. Then blow onto your hands [thereby transferring the power of the just-recited verse] and rub your hands all over yourself, to protect your entire body from possible harm.
>
> Then remain seated within the circle for as long as it takes to recite your assigned *surahs* the stipulated number of times.

I interrupted him. "And then what happens?"

"The first ten or twelve nights," he said, "nothing."

"But the dozenth night or so," he said, "if you've prayed properly, you begin to sense there's something outside the circle. You begin to sense a presence."

At this point he paused and said he had to explain something about the nature of jinns. "*Jinn azad makhluq hayn.*" Jinns are free creatures, and they value their independence. "Because they sense that someone wants to enslave them, and because they don't want to be ensnared, they try to foil your plan through various stratagems."

He detailed a typical stratagem: "Jinns can cause images of your mother, sister, wife, or any other relative to appear, and you will have the feeling someone wants to kill them. Your impulse will be to rush out of the circle to check on them and save them."

"If you give way to that impulse," he said, "the *chillah* is broken, and you have to start over from day one. But if you make it through forty consecutive nights uninterrupted, then various jinns will come under your dominion to serve you."

"And you have such dominion now?" I asked.

"Right now," he said, "at this very moment, three jinns are roaming about this room, watching over me, guarding me." He pointed to the ceiling.

Naturally I looked up. Naturally I saw nothing.

I asked whether he—as someone who'd successfully completed the *chillah*—was ever able to behold these jinns and see what they look like.

The answer was yes. "They take various shapes, animal shapes, at various times for various needs."

Could he give me an example, I said, of one of the shapes they typically take. I visualized tigers, or perhaps dragons of some kind. Something fearsome.

At home, he said, when they're guarding his family's house and property, they typically take the shape of *chhipkalian*.

Chhipkalian. The word was new to me. My hands flew to the Urdu dictionary on the table between us.

Chhipkalian: plural of *chhipkali*: lizard. The accompanying illustration showed a picture of a cute little gecko.

Gecko lizards?

That was precisely what he meant.

Geckos I knew about. Every home, guesthouse, and hotel room I've ever inhabited in the subcontinent always had its share of them. They hide behind the toilet bowl and draperies and at night race along the walls and eat mosquitoes. I've always thought of them as friendly presences, but not, I admit, as awe-inspiring jinns.

The puzzlement on my face must have been plain to see. "You want to know," Tariq said, "why my jinns take the shape of geckos."

I admitted yes I did.

The reason, he said, is that geckos are so useful. They're small, they're common, they're everywhere—to such an extent that people don't pay them any attention.

Geckos come and go in and out of houses easily and unnoticed, he said. So they're perfect as spies, for collecting information useful to an *'amil*. What better shape for a jinn to take?

That gave me something to think about. Back in my room in Lahore's Cantonment neighborhood that night, I lay on my bed in the dark and listened as my favorite gecko ran along the walls. I'd seen him up close more than once, motionless behind the curtains: big (five inches long), pale green, dappled with paler translucent splotches. A benevolent roommate.

But a spy? That would depend on its attention span. For the moment it seemed more interested in chasing bugs than watching me.

Next morning I had another question for Tariq: "There are lots of geckos in your house, aren't there? So how do you know whether one gecko is your jinn, and whether another gecko is just some ordinary gecko?"

He agreed this was a good question. By way of answer he told me a story:

> One day [he said], my jinns said to me, "We have to go out and bury one of our comrades in the cemetery." I asked, "How did he die?"

They said, "He was protecting you, positioned on a wall outside, beside the main gate of your house, facing the alley." [Tariq paused to explain that this jinn was in the shape of a gecko.] "A boy in the alley," they said, "came up and threw a stone and killed the gecko—and thereby he killed the jinn."

The surviving jinns told me what I should do. "Tell everyone in the neighborhood not to kill any geckos on the wall beside the gate, or next time we'll take vengeance on the boys in the alley."

So I told everyone in the neighborhood. That's how my jinns let me know what wall and portion of wall they occupy, so I won't kill them by mistake, and no one else will harm them."

His anecdote reminded me of an *Arabian Nights* story, in which a traveling merchant who is eating lunch outdoors carelessly tosses away a date-stone and in the process accidentally kills an unseen jinn. The jinn's father then comes storming up, ready to kill the merchant in revenge. But the father's anger is assuaged by three aged travelers who happen by. Each of them tells the demon a pleasing tale as ransom for the merchant's life.[22]

In the *Arabian Nights* as in Tariq Akhtar's Lahore, the jinns are of a quicksilver temperament, as volatile and unpredictable as the wasteland-sprites of the ancient pagan world.

"The Night the Jinns Besieged My House": Or, the Need for Precautionary Measures When Passing by a Graveyard

But jinns are not limited to the form of geckos when they choose to manifest themselves. In fact, said Tariq, a good *'amil* will detect the presence of jinns in phenomena ordinary folks dismiss as random.

This led to another anecdote:

My *ustad* [spiritual teacher] had always warned me, "When you go by a cemetery, be sure to recite the Throne Verse." That's because such places are pleasing to jinns and other spirits as places to inhabit. Without the Throne Verse or another such Quran verse to protect you, you will be vulnerable to jinns.

But one day I was driving by a cemetery on my motorbike, and I was *ghaflan* [forgetful, negligent]. Suddenly my left arm became heavy and useless, so I had trouble driving my motorbike. I reached my *ustad*'s house. He breathed on my arm and I felt better and could lift my arm again.

---

22. Muhsin Mahdi, ed., *The Thousand and One Nights* (Leiden: E. J. Brill, 1984), vol. 1, 72-73.

But once I was back on the road, I had the same numbness. Now it was spreading over my whole body.

I got to my house. My whole family was home. I had just enough strength to summon one of my own jinns. I asked if we were under attack. It said yes we were.

I commanded it to show us the *'ifrits* that were besieging us.

At once the room was filled everywhere with ants, *lakhs* [hundreds of thousands] upon *lakhs*. The whole house swarmed with them.

So everyone in my family, all of us, we started crushing them. We used sandals, whatever we could [here Tariq smashed his hand onto the table, miming destruction].

Every time we crushed an ant, it spurted blood, then disappeared. This went on for hours. Finally they were all gone.

Afterwards my *ustad* came over and drew a circle around the whole house, to keep any more jinns from entering.

The night the jinns besieged my house: this taught me the importance of the Throne Verse.

Numbness in the arm; an infestation of ants: to other people these might seem like the stray annoyances of day-to-day life. Not to Tariq Akhtar. As a sorcerer, as a "spiritual practitioner," he inhabits a world where nothing is random, where everything and every incident are assigned a deeper meaning.

Ordinary folks miss the signs, but the *'amil* is at the nexus, at the center of the whirl of phenomena, the center around which the phenomena crystallize into patterns.

Responding to these events, recognizing their hidden significances: this is the sorcerer's job. The other key players in this cosmic drama are the jinns, who—like the *'amil*—have the potential to act as agents of pattern-integration.

Knowing When to Take Two Aspirins:
Jinns and the Field of Medical Sorcery

A significant percentage of the cases handled by *'amils* such as Tariq Akhtar involve various symptoms of sickness. In an impoverished country like Pakistan, where medical facilities are few and poverty is widespread, both sorcerers and mullahs are called on as ad hoc physicians.

In Lahore's poorer neighborhoods as in many other Pakistani cities, local mosques often serve as first-resort health clinics for neighborhood residents suffering from any one of a myriad aches and sufferings. If a prayer or amulet suffices to relieve the pain, well and good; but the responsible and ethically minded healer (and this I heard from several sources) will know when to send a patient on to a medical facility.

Tariq told me he had several diagnostic tools for discerning the cause of a patient's troubles. Among them: he'd send one of his jinns into the patient's body to study the person's organs, bloodstream, etc. Such an examination, he claimed, would quickly tell him whether the individual was suffering from a mere bodily affliction or from the onslaught of some spirit. And he knew precisely which type of *ta'wiz* (amulet or charm) to write for exorcising any one of a number of satanic forces.

The day we talked about his work as a healer, I'd just come back from Rawalpindi. There, at the Ganjmandi Bridge, in the vicinity of Raja Bazaar, I'd met a parrot-master who—in addition to using his parrot to tell fortunes—also sold little jars of medical remedies that he made up himself. Each jar, the man assured me, was good for a number of ailments.

I told Tariq this, and I also mentioned that the parrot-master sold talismans to guard people from sickness. I wondered what his assessment would be of someone who was more or less in the same line of work as he was.

Tariq's response was immediate and fierce. First of all, he said, these *totevale log* (parrot-people) get their practices from Hinduism. Everyone knows, he said, that the *tota-fal* (parrot oracle) comes from the Hindus. So what they do is worthless.

Second, he said, these people have no training. So they have no business dabbling in healing and medicine.

Third, they don't have a diploma. Whereas, he said, he *did* have training, and he did have a diploma. He reminded me of the certificate he'd shown me earlier. The more time I spent with him, the more aware I became of how competitively-minded Tariq was in assessing fellow healers.

I had a chance to watch him in action one night after evening prayer. He had a small mosque of his own, and neighborhood residents came to him with complaints and ailments of various kinds.

During a lull, my driver Imtiyaz asked Tariq for help with a small complaint of his own: a headache he'd been having all day. Tariq sat him down and asked him where precisely the pain was. Imtiyaz pointed to his left temple. Tariq began whispering something, over and over, while tracing whorl-patterns of some kind with his right index finger over my driver's temple. This went on for several minutes.

Later I asked Tariq what he'd been doing. He told me he'd traced onto Imtiyaz's temple the Arabic phrase *li-yu'adhdhibahum* ("He will punish them" or "that He might punish them"). The words appear in the Quran (9.55): "God's intention is that He will punish them in this life, and that they will die in a state of unbelief." It is one of a number of scriptural passages detailing Allah's coercive power to dominate the spiritually unruly.

Fascinating to me was to see how Tariq adapted this decontextualized Quranic verse-fragment for the purpose of "spiritual healing." He explained he hadn't had time to do a thorough diagnosis on Imtiyaz, but that if a jinn had in fact been causing the ache, then threatening it with God's punishment would have been enough to drive it away.

The next morning when I got in the car I asked Imtiyaz how he was feeling. Much better, he said.

I asked whether Tariq's treatment had helped.

He said he thought so. A little bit, at least.

Then he turned to me and grinned.

"But as soon as I got home," he added, "I helped myself to some aspirin."

8

A COMPARISON OF MUSLIM AND HINDU PERSPECTIVES ON THE REALM OF THE JINNS

The Jinn in the Elephant:
A Muslim Sorcerer's View of Hindu Gods

In his capacity as my driver, Imtiyaz Yusuf accompanied me on trips to many parts of Pakistan—not just drives within Lahore, but expeditions to Islamabad and Rawalpindi, and eight-hour hauls to Peshawar. This gave him plenty of opportunities to tell me anecdotes; and one of his favorite topics was the activity of jinns.

Some of his remarks were simply brief comments on locales in our vicinity as we traveled about. For example, during a trip to Khyber Agency in December 2002, on a drive through the Khyber Pass, he said of Landi Kotal (a nearby site): "There are many jinns there." When I asked why, he said, "It's wild and lonely, and jinns like *viran jaghayn* [empty/deserted places]."

Jinns also arose one evening over dinner in Lahore at a Pizza Hut (eating there was not my idea, by the way: the tomato-and-cardboard-flavored slices were just as bad as I'd feared; still, I chewed gamely under the beaming gaze of smiling Pakistani hosts, who imagined they knew what would appeal to an American).

Among those seated at the table was Imtiyaz, and he talked about how jinns can cause car trouble.

One night while driving in the Northern Areas, his car broke down on a lonely mountain road near Gilgit. No houses nearby, no lights anywhere, no other cars on the road. He and his passengers were stuck there in the dark for hours.

Finally a car came by and a man stepped out, "a Sufi-like man, with a long beard," according to Imtiyaz's description.

The Sufi came up to the car and rested one hand on the hood. He bent over and said, *"Tum in logon ko bahut tang kar rahe ho"* (You're causing these people much annoyance). Then the man told Imtiyaz and his passengers to get back into the car.

The car, said Imtiyaz, started right up.

The Sufi's car drove off, preceding them, in the same direction they were headed. After ten minutes the man's car disappeared from view.

Imtiyaz was convinced his car's engine had been plagued by jinns, and that the mysterious stranger who intervened had been some sort of *bozorg* (holy man). The other people around our table at Pizza Hut concurred. Several diners then matched his tale with similar ones of their own.

Imtiyaz also had firm and outspoken opinions about the religious denominational identity of jinns. In March 2004 he accompanied me on a trip from Lahore to Peshawar. At a truck-stop off the Grand Trunk Road near Attock, we sat and ate lentils and Afghan bread.

I brushed away the flies that buzzed over our food and made some joke about their being as bothersome as jinns.

As far as Imtiyaz was concerned this was no topic for joking. As he waved flies away he said, "Most jinns are Hindus. Very few jinns are good."

What about Muslims, I asked. Weren't there also Muslim jinns?

A few, he said. But his *maulvi* had told him God created ten times as many jinns as humans in our world, and almost all these jinns were *kafirs*. And these *kafir* jinns were almost all Hindus.

But wasn't it possible, I persisted, that some jinns might be Sikh or Christian or Jewish?

He agreed it was at least possible. "But my *maulvi* told me almost all jinns are Hindu."

And Hindu, I learned from Imtiyaz and many other Pakistani Muslims, was all too often conceptually interchangeable with *kafir*, which in turn was interchangeable with *bura* (bad, evil).

The young sorcerer Tariq Akhtar told me he'd had plenty of dealings with Hindu members of the spirit world. One morning in March 2004, he told me that the night before he'd had to rush on his motorbike to a Muslim home in Lahore in response to an "emergency call" on his cellphone.

When he arrived, the lady of the house told him her daughter-in-law was "feeling afflicted" every evening. He walked about and studied the house and found out that "Hindu jinns" were living in a tree in the family's yard.

The Hindu jinns conveyed a message to him: "We've lived here a long time. We don't like her. She has to go."

Tariq's response: first, he wrote out a *ta'wiz* (a protective text, to be folded up and inserted into an amulet to be worn by the person to be protected). Standing in the yard near the tree, he announced out loud that he'd return in eleven days. If the *ta'wiz* wasn't enough to drive off the jinns, then he'd draw a circle around the tree and begin a series of conjurations that would either expel the jinns or kill them.

On hearing this, I thought of the stories told me by my Pakistani female students at Santa Clara University: of childhood in Karachi, and how their mothers warned them of jinns roosting in treetops, jinns who were hungrily waiting to pounce onto attractive young girls.

Then an obvious question occurred to me: how did Tariq know these jinns were Hindu?

"I didn't find that out; my jinn did," he said. He'd summoned one of his domesticated genies and dispatched it around the house. It was his jinn, he said, that spotted the troublesome beings in the tree and interrogated them and discovered they were Hindu.

House calls were part of his job, Tariq explained. He seemed to see himself as a door-to-door exterminator. He was proud of the number of Hindu demons he'd hunted down and expelled from homes in Lahore.

But a phrase haunted my mind, a statement Tariq said the defiant jinns had made. "We've lived here a long time."

Hindu people, after all, were known to have lived in Lahore for centuries, long before the creation of Pakistan and the forced exodus of Hindus from Lahore in 1947. So it seemed only natural that today's Lahori residents would imagine there to be Hindu spirits still lingering in a population center that had been Hindu for so long.

As Tariq the sorcerer told me his stories, I had a sudden sad vision of what one could call sectarian cleansing in the spirit world, of an expulsion of genies to match the expulsion of people at the time of Partition.

My impression was reinforced by a story told me in March 2004 by Tariq's father, Mustafa. This involved something that happened to Mustafa's uncle. The man was a professional singer; and Mustafa made clear at the outset of this anecdote that in his own opinion singing, like dancing (I recalled the story about Tariq dancing at the wedding), is something unislamic.

His uncle's habit, said Mustafa, was to ride his bicycle early every morning along the banks of the Ravi River, then over the Ravi bridge and back again, pedaling slowly and taking his time and practicing his singing in a very loud voice.

One morning while out bicycling, the uncle was surprised to see a beautiful little lamb, all by itself in the middle of the deserted bridge. The lamb seemed to be staring right at him.

He decided to appropriate the lamb for himself and take it home. He stopped the bike and put the lamb in a carrier-basket mounted above the rear fender. Then he started to pedal off.

He hadn't gotten clear of the bridge when he heard what sounded like something scraping along on the ground behind him. The sound followed him as he pedaled.

He turned and saw that somehow one of the lamb's legs had grown and become so long it was dragging on the ground behind the bicycle. The lamb itself was staring fixedly at him, opening its mouth as if it were about to speak.

Sheer terror: the uncle realized he'd taken on board something unnatural. He pitched the lamb from the basket and flung it behind the bike.

At once it changed into a woman. She ran after him, crying *Thairo, thairo*: Wait, wait! The man peddled home for all he was worth. And soon after reaching safety, he collapsed and came down with a fever.

The lamb, explained Mustafa, must have been a *churail* (the ghost of a woman who dies in pregnancy or childbirth). Such creatures often roam the earth looking for mates.

Mustafa's way of concluding the story was to say that from that time on, his uncle has never returned to the Ravi to do any more bellowing. Now he practices all his singing indoors, at home. Something like satisfaction—or vindication—shone in Mustafa's face as he said this: unislamic behavior had earned its comeuppance.

As he told me all this I thought about other data I'd collected about the Ravi River: of pariah-kite rituals, *chillah*-meditations by night on the shore, of spirits rising up out of the water.

I remarked that the area around the Ravi and its bridge seemed to be a magnet for stories of the kind he'd just told me. I asked if he knew why that might be.

At once he replied, "The Hindus used to cremate bodies there, on the riverbank. Perhaps there are *bhuts* [ghosts] there. Perhaps there's simply some left-over *bura ta'assur* from the time of the Hindus."

An interesting choice of words. *Bura ta'assur*: "bad feeling," "evil sensation," "ugly mark." *Ta'assur* is a word derived from the Arabic term *athar*: vestige, relic, or ancient monument.

Ancient monuments: Lahore, it seems to me, is haunted today by the vestiges of its Hindu legacy. This is a legacy about which there is apparently a lingering and subliminal collective guilt—a (largely unacknowledged and conflicted) feeling that Pakistan has impoverished itself through the various sectarian explosions that have marred its history. This is a legacy Islamic Pakistan has tried to exorcise, sometimes by expelling Hindu demon-jinns, sometimes by acts of physical destruction—as Lahori Muslims did in December 1992, when they tore down the Hindu temples that formed some of the last visible reminders of the city's pluralistic past.

But Mustafa was not done telling me about the realm of *kafir* spirits. He told me of an Indian Muslim *'amil* named Yusuf Bhai who lived in Delhi and who had succeeded in gaining mastery over many genies. Among them were a number of Hindu jinns.

Through them, Yusuf Bhai reported to Mustafa, he'd learned that some Hindu jinns take on the form of the deity Ganesha: an elephant's body, with a long elephant-trunk. Other Hindu jinns take on the shapes of other assorted Hindu divinities. These disguised jinns are what India's Hindus mistakenly worship as gods.

I see this as an explanatory model by means of which some Muslims of the subcontinent come to terms with what they perceive as the very evident power of Hindu idolatry. Yusuf Bhai's claim is reminiscent of the "City of Brass" story mentioned earlier from the *Arabian Nights*: a genie speaks through the mouth of a statue and overawes people into false worship. So too with the Christian Church father Justin Martyr, whom I also mentioned earlier: he accounted for Roman paganism by describing Zeus-Jupiter and the other Olympian gods as the offspring of the biblical "sons of God" and daughters of men.

And in Pakistan today many Muslims account for the palpable power and attractiveness of Hinduism—and reduce it to something manageable, something less terrifying—by describing it as a religion animated by a gang of unruly *kafir* jinns.

Lahore's unseen world of malevolent spirits is troubling to its Muslim residents, to be sure. But calling these forces "Hindu jinns" fits them into a historical and Quranic framework over which Pakistani Muslims can claim some mastery—even if this mastery is perpetually unstable.

Krishna, the Jinns, and "Suitable Punishments": A Rajasthani Hindu Explanation of Islamic Demonology

I had the good fortune to get a completely different perspective on demonic presences in our world when I visited the province of Rajasthan in August–September 2004 (Rajasthan, in western India, is located just over the border from Pakistan; the bulk of its population is devoutly Hindu).

I toured the Rajasthani city of Jodhpur with an elderly Hindu gentleman named Narayan Gupta. Mr. Gupta described himself as a Vaishnavite (devotee of the god Vishnu). He knew the city's history and its monuments well; but his passion, he said, was "philosophical discourse on religion," which he studied with a local guru.

One morning while touring Jodhpur's Mandore Gardens and its gallery of deity-statues, I told Mr. Gupta what I'd been told in Lahore earlier that year: that Hindu worship could be explained as the product of a colossal act of deception by *kafir* jinns. I repeated the assertions I'd heard from Lahori *'amils*: that Hindu jinns defy Allah by assuming elephant shapes and the like, thereby luring Indians into idolatry.

My guide considered this calmly and then replied: "Muslims typically have things all wrong in their heads. Krishna explains all these things properly in the *Bhagavad-Gita*."

The *Bhagavad-Gita* (composed c. first century AD) is a devotional text that honors Krishna, an avatar of Vishnu. For centuries it has been one of the most popular and widely known texts in Hinduism.

The *Gita*'s "Ninth Teaching" expounds the concept of what can be termed "temporary heaven." Individuals who have accrued a measure of karmic merit in their lifetimes (but who haven't yet reached the state of passionless detachment that permits *moksha* or eternal deliverance from the cycle of reincarnation) will in their afterlife enjoy a limited period of reward in "the world of heaven." Thereafter, however, they will eventually be reincarnated on earth to continue their spiritual education. Krishna speaks as follows in the *Gita*:

> They savor the heavenly delights
> Of the gods in the celestial sphere.
> When they have long enjoyed
> The world of heaven
> And their merit is exhausted
> They enter [once more] the mortal world.
>
> As for the fate of "demonic men":
> Confused by endless thoughts
> Caught in the net of delusion,
> Given to satisfying their desires,
> They fall into hell's foul abyss…
>
> These hateful, cruel, vile
> Men of misfortune, I cast
> Into demonic wombs
>   Through cycles of rebirth.[1]

My Rajasthani guide applied the *Gita*'s concept of reincarnation and temporary heavens and hells to reinterpret Lahore's Islamic demonology:

---

1. Barbara Stoler Miller, trans., *The Bhagavad-Gita: Krishna's Counsel in Time of War* (New York: Bantam, 1986), 85-86, 135.

> Normally [Mr. Gupta said], people after death enjoy rewards in some heaven. Then after their account is used up, they return to earth. Bad people likewise are reincarnated after suitable punishments. But if someone is *very* bad, then Krishna causes him to come back as a *pret*. [The *pret* is variously defined as "the malicious ghost of someone dead" or as a "ghost, goblin, sprite, evil spirit, fiend."[2]] Krishna makes souls that have done great evil experience a cycle of existence as a *pret*, in a life as a special kind of evil ghost. These jinns you talk about: they're simply one type of demons from among the *prets*.

In other words, Mr. Gupta had drawn on the *Gita* to construct a demonology that countered the system propounded by Muslim sorcerers across the border in Lahore. My Lahori informants explained away Hinduism's genesis in terms of sinful jinns defying Allah; my Rajasthani informant explained Islam's spirit-world in terms of reincarnational cycles imposed by Krishna. Each demonology swallows up the religious phenomena of the other faith and subordinates these things within its own explanatory framework.

Conclusion:
Siege Mentalities and the World of Jinns

In his study of Muslim–Hindu devotionalism at sacred sites in the religiously mixed Indian village of Arampur, Peter Gottschalk raised the question "whether the recent national tensions exacerbated by Hindu and Muslim chauvinists had penetrated even the realm of the dead, such as *bhut-pret* and jinn." Despite the evidence for a certain amount of polarizing, Gottschalk was guardedly optimistic in asserting that "area residents" had managed to "create an intercommunal public sphere."[3]

The issue is relevant to Lahore, where, it seems to me, "Muslim chauvinists" have in fact polarized "the realm of the dead" and the world of jinns, through the process of labeling hostile spirit forces as not only *kafir* but Hindu.

The politics underlying such polarization become clearer when we take into account the terms used by one such chauvinist—the Lahori sorcerer, Tariq Akhtar—to describe himself.

One afternoon in December 2002 I arrived a few minutes late for a meeting with him. I apologized, explaining I'd just come from down-

---

2. Peter Gottschalk, *Beyond Hindu and Muslim: Multiple Identity in Narratives from Village India* (New York: Oxford University Press, 2000), 192; John T. Platts, *A Dictionary of Urdu, Classical Hindi, and English* (Delhi: Munshiram Manoharlal, 1993), 259.

3. Gottschalk, *Beyond Hindu and Muslim*, 137.

town and the Shia shrine of Karbala Gamay-Shah, where I'd bought some posters from a kiosk near the entrance.

Curious to get his reaction, I unrolled the posters—all of them pictures of a bloodstained Zuljenah, the arrow-pierced "Horse of Karbala," one of the most prominent icons of South Asian Shia Islam.

He did no more than glance at the posters before looking away. Easy to see the man was displeased. Abruptly he announced he was Deobandi.

As discussed in a previous chapter, Deobandism—a reform movement that inspired the Taliban—seeks to purify the faith of "unislamic" influences. Tariq didn't define for me in so many words what he understood Deobandism to be. But he gave me a pretty good idea by the turn the conversation took next.

He told me a story about a healer in the Pakistani province of Sindh named Ali Sher Haydari. He described the man as "an ex-Shia who's now become a Muslim" (a description that implies a great deal about Tariq's view of Shias). A boy was brought to this Ali Haydari. The boy had fallen from a roof and was about to die. Ali wrote out a *ta'wiz*-spell, the gist of which was a sentence—repeated numerous times—stating that "the Shias are *kafirs*." God was so pleased with this spell, Tariq told me, that He allowed the boy to be healed.

In his own opinion, Tariq added, the term *kafir* applied to both the Shias and the Ismailis. (Ismailism is actually a sub-sect of Shia Islam, but Tariq, like most Pakistani Muslims I've met, used the term Shia specifically to designate "Twelver" Shiism. Most Shias, in Pakistan as in Iran, are Twelvers. They revere a succession of twelve Imams, the last of whom they believe disappeared from the earth in the ninth century. Ismailis, however, revere a "living Imam" known as the Agha Khan.)

I asked Tariq why he considered Shias *kafirs*. First, he said, they insult the *Sahaba* (the Prophet's Companions) and consider the *Sahaba*'s actions wrong. Second, they believe there are forty *siparahs* (sections) to the Quran (the Quran actually has thirty), the missing ten of which are supposedly in the possession of the Shias' Imam Mahdi. "This makes the Shias think we Sunnis have copies of the Quran that are incomplete."

His third objection had to do with the posters I'd shown him. "These posters of Zuljenah: this is all part of Shias' practice of *but-parasti* (idol-worship/idolatry). This makes the Shias more like Hindus than Muslims."

In a subsequent meeting Tariq expanded on the list of Muslim denominations whose practices he condemned. He was explaining his view of the difference between Deobandis and Barelvis (Barelvism is a form of South Asian Sunni Islam that—compared with Deobandism—is much more accommodating of traditional folk religion).

He said the biggest difference between Deobandism and Barelvism is that the Deobandis are strict in upholding *tawhid* (God's divine oneness), whereas the Barelvis violate *tawhid* by claiming that the *awliya'* ("friends" of God, or Sufi saints) can receive our prayers and thereby act as intercessors with God. Also, he said, the Barelvis claim the talismans they write have a power that is independent of God and always effective. By neglecting *tawhid*, he said, the Barelvis behave like Hindus.

As diplomatically as I could, I pointed out to Tariq that he himself belonged to a Sufi order and wrote amulet-spells for clients every day.

He was quick to point out the difference. "As a Deobandi I acknowledge that sometimes the *ta'wiz* and *dam* (breathing on a person in prayer) are ineffective, because God decides not to help. These things I do are effective only *bi-idhni Allah* ('with God's permission')."

I was skeptical. I've talked to Sufis in many countries, and all of them, I'm sure, would agree that the healings and miracles for which Sufi masters are famous can take place only *bi-idhni Allah*.

Nevertheless I thought I saw a pattern emerge in Tariq Akhtar's worldview. In an earlier chapter I argued that many Pakistani Muslims see themselves as a beleaguered minority—a notion that makes sense, despite the fact that Pakistan's population is 97% Muslim, if one recalls that until relatively recently (1947: still within living memory for many Pakistanis) Pakistan was part of India, a country much larger than Pakistan that is also overwhelmingly Hindu.

Pakistani Deobandism can be seen as an ideological expression of this siege mentality. Tariq's complaints—at various times he identified himself to me as anti-Shia, anti-Ismaili, anti-Barelvi, anti-Hindu, and even anti-parrot-fortune-teller—all have to do with safeguarding a collective Islamic identity that is perceived to be under attack.

Deobandism, as articulated by this *'amil*, is a way of safeguarding Pakistani Islamic identity. It does so—to borrow a term from Tariq's line of work—by drawing a "safety ring," a magic circle, around Pakistani Islam, to exclude whatever has been "tainted" by Hinduism.

So too in the spirit world. For many of the Pakistani Muslims I met, the sense of being an imperiled minority applies also to the unseen demonic realm that presses in on us from all sides, where helpful (Muslim) genies are few and harmful (Hindu) ones are in the vast majority. The solution: taking refuge within a magic circle, and using purity and prayer to keep the spirit-forces at bay.

For someone like Tariq Akhtar, perhaps, what sorcery and Deobandism share as attractive qualities is a promise of survival in a world that is perceived as swarming with hostile and impure forces. This survival is achieved via a process of exclusion, demarcation, and the assertion of absolute control over boundaries.

The worldview of an *'amil* like Tariq, then, becomes sectarian in its hostility to Shias and other minorities in Pakistan; it becomes political in its embrace of Deobandism; and it becomes harmful in its rejection of any form of pluralism.

LAHORI PULP FICTION:
THE WORLD OF *KHOFNAK DIJAST* ("FRIGHT DIGEST")

Grinning skulls that drip blood tend to grab one's attention. It worked for me.

I was following my usual early-morning routine in Lahore's Cantonment. A walk before breakfast down the block to shop at Rahat Bakery, then a stop at the newsstand to pick up the day's papers.

I was hefting a loaf of fresh bread and a copy of *The Friday Times* and a couple of Urdu-language dailies, *Jang* and *Khabareyn*—reassuring parts of ordinary day-to-day normality.

That's when I spotted it, on a rack behind the kiosk's pile of papers: the cover of *Khofnak Dijast* ("Fright Digest").

The blood-dripping death's-head filled one corner of the illustration. But what dominated the cover was the picture of a young woman. Big blue eyes, soft glowing skin, flowing hair and pouty red lips: beautiful enough to kiss.

But that was just half her face. The other half: fangs, and a scalp of bleeding raw flesh, flesh that oozed and was held together by Frankenstein-monster stitching. She wore a burgundy-colored gown—but the gown's brocade-work was an ocean of skulls, each impaled on a stake. Above the skulls flitted an upsurge of bats.

The cover did its job. I asked the kiosk man how much.

Thirty-five rupees. About half a buck.

I added *Fright Digest* to my day's reading.

As he handed me a copy the vendor grunted. Disapproval? In any case I saw he had quite a stack of them for sale.

I asked who bought them. Young men, was all he had to say.

I opened to the first page and saw that this magazine is published in Lahore, in the city's Gulbarg quarter. So: this was very much a local publication (although later I found copies on sale at newsstands in Islamabad, Rawalpindi, and Peshawar).

At breakfast *The Friday Times* lost out to the girl in the skull-brocade dress. She was my introduction to the world of *Fright Digest*.

Pulp Fiction in the Pakistani Context

Fright Digest is a good example of what I'll call Lahori pulp fiction (other Urdu-language magazines of this genre that I saw on sale in Lahore included titles like *Spy Digest* and *True Story*). To appreciate what I mean by pulp, let's define the term in its American context. Later we can test how applicable the label is with regard to Pakistani publications like *Khofnak Dijast*.

Robert Lesser's study, *Pulp Art*, reviews the heyday of American pulp fiction in the 1930s and '40s. An essay in this volume by Roger T. Reed describes the kind of stories that were printed in magazines such as *Spicy Adventure*, *Dime Detective*, and *Weird Tales*. They were "generated by formula and printed on below-newsprint-grade 'pulp' paper. They were cheap in every meaning of the word. Yet their weaknesses were also their strengths."[1]

This weakness–strength duality is linked, I believe, to the fact that these stories were, as Reed says, "generated by formula." In other words, pulp fiction is genre fiction, keyed to the widest possible audience. In general, genre fiction indulges rather than challenges its readers, which is another way of saying that genre writing—whether romance or western or (as in the case of *Khofnak*) horror—offers a satisfying and reassuring degree of predictability.

To illustrate: as a teen I faithfully bought issues of the Marvel comic *Tales to Astonish*. Of course I wanted these stories to be startling and terrifying and—as the title promised—astonishing. At the same time in buying such a comic I was secure in the knowledge it would furnish the quota I wanted of monsters and heroes and close-call escapes. That I could count on. That much was predictable.

Reed's essay emphasizes the salient feature of this kind of fiction: "It was action, above all, that sold the pulps." Character development, soul-searching dialogue, sustained philosophical speculation, introspective asides? Not a chance. As Reed says, "The pulps' contents tap directly into our primal nervous system: the fight-or-flight reflex, the pleasure center, the gut and the tearducts—places where violence, power, awe, sex, horror, hero worship and xenophobia stir our impulses."[2]

One can see an example of American xenophobia at work in stories from the 1930s that featured villains like "the mysterious Wu Fang"—a

---

1. Roger T. Reed, "The Pulps: Their Weaknesses Were Their Strengths," in Robert Lesser, ed., *Pulp Art: Original Cover Paintings for the Great American Pulp Magazines* (New York: Castle Books, 1997), 8.
2. Reed, "The Pulps," 9.

mirror of the racial preoccupations and anti-Chinese prejudice of the time.[3] When we examine Lahore's *Fright Digest* stories, we can check to see whether xenophobia is likewise tapped to "stir our impulses."

Khofnak Tota *("The Frightful Parrot")*

My first example of a story from *Khofnak Dijast* is a tale called *Khofnak Tota*: "The Frightful Parrot."[4] It appeared in the February 2005 issue, the cover of which features a beautiful young woman, big-eyed, with lots of makeup (the standard look for *Khofnak*'s cover art, to judge from the issues I've collected over the past four years). But the girl's mouth gapes open, to reveal vampire fangs; and behind her are ranged skeletal corpses with staring eyes and bloodstained teeth.

A curious thing about these skeletal figures: they grin in a crazed and jovial way that, for an American reader like me, is distinctly reminiscent of the 1960s-era "Rat Fink" cartoons of Ed "Big Daddy" Roth.

Which points to an interesting feature of *Khofnak Dijast*. Its stories draw heavily (as we will see) on localized forms of South Asian folk religion; but its illustrations are heavily indebted to the Halloween-conventions of American pop-culture monster-art. Sometimes the borrowings are so overt as to be inescapable: a Wolfman-drawing looking like a copy of a movie poster for the actor Lon Chaney; a gnome that resembles Andy Serkis's Gollum from Peter Jackson's film version of *Lord of the Rings*. Thus the pictures serve to update and "westernize" (however superficially) stories that draw on centuries-old Islamic narrative figures such as the jinns.

As for the "Frightful Parrot" story itself: like most of the *Khofnak* tales I've encountered, it's told in the first person. The author, Ghulam Mustafa 'Arabani, is said to be a resident of the Pakistani province of Sindh (typically, the authors are Pakistani men who often describe themselves, in the opening lines of their stories, as regular readers of the magazine).

Now to the action:

The narrator (who refers to himself as Mustafa, thereby appropriating the author's own name) says the incidents he's about to describe, involving himself and his friend Mir Muhammad, occurred six or seven years ago. At that time, he explains, "We were young men, but in our actions we were children"—the first hint that this will be a tale with a strong moralizing and didactic dimension.

3. Lesser, *Pulp Art*, 104-107.
4. Ghulam Mustafa 'Arabani, "Khofnak Tota," *Khofnak Dijast* (Lahore) 8.15 (February 2005): 132-34.

As the story opens, Mustafa describes the young men's idea of recreation: shooting birds with a pellet-gun, and capturing those they don't kill to raise for their own amusement. "It was lots of fun," he confesses, "but we did this to the point of madness." Their parents disapprove, but the two young men do it anyway.

One day the youngsters go bird-hunting in a jungle at some distance from their village. The jungle, notes Mustafa, is beside a *qabaristan*—a graveyard.

They fire their guns and make a lot of noise; they sit and eat and chat in the shade of a tree—which happens to be right beside the cemetery.

Any fairytale-reader can guess that the place the young men have chosen for sitting—the shade of a tree at the jungle's edge, beside a graveyard—is a liminal zone, on the threshold between the civilized world of humans and the untamed world of the uncanny.

More important is the way these two have approached the border zone. They make noise and fire guns and carelessly eat and chat. In other words, like Tariq Akhtar (the sorcerer we met in a previous chapter), in passing by a graveyard they are *ghaflat-zade*: heedless, unmindful. For Tariq, as we saw earlier, the consequences entailed a temporarily paralyzed arm and a swarming onset of jinn-ants. For the two trespassers in this story, the consequences will be worse.

While seated in the tree-shade, they hear the "sweet voices" of parrots. Looking up, they glimpse the birds' "noble and beautiful" appearance.

And they spot something else, something enticing, high above their heads: a hole in the tree-trunk, a hole that must serve as a nest. The two decide to raid the nest and capture some parrots for sport.

The narrator's friend Mir Muhammad climbs the tree and easily reaches the nest. So far, so good. Then he sticks his hand into the hole. And that's when the trouble starts.

From below Mustafa hears his friend scream for help. In a flash the nest-raider tumbles unconscious to the ground.

The narrator rushes to his friend and sees what's happened: "The parrot had mercilessly bitten off Mir's index finger."

For an instant the bird perches on Mir Muhammad's motionless body. Then the story tips over into the supernatural: the bird bobs its head and mysteriously disappears within the chest of the offending human.

Thus we face a sudden reversal: within the space of a paragraph, that which was originally presented as sweet, noble, and beautiful becomes a devouring menace. Things happen fast in the pages of *Fright Digest*.

Mir Muhammad wakes up, and for a second it seems he'll be fine. But when he opens his eyes they're a glaring inhuman red.

Worse is to come. He runs off to the nearby village and mindlessly attacks a herd of water buffaloes and cows. He leaps onto an ox and with his hands and teeth kills it and gobbles it down to the bones. Mustafa tries to intervene but is shoved to the ground. Mir Muhammad dashes away, "emitting cries like a parrot."

For days the bird-possessed Mir roams the environs of the village, preying on the cattle. Together, the narrator and the villagers capture and briefly restrain Mir Muhammad. They urge the youngster's family to consult with the local *'amil baba* (spiritual practitioner). To no avail: "They were educated people," reports Mustafa, "and they had no regard for such things."

Instead, the family insists on bringing in a physician, who tries to inject the captured Mir Muhammad with a sedative. But the poor doctor isn't equipped to deal with a parrot-man. Mir squawks and screeches, and the hypodermic needle goes flying from the startled doctor's hand before he can give his intended patient the injection.

The needle flies up into the air and hits the physician himself in the arm. The result: "The doctor became altogether as rigid as a statue." That's the last we see of the doctor in this story. So much for modern medicine.

For days the ravenous Mir Muhammad attacks one cattle-herd after another. The villagers approach his family and threaten to confine him to a *pagal-khana* (insane asylum). Desperate, the narrator makes a *du'a* (petitionary prayer) to "Allah most exalted": "O my Lord, restore the health of my friend and brother."

And that's when order begins to be restored.

The morning following the *du'a*, a new character enters the story: the possessed youngster's older brother Rashid. He tells the narrator that last night he had a dream in which there appeared to him a *bozorg* ("great one" or holy man). In the dream the *bozorg* instructed the older brother to come to him on Thursday night. "Then," promised the holy man in the dream, "I will heal your brother."

On Thursday night Rashid and Mustafa go to the cemetery. Unstated in the narrative (because these things are presumably well known to *Khofnak*'s readers) are the following points. First, the most powerful *bozorgs* are often those that are dead, and the place to contact such beings is the graveyard. Second, the cemetery–jungle boundary is where the initial offense occurred, so it makes sense for the healing to commence there. And third, Thursday night is an auspicious time for healings, as this is the eve of Islam's Sabbath and the favorite night for Sufi mystical gatherings.

At the cemetery they find an old man with a long white beard. He's wearing robes and a turban that are green (a color associated with paradise and the Islamic faith).

The *bozorg* says he's been waiting for them and they take him to the house where the parrot-man is currently a prisoner. He demands a black goat and says he's going to enter the room alone where Mir Muhammad is confined. The holy man instructs Rashid to stay outside and slaughter the goat the moment he enters the room. (Animal-slaughter for cures is not unfamiliar in Pakistani folk Islam: Katherine Ewing's study of Lahori religious practices analyzes goat-sacrifice as a way of "ritually transferring harmful influence to an animal."[5])

Rashid follows his orders and kills the goat as the *bozorg* enters the room. The agitated family and other onlookers make *du'as* of entreaty on the possessed youngster's behalf.

And then:

> Immediately thereafter the sound of the parrot's screeches came forth from the room. Then the *baba* came out and in his hand was the very same parrot, dead—the very parrot that had entered my friend's body. The *baba* said, "Don't be afraid. Now Mir Muhammad is completely well. Soon he'll regain consciousness." He said this and then vanished.[6]

Things are now back to normal. But tokens remain of the experience: "The villagers said that on the night the holy one appeared, the jungle around the cemetery caught fire. It was reduced to ashes"—a nice way of symbolizing the *bozorg*'s mastery of the jungly forces of chaos.

And then there's this:

> After what he went through, my friend has learned his lesson. In accordance with his request, I'm writing this story… And the remaining mark of the tale is this: my friend Mir Muhammad's finger, which the cruel parrot cut off and ate up, remains cut off to this day. For this reason I ask all my friends to give up this passion for hunting.[7]

In reviewing the story I'm struck by its folkloric quality. The narrator begins by describing the obsessive bird-hunting he and his friend do as something they pursue "to the point of madness." They insist on doing this hunting even at the border of a graveyard—thereby signaling the reader they've reached the boundary of the forbidden. They then cross the boundary and commit a transgression. Thereby *Khofnak Tota* conforms

---

5. Katherine Pratt Ewing, *Arguing Sainthood: Modernity, Psychoanalysis, and Islam* (Durham: Duke University Press, 1997), 97-103.

6. 'Arabani, "Khofnak Tota," 134.

7. 'Arabani, "Khofnak Tota," 134.

to one of the traditional narrative patterns outlined by Vladimir Propp in his *Morphology of the Folktale*: "interdiction/the interdiction violated/ bodily injury–mutilation."[8]

Folkloric, too, is the story's conclusion. Mir Muhammad loses a finger but "has learned his lesson" and swears off shooting birds. *Pathei mathos*, Aeschylus tells us: "Through suffering, understanding." Loss of a body part, coupled with a compensatory gift: think of the Norse god Odin, who sacrificed an eye to gain wisdom, or Teiresias the blind seer, or Hephaestus the smith, who walks with a limp.[9]

Another transgression is on display in this story, one that would be familiar to many Pakistani readers: carelessly lounging at the foot of an inhabited tree. The inhabitants appear to be parrots—their appearance is sweet and attractive; but their behavior is demonic. Carelessness is punished, and the hunting-tale turns into a narrative of uncanny possession.

So that ultimately this becomes a story of healing—or more precisely, a tale of two competing forms of healing. Those who put their faith in secular medicine get jabbed with their own needle: the doctor can't handle a crazed parrot-boy. But those who put their faith in *bozorgs* and *'amil baba*-types are vindicated: their petitionary *du'as* are answered.

In the end this story demonstrates the efficacy of heartfelt prayer to Allah—and that's a cure that's within the reach of any reader of *Fright Digest*.

Ayat al-kursi ki barakat
("The Blessing Associated with the Throne-Verse")

The author of this story, one Qaysar Jamil Parwana of Rafiqabad, begins like this: "The incident I'm going to tell you happened to me and is 100% true. My cousin, Khalid Salim Diwana, was present, too."[10]

The story (which appeared in *Fright Digest*'s March 2004 issue) is simple and brief enough. Qaysar Parwana eases into his tale by describing the setting (which happens to be his home town—thereby adding to the narrative's verisimilitude): "I live in a neighborhood in Rafiqabad. Beside the village of Rafiqabad is a well. Near it is a very big massive tree."

A prominent tree at the margin of a town: this is familiar enough to us now as a potential lurking place for things supernatural.

8. Vladimir Propp, *Morphology of the Folktale* (Bloomington: Indiana University Press, 1958), 26-36.

9. The phrase *pathei mathos* is from Aeschylus's drama *Agamemnon*. See Arthur Sidgwick, ed., *Aeschyli Tragoediae* (London: Clarendon Press, 1902), vol. 1, 177.

10. Qaysar Jamil Parwana, "Ayat al-kursi ki barakat," *Khofnak Dijast* 7.11 (March 2004): 65.

Qaysar says originally he was a skeptic about such matters: "I'd heard that at night jinns, *churails*, et cetera come here. But I'd never put any faith in these things."

Then comes the incident that upends his worldview.

One night his cousin Khalid drops by to borrow a video. The film is with Qaysar's uncle, who happens to live near the well.

Even though it's ten-thirty at night, says the narrator, he and his cousin set out for the uncle's house "without any fear or timidity." But when they reach the well and pass by the tree, they both suddenly feel frightened. And then they hear something: "Wondrous and strange voices began coming forth."

That's when they see an apparition—a woman, dressed in white and carrying a club. "Her teeth were very big." Looking at her feet, says Qaysar, made the cousins realize: "This was a *churail*." (Such beings are said to have feet that are turned backward—reverse-order anatomy being a telltale trait of quasi-human visitors from the other world.[11])

The men forget about watching their movie:

> We began running away from there. In our hearts we kept reciting the Throne-Verse. The *churail* followed us for a while. Then all of a sudden it disappeared. This was due to the excellence of the Throne-Verse. We gave thanks to Allah, who had saved our lives. Today, whenever we remember this incident, our hair stands on end. After that, we've never gone there again at night.[12]

A short and simple enough story, yet remarkable for what it accomplishes within the space of a few paragraphs. Note how it begins with a family member dropping by to borrow a video—a homey touch that offers us something convincingly familiar before things get weird. In both its described predicament (the presence of *churails*, jinns, and haunted trees) and its prescribed solution (recitation of the Quranic Throne-Verse), the world visualized here is recognizably that of present-day Lahore as recounted to me by the sorcerers I've encountered.

The story does more. It rebukes doubters and shows skeptics turning into believers. In short, it vindicates traditional beliefs, with regard to both spiritual menaces and defensive countermeasures against such threats. The "100% true" quality insisted on at the story's beginning thus applies not just to the anecdote itself but to the whole spirit-universe *Khofnak* readers are invited to share.

---

11.   Helle Hinge, "Islamic Magic in Contemporary Egypt," *Temenos* 31 (1995): 93-112.

12.   Parwana, "Ayat al-kursi ki barakat," 65.

Khofnak Jinnat ("Frightful Jinns")

The same March 2004 issue of *Fright Digest* featured a second and much longer story by Qaysar Jamil Parwana. It offers some of the same narrative elements found in the *Ayat al-Kursi* tale but emphasizes substantially different themes.

Qaysar Parwana gives a bit more information about himself at the beginning of this story, saying he's been a *Khofnak Dijast* reader since 1998 and expressing the hope his story will be accepted for publication. Then he gets down to business:

> I live in the village of Rafiqabad, in Mamun ka Najn (district). Across the street from our house is a school. Near the school is a date-palm tree. On this tree jinns and other such creatures have been roosting for centuries. In fact these are Hindu jinns. They harass every passer-by.[13]

Parwana packs a lot into a few lines. The scenario he offers would be instantly familiar to the Lahori sorcerer Tariq Akhtar—Hindu jinns perched atop trees, causing trouble to inoffensive humans. And—again, like the bothersome genies described to me by Tariq—these jinns have been around a long time, "for centuries." This narrative aside can be construed as a storyteller's acknowledgment of Pakistan's enduring— and, for many, disturbing—Hindu legacy.

The action gets underway when a newcomer to the village, a man named Thaqib Rahman, befriends Qaysar Parwana (as in the other story, the tale is told in the first person and the narrator is given the author's name). One day Thaqib suggests they go pluck dates from the palm tree near the school.

Qaysar knows this is unwise and tries to talk him out of it: "The jinns vex and beat anyone that plucks dates from that tree." Against his better judgment, our narrator allows himself to be persuaded.

They approach the tree. Voices issue from it, voices that get louder as they draw near. Like the "Frightful Parrot" story, this narrative has a fairytale quality to it: right at the beginning, the interdiction is announced, the warning given.

Which of course the two men disregard. They climb up and pluck dates and eat and eat. And once they've brushed aside the warning and become trespassers, punishment swiftly follows.

Voices all around them come forth: "Now that they've plucked the fruit, they've earned our enmity. Why don't we teach them such a lesson

---

13. Qaysar Jamil Parwana, "Khofnak Jinnat," *Khofnak Dijast* 7.11 (March 2004): 91.

that for the rest of their lives they'll never bother us again? For centuries we've been the ones who have eaten the fruit. We'll seize them by the throat."

Frightened, the men stop eating and recite the Quranic Throne-Verse. But in this tale—unlike the *Ayat al-Kursi* story previously described—the words do no good. The jinns "assumed an enraged form and began to terrify us."

The men try another defense: reciting *Surat al-Nas* (surah 114 of the Quran, a talismanic chapter specifically designed to repel jinns) as loudly as they can. But they chant in vain.

Then a jinn becomes visible and lunges at Thaqib Rahman. We're given an incomplete but nonetheless vivid description of the demon: "From its body a long sharp tongue, like the blade of a knife, extended outwards. Blood dripped from the tongue."

The narrator lingers over the next part: how the jinn seizes his friend and kills him and plucks out and eats his liver and heart and eyeballs. We're given piles of detail that can best be described as disgusting. Here the magazine earns its title: *Khofnak*. Frightful.

Capriciously, the jinn then spares Qaysar, who runs off, vowing vengeance.

But a few days later he returns to the tree to confront the killer-jinn. When he threatens retaliation, the genie only laughs. "You people can't harm me. Muslims can't do anything to Hindu jinns. Get out of here." Then it makes a threat of its own: it will dispatch a snake to attack this insolent human.

Sure enough, on the way home Qaysar gets into life-and-death combat with a cobra. Using sticks and rocks, he finally manages to crush the thing dead.

But that's not the end of his serpent-worries. He makes it home and goes to bed. Then: "I fell asleep but had the feeling there was something suspended above my head." He opens his eyes, to see a second snake before him, poised to strike. It springs; he runs; and amid his screams, it disappears.

In the morning he comes to a decision: he needs to consult "some good spiritual practitioner." He goes to the home of one such *'amil*, where he finds "people standing about and waiting their turn." Then "my turn came and I gave my salaams to the *'amil baba*. I sat down and told him the whole matter from start to finish." All these details feel real enough and resemble the kind of interactions one can witness during consulting hours in the office of any Lahori sorcerer.

The *'amil baba* listens. "For some time he remained in thought. Then he said, 'My son, this is the female mate of the snake you killed. For this reason it will take vengeance on you.'" To counter this jinn-inspired snake, says the *'amil*, Qaysar will have to undergo a five-day *chillah* (spiritual retreat).

Our hero follows the sorcerer's instructions precisely. At night he leaves home and goes out to a *viran jagah* ("deserted place"). He draws a circle around himself and, all night long, until he hears the dawn call to prayer, he sits up reciting the Quranic Throne-Verse. Again, these details match the actual rituals of the *chillah* as described to me by informants in Lahore.

The first night, nothing happens. But things begin to get alarming on the second:

> As I sat there and spent time in the *chillah*, a bird passed over my head. When I looked up, I had the feeling that thousands of birds were flying by. I heard their voices and my eardrums began to burst. I began to pray in a very loud voice. Then the birds grew less, and after that the dawn call to prayer [*fajr ki azan*] began to sound.[14]

So Qaysar has survived the second night. When I first read this passage I recalled the words of the Lahori sorcerers I interviewed: demon-forces don't want to be tamed, so they'll press up against the circle and try to disrupt the *chillah* by creating distractions in any way they can.

On the third night Qaysar finds his safety-ring under attack:

> A half-hour before the end of the *chillah*, in the distance there came into view a number of snakes. They came right up to me and then stopped, exactly as if they had come to besiege me. I screamed, and they disappeared, just as there came forth the sound of the call to dawn prayers [*fajr ki azan*].[15]

Consider, for a moment, the role played here by the *fajr ki azan* (the dawn prayer-summons, which in Pakistani cities is broadcast from loudspeakered minarets all over town). In this story the *azan* is more than a wake-up call. It demarcates day and night, separating the familiar human-dominated workaday world of sunlit time from the dark hours when demonic forces are abroad. Like a shaft of light in vampire movies, the *azan* rescues sleepers from the things that press round at night.

The fourth evening of the chillah passes uneventfully. But with the fifth and final night comes the payoff.

---

14. Parwana, "Khofnak Jinnat," 92.
15. Parwana, "Khofnak Jinnat," 92.

> Just as I was finishing the *chillah*, a *nagin* [female snake] appeared. It began to writhe on the ground. Fire surrounded it on all sides. The snake burned up and was reduced to ashes.
>
> So I went home happily and gave my family the good news. They, too, were happy.
>
> But we had one worry. The jinn itself might harm my family.[16]

So Qaysar returns to the date-palm tree once more to confront the jinn with news of his triumph. He's ready for any one of a number of possible fresh assaults.

Instead the jinn surprises him, announcing, "Now I consider you my friend."

Here the plot twists in a curious and interesting fashion. Qaysar allows himself to be seduced by the promise of friendship with this alien being. For days he is the jinn's companion, wandering about with it, eating food in the company of jinns, chatting with them. His mother forbids him to keep returning to the tree; but he disregards her words. Moral corruption has set in.

One day the narrator's new "friend" announces it's hungry. Obligingly the human climbs a mango tree and gathers fruit for it. But this doesn't satisfy the demon for long.

It says it's thirsty for blood and—with Qaysar as a helpless onlooker— it pounces on two wayfarers who happen along at that moment. The genie rips out their hearts and drinks their blood.

So much for the try at jinn–human friendship.

Qaysar flees and retreats to his family's house. But at night the jinn appears in his room and threatens him. Our hero tries defending himself again with the recitation of the Throne-Verse, but, as was the case before, this proves a waste of effort.

The genie laughs in his face and says, "We're Hindu jinns. These Quranic verses will have absolutely no effect on us."

The narrator describes himself as turning red with "anger, contempt, and hatred." But he's powerless, and the jinn maliciously emphasizes the sectarian divide that separates them:

"You are Muslim. We are Hindu jinns. There's a big difference between you and us. Well, don't talk nonsense now. I will not leave you in peace."

Then the demon vanishes from sight.

The next day a desperate Qaysar Parwana visits the *'amil* again. Once more the narrative emphasizes the religious-denominational identities of the antagonists, this time via the words of the *'amil*: "My son, what we

16.   Parwana, "Khofnak Jinnat," 92-93.

have here is a very difficult case. This is a Hindu jinn. You are Muslim. How can you match him? Quranic verses have no effect on him."

The sorcerer tries an alternative strategy, giving Qaysar a magic sword and kerchief. The latter, when wrapped around our hero's head, renders him invisible.

At first he lacks the moral discipline to employ his gifts properly. He uses his invisibility to steal fruit and cash and play pranks on his mother and generally indulge himself. "A wickedness overcame my mind."

But things get more serious when he returns to the tree and the jinns assembled there laugh at him and his sword. "Why does he keep forgetting," one of them says, "that we're so powerful that not even an *'amil* can kill us? He's Muslim. We're Hindu. There's a big difference between us and these Muslims. Now go!"

But Qaysar won't back off. He singles out his former "friend" and "then I ran up and struck him in the head with the sword. The head fell a long way away."

The end of our hero's problems? Not yet. These are die-hard jinns: "The head flew up again and reattached itself to the jinn's neck."

Then the demon laughs and says, "Who's the fool that's trying to kill us?"

Qaysar's reply impressed me as particularly chilling, for the way his words reverberate far beyond the confines of this tale: *Mayn chikha mayn tum logon ko marna chahta hum aur tumhayn khatm karna chahta hum* ("I screamed, 'I want to kill you people, and I want to finish you off'.")

More episodes intervene, but—to cut to the climax—Qaysar achieves victory as follows. First, he asks his mother to perform *du'a* (petitionary prayer) for the success of his attempt to "finish off" the date-palm jinns. Then he returns once more to the *'amil* for help. The sorcerer tells him to use again the weapon he gave him, but he adds a further stipulation: this time, before engaging in combat, recite the Throne-Verse over the sword.

And that makes all the difference.

Qaysar dashes back to the troublesome tree and chops it down with the sword. It topples to the ground. The genie that once "befriended" him now shows itself.

Our hero wastes no time. He recites the Throne-Verse ten times over the sword, then quickly strikes the jinn in the head and chest. Jinn and tree burst into flames and are reduced to ashes.

Qaysar returns home in triumph, to find his mother still at prayer, faithfully persisting in her *du'as*.

And the story ends with a happy family reunion.

Some thoughts in response to this tale:

First, it offers plenty of lurid detail—heads flying, eyeballs and livers eaten, snakes rearing up in the dark—enough to situate the story firmly in the genre of pulp horror.

But more disturbing than the head-lopping and blood-spurting is the religious-denominational labeling throughout the tale. The only Hindus in this story are jinns, and when one of them offers Qaysar friendship, it leads to treachery and violence and the incipient moral corruption that begins to corrode our hero's soul.

Islamic scripture says nothing about Hindus, but it does advise this when it comes to dealing with non-Muslims: "O you who believe! Do not take the Jews and Christians as friends. They are friends only of each other."[17] It is as if our author substituted "Hindus" for "Jews and Christians."

Again and again, this narrative emphasizes the hostility and the *bara farq* ("big difference") dividing Muslims and Hindus. The fact that the Throne-Verse is inoperative for most of the story adds yet another disquieting element. Nor does the *'amil's* sword do any good, at least when used alone.

What does work in the end is a combined prayer-and-sword offensive: religion paired with violence. The story exalts jihad of the most physical kind, directed against demonic Hindu enemies of Islam.

What we're left with are the words screamed by Qaysar at his one-time friend: "I want to kill you people, and I want to finish you off." In other words, we're looking at "sectarian cleansing" in the spirit world, much like what I encountered in my talks with Lahori sorcerers.

For me, one image in particular lingers from the story: a tree toppling and bursting in flames, a tree that had housed Hindu spirits "for centuries." As I reviewed those lines, I remembered a *New York Times* photo from December 1992: rioters swarming over the spire of an old Hindu temple in Lahore, making ready to send it crashing to the ground.

Purana Mandir *("The Old Temple")*

This tale, authored by one Minwar Nadhir (who is listed as residing in Vihari, in the Punjab), appeared in *Khofnak Dijast*'s March 2003 issue. Of all the *Fright Digest* stories I've read, this one is the most closely grounded in discernible events of recent Pakistani history. Here's how it starts:

17. Quran 5.51.

In our city is a temple that extends over a large area. When the Hindus conspired to demolish the Babri Masjid, then we in turn unleashed our anger against the temple and set it on fire. From that time until today, this place has become an abode of desolation, depopulation and ruin.

But even before this, it was uninhabited. Nor did any Hindus come here to offer *puja*-worship rituals. Yet even the stories from the time of its being populated are remote and few and far between. What did the Hindus once do here?

Its time as a school is also finished. When was this school built, and why did it come to an end?

We can hear the school's strange and wondrous story in detail from the school's *chaprassi* (caretaker/watchman), Shafi' Muhammad. After much insistence on my part, he told the story with his own lips.[18]

This introduction closely parallels the actual history of one of Lahore's best-known non-Muslim religious monuments—the Jain Mandir. Like the "old temple" in this story, the Jain Mandir was destroyed by Muslim rioters in December 1992 in retaliation for the destruction by Hindu militants of the Indian mosque known as the Babri Masjid. Also like the ruined temple in the story, after the 1992 riot the Jain Mandir in fact became "an abode of desolation, depopulation, and ruin" (although, as I noted in an earlier chapter, when I visited the ruins in 2004 I saw that squatters had recently taken over the site and made it part of a rickshaw-repair shop).

Again, like the temple in the story, the Jain Mandir had served as a Muslim school for some years before the 1992 riots. (At Partition, in 1947, the Mandir had been abandoned by its original worshippers, who fled to India, and for some years the temple had simply stood empty.) The close correspondence to actual events in Lahore's religious history makes this story especially compelling.

After the introduction quoted above, the story's narrative shifts to the voice of Shafi' Muhammad the watchman. The action begins in 1954, several years after Partition and the Hindus' abandonment of the "*Purana Mandir*." Local Muslims decide to convert the temple to a school, and Shafi' is one of the men hired to enter the empty shrine and tidy things up in preparation for its first day as an academy.

"We cleaned it and made it ready for use," he says. But the place makes him uncomfortable: "From the cavernous chambers, something akin to hatred could be felt."

Despite his unease, Shafi' accepts the job when he's hired as a live-in watchman. He brings his luggage and establishes his bed in one corner of the structure. He notes that the temple has three towers, but the towers

18. Minwar Nadhir, "Purana Mandir," *Khofnak Dijast* 6.11 (March 2003): 161.

are kept locked. In any case he avoids this part of the temple on his rounds; he doesn't like the feeling emanating from there.

He has time on his hands: the academic year hasn't started yet, and he's all alone in the vastness of this dead space.

This is how his first night on the job goes: at twilight the air becomes suddenly chill. Bats come swooping from the top of the towers and fly about the halls. At the same time he senses a "great terror" radiating from the towers.

Sleep seems out of the question. He lies awake in the dark watching a "yellowish glow shining from the eyes of the bats." Then he hears a pounding on a door somewhere and the indistinct growl of voices. The tone is menacing. "I was completely overcome with fear," confesses the watchman, "even though I'm a brave man."

The pounding and the voices grow in volume, and his fear increases along with them, until there comes a welcome interruption: the sound from outdoors of the dawn *azan*. "As I regained consciousness and returned to the world," he says, "all this felt like a dream… I didn't know what all this was, but I decided my imagination had overcome my reason. The morning sunlight was shining on the horizon." As in the "Frightful Jinns" story, the dawn *azan* divides the rational world of Muslim daylight from the unislamic shadow-realm of night.

A week passes. Classes have not yet begun, and Shafi' Muhammad is still alone in the temple. At night he begins to hear the sound of someone weeping. It seems to come from a sealed room at the foot of one of the towers in the locked quadrant of the shrine. But he has yet to venture forth to solve the mystery.

All this changes one night when he wakes up suddenly and feels thirsty and goes to the sink by his bed for a drink. He turns the faucet. No water.

This leads him to climb a ladder in the dark to the roof to check on the building's water tank. (Like the video-loan in the "Throne-Verse" story, this is a convincing and homey detail: I myself have had the experience of clambering up to Lahori rooftops at night to see what's wrong with the water tank.)

But quickly Shafi' Muhammad forgets all about the water. From the roof he has a view through one of the tower windows. A glimpse, nothing more: "Something black showed itself." He decides to investigate.

He uses the ladder to descend and try to inspect the locked towers. But he slips and falls and hits the floor. He's barely picked himself up before he hears a voice in the dark bark an order: "Seize that bastard!" Unseen hands grab him and haul him off. He's brought to a torch-lit chamber:

> In its yellow radiance I saw a frightful sight. I shivered all down my backbone.
>
> The creature that had seized me was a skeleton of white bones. They gleamed all the more brightly in the torchlight. The skeleton squatted in front of me in the manner of a yogi and then began drawing near to me.
>
> There was a small platform on which there was a black idol. It was a dreadful, awe-inspiring black; but it glittered and shone. From its mouth hung a red tongue that protruded all the way down to its chest.[19]

Good lurid stuff, worthy of the 1939 movie version of *Gunga Din*: the description of the idol (black skin, protruding red tongue) is detailed enough to identify this as a shrine of the goddess Kali (who will be referred to by name later in the tale).

The story's principal villain emerges from the shadows: a knife-wielding skeleton named Ram Das ("slave of the god Rama"). Mysteriously, its skull is half-crushed. Only later will Shafi' Muhammad—and we the readers—be allowed to discover the reason for the damage to its skull.

Right now the poor watchman has more pressing problems. Ram Das announces to the other skeletons that their prisoner is to be offered as a sacrifice: "We'll be able to obtain his spirit easily. Then we can restore the splendors and beauties of this temple. These Muslims thoroughly trampled underfoot our Hindu teachings and religion. Now we will take revenge. Bring him here."

We are then treated to several paragraphs' worth of suspenseful build-up before the sacrifice: Shafi' Muhammad's futile attempts to resist; his being trussed and dragged before the Kali statue; the behavior of the ghoulish onlookers ("The other skeletons stood before the platform with its idol and joined their hands and babbled"—an unflattering caricature of pious Hindus at prayer); and the watchman's frantic emotional state ("My heart was pounding like a petrol engine").

Our hearts are pounding, too. We readers are as eager as he is to know if there's any way to fend off the skeleton's knife. This—as Roger Reed reminds us in his essay—is what pulp fiction is all about: action, and primal emotions.

And here's what happens next:

> With both hands Ram Dass raised the dagger. He came round behind me. His dark eye-sockets were fixed on my neck. With one violent stroke, he was about to cut off my head and imprison my soul and accomplish this black sacrifice to his *shaitan* (Satan).

---

19. Nadhir, "Purana Mandir," 163.

> My eyes failed. I didn't want to die in this way.
> My heart stopped and my senses failed. Maybe I was already dead, and
> their foul and impure incantations had succeeded.[20]

When he wakes up, the hero finds the skeletons have mysteriously retreated. His attention is drawn to something he's heard before: the sound of weeping, issuing from a room at the base of one of the towers. Curiosity leads him to find a way inside the chamber, the walls of which are covered with "beautiful decorations" and painted female figures (a description evoking the interior of Hindu shrines).

But the author focuses our attention on the person Shafi' Muhammad discovers in this chamber: a young woman, seated in a chair, her face in her hands, weeping. Nearby is a bed.

Beside her is something that alarms him: "A knife, a bloodstained knife, looking exactly as if it had just been pulled from a body."

Frightened, he backs away. But the young woman lifts her face and speaks reassuringly. Her name is Lakshmi, she says, and she's been waiting for him for a long time. "I was sure you would come," she says, "in order to hear my story."

"What story is that?" asks the watchman.

Now we know he's hooked. Just as in the medieval *Arabian Nights*, where the discovery of strange objects and strange behavior makes one character demand from another the story behind the oddities, a similar scene occurs here in the twenty-first-century genre of Lahori pulp fiction.[21] The watchman gives up any attempt at flight and stays to hear the story that will explain the mysteries: why the knife, why the weeping, why the skeleton with the crushed skull. He wants to know, and so do we the readers.

Lakshmi explains she's from a village called Rajunpura. Years ago she fell in love with a young man named Deepak. Her family, however, had already arranged a marriage with someone else. Escaping the arranged marriage, Lakshmi fled with her lover here to the city and took refuge in this temple.

"At first," says Lakshmi, "we thought we were in a safe place." Ram Das, the guru in charge of the temple, had his disciples offer the couple hospitality and a room in the temple precincts. But he coveted the beautiful Lakshmi for himself. Late one night he crept into their room while the young lovers slept. He awakened her and tried to seduce her.

---

20. Nadhir, "Purana Mandir," 163.

21. For a discussion of such scenes in medieval Arabic literature, see David Pinault, *Story-Telling Techniques in the Arabian Nights* (Leiden: E. J. Brill, 1992), 118-29.

She refused him, and the angry guru knifed Deepak where he slept. In turn Lakshmi picked up a jar and broke it over Ram Das's head and crushed his skull. With his last strength the dying villain stabbed her between the ribs.

Concluding her story, Lakshmi tells the watchman she has something to show him. She steps to the bed and pushes it aside. Underneath is a skeleton. Things are crawling on it: "Maggots were writhing all over. The maggots were fat, very fat. They crawled out of its vacant eye-sockets and into its hollow jaws."

A satisfyingly horrific revelation.

Then Shafi' Muhammad glances back at the beautiful young Lakshmi:

> My gaze fell on her, and she, too, suddenly became a skeleton. It stood there, elegantly dressed in a sari. On its sari, near the ribs, were stains of dried blood. The sari was torn. The knife, too, was still there, near the black stains of dried blood.
>
> I saw everything as if in an evil trance.
>
> "Come, Stranger," she said. "We'll offer you as a gift to Kali and fulfill her command."
>
> She advanced on me with her withered legs.[22]

Shafi' Muhammad does what any of us in the reading audience would do. He runs like mad. He rushes to the roof "while death advanced on me, from behind and from beneath me."

He jumps from the roof and picks himself up. Then he runs and runs.

Here are the story's closing lines: "But soon I felt one of my legs become paralyzed. I fell down on the spot. I woke up in the hospital. One of my legs had been cut off."

And that's the end. An abrupt conclusion, and not altogether satisfying (did he lose his leg in the hospital or at the bony hands of the ravenous ghouls?). But the tale does at least share a formal symmetry with the "Frightful Parrot" story. In each case a Muslim victim is rescued from satanic forces, but at the price of a limb or other body part. Walter Burkert's study of "escape and offerings" in his book on the archaic origins of world religions explores the persistent popularity of this motif in ancient myth and ritual from Paleolithic times to the present: to evade the jaws of a hungry demon or predatory beast, individuals sacrifice a leg or finger.[23]

Note *Purana Mandir*'s overwhelming sense of claustrophobia and iso-lation. Amid a menagerie of bats and animate skeletons and cadaverous

---

22. Nadhir, "Purana Mandir," 165, 172.

23. Walter Burkert, *Creation of the Sacred: Tracks of Biology in Early Religions* (Cambridge, MA: Harvard University Press, 1996), 34-55.

Hindu phantoms, Shafi' Muhammad is the only character who is both Muslim and fully human. Naturally this is the figure with whom Pakistani (and presumably Muslim) readers are likely to feel some kinship. His situation is theirs. A threat to his life is (imaginatively, for as long as the story's spell lasts) a threat to theirs.

Earlier we noted the similarities between the fictional Purana Mandir of this story and the actual Jain Mandir of Lahore. Both temples stood abandoned for some time, were reoccupied for use as Muslim schools, and were destroyed in the wake of the Babri Masjid riots. Given the fact that this story was published in Lahore, it seems fair to regard it as an explanatory fable. The tale's author imagined a fantasy-horror story to explain why Lahore's Jain Mandir had stood empty for so many years.

Underlying this horror-fantasy, it seems to me, is a certain air of defensiveness and self-justification. Some Lahori Muslims I interviewed in 2004, as I noted in an earlier chapter, voiced regret for the retaliatory destruction of the city's Hindu legacy. This *Purana Mandir* story amounts to a rebuttal and a refusal of any such regret. See what such *kafir* places were really like, implies this story.

After the revelation of what lurked within the empty temple—writhing maggots, vicious gurus, red-tongued Kali idols—Muslim readers are tacitly invited to come to one inescapable conclusion. If *that's* what had been going on in the temple, then thank Allah we tore it down in '92.

At the same time, the author permits a note of pathos: star-crossed lovers, fleeing a disapproving family and an arranged marriage. This is a situation with which South Asian readers of any religious persuasion might identify.

But just when we begin to feel sorry for Lakshmi, she reveals her true, skeletal self and orders our hero served up to Kali.

So: sympathy for Hindus, like friendship with them in the "Frightful Jinns" story, can prove fatal. The message seems to be: best to shun them altogether.

A Note on Style and Theme in Fright Digest *Stories*

Characteristic of these tales is their mix of three sets of motifs: South Asian (Kali idols, *churails*, saris, *'amils*), Arab/Islamic (jinns and Throne-Verses), and American/cinematic (knife-wielding skeletons and eye-crawling maggots, served up with B-grade Hollywood panache). Heterogeneously jumbled, these elements are each described vividly enough to give us a thrill. Then we're hurtled forward to the next lurid scene.

Pulp-fiction readers demand action, and *Khofnak* stories certainly deliver. How to describe this magazine's narrative style? To borrow the breathless title of one of Japanese artist Takashi Murakami's postmodern pop-art paintings, call the style "And Then And Then And Then And Then": linearity and nonstop forward propulsion.[24]

What the literary critic Tzvetan Todorov says of *Arabian Nights* characters also applies to *Fright Digest* heroes. They are generally stick-figure "narrative-men," barely individualized or given distinguishing characteristics except insofar as such traits serve to advance the action.[25]

But note what does characterize *Khofnak*'s "narrative-men": their most consistently distinguishing feature is that they are Muslim. Either they use their Islamic faith and Islamic resources to confront the Other (Throne-Verses and spells supplied by Muslim *'amils*), or else their Islamic identity makes them the target of demonic non-Muslims.

Hence *Khofnak*'s heroes offer a persona that any reader can inhabit, and a mask that any reader can wear, as long as such readers identify with Islam as a constituent and conscious part of their identity. Such identification emphasizes the collective and the sectarian rather than the individual.

Khofnak offers action-oriented pulp fiction, but it also belongs to the genre of horror. One way to appreciate the four stories outlined above is via consideration of Victoria Nelson's book *The Secret Life of Puppets*, which explores the spiritual motifs latent in various forms of modern literary works.

Nelson focuses on stories she labels "grotesque." As a visual art form, the term describes paintings in which hybrid-shaped fantasy creatures (men with fishtails, serpents with lions' heads) share the canvas with the normal inhabitants of our day-to-day world (and in fact the half-human half-monster females of *Khofnak*'s cover art certainly conform to this definition).

As background to her analysis of the grotesque in literature, Nelson locates the origin of this term in the Italian Renaissance. Craftsmen of the fifteenth and sixteenth centuries created grotto-art (hence the term *grottesca*): garden-paths leading to caves within which lurked carved gaping mouths and monstrous forms of various kinds. Strollers could thus engage in a visit to the netherworld, following a primordial pattern: leaving the daylight of ordinary life, crossing the threshold to an

---

24. Arthur Lubow, "Tokyo Spring!: The Murakami Method," *The New York Times*, April 3, 2005.

25. Tzvetan Todorov, *The Poetics of Prose* (Ithaca: Cornell University Press, 1977), 66-79.

alternate realm, and thereby experiencing a revelation, glimpsing the grotto-esque/grotesque unveiling of a reality that ordinarily remains unseen. Because such excursions took place within the framework of a safely managed structure—in the gardens of some nobleman's estate—it could be classed as entertainment.[26]

Grotesque entertainments in the literary genre of horror tend to follow one of two possible narrative paths. The monstrous may seek out victims, when the latter stray near the liminal zone between the everyday and the unseen. An example is *Khofnak Tota*, where the parrot bites an individual near a graveyard at the margin of a village. Or—following the footsteps of Renaissance strollers—a hero may cross the threshold from daylight reality into the grotto-esque lair of the monstrous. The best example here is *Purana Mandir*, where the Hindu temple functions as a kind of twilit cave leading the watchman-protagonist to an unislamic underworld.

Temple as grotto and place of uncanny encounters: this is a concept with a long history. Think of the subterranean Mithra-vaults once frequented by Roman legionary troops in sun-scorched Parthia and darkest Britain.

"Light upon light": this is how the Quran describes Allah's pervasive presence in our world.[27] Blinding radiance drives away shadows, and the theological reflection of such imagery can be found in the Quran's war on the forces of darkness as represented by satanic pagan jinns. Islam insists jinns are accountable to God: creatures of only limited power, subject to creation and death, moral choice and moral consequences, heaven and hell—much as we are. The Quran saddles jinns with ethical burdens and the need for long-range behavioral planning. That is, Islamic scripture rationalizes what is at heart capricious and irrational: the realm of the wasteland, the non-human, and the sense of unease that haunts solitary wayfarers in such realms.

But Joyce Carol Oates, in her own work on the literary genre of the grotesque, reminds us of a truth of human nature. In analyzing the persistent popularity of horror fiction, she asserts the following: "This predilection for art that promises we will be frightened by it, shaken by it, at times repulsed by it, seems to be as deeply imprinted in the human psyche as the counter-impulse toward daylight, rationality, scientific skepticism, and the 'real'."[28]

26.   Victoria Nelson, *The Secret Life of Puppets* (Cambridge, MA: Harvard University Press, 2001), 1-3.

27.   Quran 24.35.

28.   Joyce Carol Oates, *Haunted: Tales of the Grotesque* (New York: Penguin, 1995), 305.

This ambivalence in human nature is mirrored, I think, in *Khofnak Dijast*'s horror fiction. On the one hand these stories are Islamically orthodox insofar as Muslims are shown as heroes and Hindus/pagans as villains. The *'amil* kills the evil parrot; Qaysar Parwana repudiates friendship with Hindu genies and burns down the jinn-roost.

On the other hand the Muslim watchman Shafi' Muhammad in *Purana Mandir* barely escapes with his life and loses a leg to the Hindu ghouls. Hardly a triumph; and readers are left with the feeling—as I suggested earlier—that if old *kafir* temples are haunted, it's best to tear them down. The effortless divine mastery over darkness asserted so confidently in the Quran—"Light upon light"—seems eternally precarious in the pages of *Khofnak*. Consequently one could assume that, regardless of what scripture tells us, human normality is constantly threatened by forces that press in all around us.

Thus Lahori pulp fiction uses jinns and Hindu ghosts as a way to talk about those aspects of life that resist human domestication—the *viran jaghayn* (wasteland places) outside the magic safety circles we work so hard to maintain.

Advertisements, Gender and Audience
in the Pages of Fright Digest

Men as heroes, women as ghouls and skeletal ghosts. Easy enough to assume *Khofnak Dijast*'s intended audience is male. As mentioned earlier, the kiosk vendor I asked told me the buyers of such magazines are "young men." And *Khofnak*'s artwork, with its high-gloss pin-up focus on beautiful girls that are both luscious and deadly, could be construed as targeting male appetites and fears.

But such a notion wouldn't do justice to the range of *Khofnak*'s audience. I showed copies of *Fright Digest* to my Santa Clara University female Pakistani students—some of whom, as noted earlier, had much to say about the activity of jinns.

They all knew the publication and agreed it's widely circulated. One student told me, "Magazines like this are very popular—but only among the lower classes, servants, drivers, and so on. *Not* among the better classes. We take our amusements in English. Urdu is too hard to read for pleasure—especially with that tiny script." (In true pulp tradition, *Khofnak Dijast* is printed on cheap paper; the lines on each page are minuscule and squeezed together and sometimes smudged.)

Jameela, whose comments I quoted earlier on jinns, trees, and the evening call to prayer, had this to say:

> I myself don't like to read these magazines. Too scary. They give me bad dreams. And the print is so small, it's impossible to read. But my older sister used to read things from *Khofnak Dijast* out loud to me when I was little. She managed to frighten me thoroughly. Quite a few girls read these things.

Now consider the advertisements that crowd the end-pages of *Fright Digest*. Ads for *Akhbar-e Krikat* ("Cricket News"), with its sports coverage of Pakistan's favorite teams, might well be targeting young men. But what to make of this (from *Khofnak*'s November 2005 issue): an ad for a publication called *Bahurani khavvatin ka mahnama*—"Queen Bride: Ladies' Monthly." Featuring a picture of a teenaged girl resplendent in gown, brocade-shawl, and gold jewelry, the ad exclaims, "If you want to become a fine bride, then you certainly must read *Bahurani*!"

Then there's a full-page color ad on the back cover of the February 2001 issue, showing a young Punjabi male singer—smiling and clean-cut, a dreamy-eyed heartthrob—and trumpeting his new record album *Kalaj ki larki* ("High School Girl").

And the December 2005 issue highlights a blurb for a magazine called *Javab 'Arz* ("Question and Answer"). The accompanying illustration shows a young woman in high heels and a Western-style evening dress. The text describes this publication as offering "the true stories of wronged women who cannot bear to express these stories themselves"— thus implying that *Javab 'Arz* provides a voice for the voiceless female.

The ad continues: "The magazine that reveals the true stories of women and men, in which every month wholesome stories appear concerning the lives of young women and young men!" Regular features that are promised in each issue include "relations between women and men"; "unforgettable incidents of life"; "sorrows of life"; "horoscope"; and "the diary of my life."

Such ads, which seem to aim at the dreams and aspirations of a young female readership, make one go back and take a second look at *Fright Digest*'s story illustrations.

For example, a picture in the November 2005 issue shows a young woman confronting a nasty terror: a male figure holding a blood-dripping sword. The latter's face is concealed by a hockey mask (again, we see the influence of American horror-movie clichés). But the artist gives a great deal of attention to the female in the picture: flowing dark hair, lipsticked lips, plucked eyebrows, eyes rimmed generously with kohl.

Or consider this picture (from the same issue): a cadaverous humanoid beast—male—bites the luscious neck of a swooning young woman. She lies back, throat exposed. ("Swooning" is a word one doesn't get to use much nowadays. But it seems apt—the posture of the two figures conforms so well to the late-Victorian vampire-Bram Stoker mode.)

In other words: are pictures like this intended only for kiss-hungry adolescent males—or might they also offer an imaginative space within which female viewers can construct fantasies of their own?

Relevant here is an analysis of American slasher films by *New York Times* reporter Alex Williams. Entitled "Up to Her Eyes in Gore, and Loving It," the essay argues that nowadays, "Young women bond with horror films." No longer, claims this article, are young men the sole audience for this type of movie. Williams interviewed one twenty-one-year-old woman in Manhattan who felt that "the tension-and-release cycle that accompanies cinematic terror brings about something like a gambler's high." A twenty-three-year-old interviewed in Washington, DC, confessed she enjoyed the "fantastically campy and hypergritty" feel of slasher movies. " 'You're trapped in a basement with cockroaches on the floor and there's dirt,' she said. 'I feel dirty when I watch them. I like that about them'." And a twenty-year-old video editor in North Carolina admitted she especially favored movies in which alluring women tempt foolish men into gruesome deaths.[29]

Sex, power, revenge; crossing the threshold into forbidden spaces where one leaves normal everyday life behind: this is the raw material of dark fantasy in both slasher films and pulp horror fiction. To judge from the advertising, and from the Pakistanis I've talked to, it seems *Fright Digest* succeeds in offering a parade of ghouls that manages to appeal to women readers as well as men.

"The Islamic Page": Sin and Story in Fright Digest

Even more remarkable than its stories is another form of writing that appears in *Khofnak Dijast*: a monthly nonfiction column called *Islami Safhah* ("The Islamic Page"). Authored by individuals who display considerable knowledge of both scripture and *hadith*, "The Islamic Page" is a regular feature, one to two pages in length, at the beginning of almost every issue.

When I initially discovered *Khofnak*, the first thing I noticed about it—as I confessed earlier—was its sex-and-blood-skull cover. The second thing that grabbed my attention was the *Islami Safhah*. How to reconcile these two components?

---

29. Alex Williams, "Up to Her Eyes in Gore, and Loving It: Young Women Bond with Horror Films," *The New York Times*, April 30, 2006.

This made me want to figure out what makes *Khofnak Dijast* tick. My first goal was to locate every back issue of the magazine I could find. My Urdu tutor Qamar Jalil patiently accompanied me one blisteringly hot March afternoon to Lahore's Anarkali Bazaar, where we went from bookstall to bookstall hunting for old copies of *Khofnak*. We emerged with armfuls of issues dating back to the year 2000.

To convey an idea of the column's contents, here's a sampling of essay titles from the magazine's "Islamic Page." August 2000: "The Judgment Rendered Against Those That Don't Do the Prescribed Mandatory Prayer." December 2000 (a pair of essays): "The Resurrection of the Dead" and "Fear of the Grave." May 2002 (again, a pair of essays): "The Fire and Darkness of Hell" and "The Snakes and Scorpions of Hell." November 2002: "Five Sights Seen in the Grave That Brought a Sinner to Repentance."

As might be guessed from the titles, *Islami Safhah* is moralizing in tone. Its columns encourage ethical behavior via a device as old as Islam: urging the reader to remember what awaits us in the (all too rapidly approaching) afterlife.

The *Islami Safhah* column frequently drives home its themes by means of *hadith* citations. Here's how the "Fear of the Grave" essay begins:

> Hazrat Abu Sa'id Khadrami says that one day the holy Prophet entered a mosque where people were laughing and chattering idly. The holy Prophet thereupon offered the following guidance: "If you were plentifully mindful of death, which puts an end to pleasures, then it would also put an end to your busying yourself with those things that have been a source of amusement to you."[30]

The same essay also warns us what to expect in the tomb:

> Every person's [predestined] grave makes a daily announcement: "I am the abode of complete desolation; I am the abode of maggots…When an evildoer or *kafir* is buried…seventy serpent-dragons will begin biting him. They are so poisonous that if even one of them exhales its breath onto the earth, then until the Day of Resurrection no grass or crops will ever grow on that spot. These serpents will bite at him continuously until Judgment Day."[31]

More on sinners' punishments, from the "Islamic Page" column in *Khofnak*'s May 2002 issue: "Compared to hellfire, the flames of this world of ours are very cold. For this reason, earth's fire would seem relaxing and comfortable to a denizen of hell." Another afterlife tidbit,

30. Amir Husain, "Qabr ka khawf," *Khofnak Dijast* 4.8 (December 2000): 2.
31. Husain, "Qabr ka khawf," 2.

from the same issue, concerning the scorpions Allah has allowed to infest hell as a punishment for sinners: "The testimony of their poisonous power is this: when one of them stings, the denizen of hell will feel the lingering burning pain of the sting for forty years."[32]

The *Islami Safhah* column in the November 2002 issue features a *hadith* concerning a grave-robber who repents after the discovery he makes in the tombs he tries to plunder: the tortured corpses of sinners. One corpse has been transformed into a tightly fettered pig; another burns in flames; a third is pierced with "nails of fire."[33]

Worth quoting in its entirety is the "Islamic Page" essay from *Khofnak*'s March 2004 issue. Its title is "The True Fear of God and Fear of the Afterlife":

> We—thank Allah—are Muslims, and all of us believe that sooner or later we have to die, and that death has a claim on us. In the pure Quran, Allah the pure has given us this guidance, that "every soul must taste death." We believe that death conveys justice and that it can come in youth or old age, and that after death we will live again and will have to render an account to the Lord of Creation.
>
> Nevertheless, in spite of our faith in the Book of Accounts, why do we do so little in the way of good works? Why don't we prepare for death before death? Because we're so involved with life and family that we spoil the chances for our own afterlife?
>
> To these questions the answer is the following. We believe in death, life after death, and eternal life, but we don't prove our faith in these things through deeds. If we make space in our hearts for the fear of God, then we will have a cure for every one of our fears.
>
> If we followed the example of our pious ancestors, and prepared traveling provisions for the journey to the afterlife (*akhirat ke lie zad-e rah tayyar karte rahayn*), then we could be successful. If out of the twenty-four hours in the day, we sat alone for just one hour and imagined the terrors of the Day of the Resurrection of the Dead, the torments of the grave, the fire of Jehennum, and the troubles and afflictions of the afterlife, then we would be incapable of sinning the other twenty-three hours of the day.
>
> If we always kept in mind that God most exalted sees us, then we wouldn't be able to sin. We should do our *namaz* [required prayer] in the proper way. We should perform our *namaz* slowly, with humility and submissiveness.
>
> Remember, *namaz* is the key to the garden of paradise. *Namaz* is the marker that distinguishes between the believer [*mu'min*] and the infidel [*kafir*].

32. Mukhtar 'Ali Parimi, "Dozakh ki ag aur andhera," *Khofnak Dijast* 6.1 (May 2002): 3.

33. Shabnam Daoud Shinakeh, "Panj qabron ki chashmdid-e halat ne gonahgar ko tawba par amada kar diya," *Khofnak Dijast* 6.7 (November 2002): 4.

>   After this, we must give our attention to fasting in the blessed month of
>   Ramadan, offer *zakat* [mandatory alms-giving], and—if we are able—
>   undertake the *hajj* [Mecca-pilgrimage] to the Sacred Precinct. If we can-
>   not undertake the *hajj,* at least we must have the wish to do so. We should
>   also get into the habit of reciting the glorious Quran.
>
>   Jihad, too, is most intensely necessary for the recovery of occupied
>   Muslim lands. In whatever form it may be, may God most exalted pro-
>   vide us the means to fulfill all of His divine commands properly.[34]

What becomes clear as one reads *Khofnak*'s "Islamic Page" is that this
nonfiction column shares a number of features with the fictional stories
that make up the bulk of each issue.

Both have a thematic preoccupation with death and the afterlife—but
with particular attention to the punishments of Jehennum rather than the
pleasures of paradise. There's nothing surprising, of course, in the preference many writers show for hell over heaven. The devil's realm has a
way of gripping people's attention. (And of course Muslim authors aren't
alone in this preference. Think of Puritan New England and Jonathan
Edwards's 1741 sermon *Sinners in the Hands of an Angry God*: "The
God that holds you over the pit of hell, much as one holds a spider, or
some loathsome insect over the fire, abhors you, and is dreadfully
provoked."[35])

Both the fiction and nonfiction in *Fright Digest* share thematic elements (for example, maggots and darkness; revelation/disclosure after
someone enters a forbidden zone: a Hindu temple or a tomb). Fiction and
nonfiction in *Khofnak* share a taste for the vivid and visceral (a knife
between the ribs; corpses transfixed with nails of fire). Both forms of
writing, after all, are targeting the same audience, so it isn't surprising if
their style shares much in common.

Perhaps the best way to understand *Khofnak*'s "Islamic Page" in
relation to the magazine's fiction is to consider both of them forms of
entertainment. The stories provide entertainment in the form of shock-
filled revelatory narrative; *Islami Safhah*, entertainment in the form of
shock-filled revelatory sermons.

Another element that *Khofnak*'s stories and *Islami Safhah* share in
common is an emphasis on Muslim identity and communal Islamic
solidarity. *Khofnak*'s fiction employs Hindu jinns and Hindu ghouls as
villains, while pious Muslims are the heroes and victims of predatory

---

34. Muhammad Harun Chaudhry, "Haqiqi khawf-e Khoda aur andesha-ya
akhirat," *Khofnak Dijast* 7.11 (March 2004): 4.

35. Jonathan Edwards, "Sinners in the Hands of an Angry God," *The Jonathan
Edwards Center at Yale University 2005* (http://edwards.yale.edu/images/pdf/
sinners.pdf).

kafirs. The "Islamic Page" column takes for granted that its readership is entirely Islamic: as the March 2004 essay declares, "We—thank Allah—are Muslims."

The same nonfiction essay strives to encourage its readers to be not only nominal Muslims but rigorously and piously observant in their Islam: "*Namaz* is the marker that distinguishes between the believer and the infidel." The descriptions of hellfire in such essays serve to encourage the performance of rituals that mark one as Muslim and thus worthy of salvation in the afterlife.

References to contemporary politics occur in both the fiction and nonfiction writing found in *Fright Digest*. As we've seen, the *Purana Mandir* story is based on the actual destruction of India's Babri Masjid in Ayodhya and Lahore's subsequent anti-Hindu riots that occurred in December 1992. The *Islami Safhah* column quoted above from *Khofnak*'s March 2004 issue is by one Muhammad Harun Chaudhry, an author whose residence is listed as "Azad Kashmir." The term Azad Kashmir ("liberated Kashmir") is used by Pakistanis to designate that part of the disputed territory of Kashmir which is under the control of Pakistan. And many of the Islamic militant organizations that launch terrorist attacks on Kashmiri sites across the border in India are based in Azad Kashmir. So when this Kashmir-based writer states, "Jihad, too, is most intensely necessary for the recovery of occupied Muslim lands," *Khofnak*'s readers can be expected to understand exactly which "occupied Muslim lands" he has in mind.

Fright Digest's December 2005 issue begins with an essay by the magazine's editor, Shahzada 'Alamgir, in which he insists on a religio-political interpretation of a recent natural catastrophe: the October 2005 earthquake that devastated dozens of towns across Pakistan. The essay is lengthy; here I present my translation of the text's most noteworthy passages. It begins with a traditional medieval prayer, which is presented first in its original Arabic and then in Urdu: "O Allah! Your forgiveness is greater than my sin, and more is to be expected from Your mercy than from my deeds."

'Alamgir continues as follows:

> On October 8, 2005, at a few minutes before nine in the morning, there was a strong earthquake. This earthquake was the biggest disaster in the fifty-seven years of Pakistan's history. In this earthquake, hundreds of thousands of persons were injured and martyred, and hundreds of thousands were made homeless. O God, be merciful!
>
> Today, I'm weeping, and my heart is weeping, because I have seen the biggest disaster of my lifetime. In this disaster hundreds of thousands of my own Muslim sisters and brothers, mothers and fathers, boys and girls,

sons and daughters, have seen all their goals and dreams—the same goals and dreams we all long for with our hearts and souls—become nullified...

Why did Allah most exalted inflict this disaster on the *ummah* [community of believers] of his dear and beloved Muhammad (may God bless him and his family)?

Why Allah did this, Allah knows best. But this matter surely must be in accordance with the divine plan.

Allah most exalted created this world to be temporary. Some day everything will be swept away... At one time or another everyone becomes tied up in relations with dear ones and dear things, and every life becomes entangled in the threads of those relations.

But Time the tyrant slowly strips away the threads of these relations... Death is a truth that can never be denied. Death must come to every living being, to some quickly, to others later. Allah most exalted has determined the time of death for every living being...

Readers! Because of this earthquake, the whole world has seen the zeal and passion, the compassion and brotherly help demonstrated by the Pakistani nation. The whole world has come to recognize that this nation is a living nation. Its energy and courage are as big as the disaster itself.

Today the Muslim nation [*Musulman-e qawm*] is displaying a devotion and zeal that will be inscribed with golden letters in the history of Muslims. Under the influence of such devotion and fervor, the Muslim nation defeated even the greatest power in the past. History is a witness of this.

Today I praise the young soldiers of my country who risked their lives to rescue earthquake victims. I praise the president of my country—the Islamic Republic of Pakistan—Pervez Musharraf, under whose outstanding leadership the army supported the people with great courage and energy.

The younger generation has also taken part. I salute each person that has participated in aiding the brother-Muslims of his country...

Readers! Today I especially ask each of you that you, too, take part in this pious task of aiding your Muslim sisters and brothers...

Allah most exalted is compassionate and noble. He is the dispenser of mercy. May Allah most exalted show us forgiveness for our sins.[36]

Three things impress me as remarkable in this essay by *Khofnak*'s editor. First, it bears the hallmark of conventional Islamic devotionalism: the emphasis on divine mercy, the forgiveness of sins, and the need for pious fatalism in the face of God's will as manifested in natural catastrophes.

Second, 'Alamgir reiterates the death-in-the-midst-of-life motif that occurs so frequently in both the fiction and nonfiction sections of *Khofnak*.

---

36.   Shahzada 'Alamgir, "Ya Allah rahm farma!," *Khofnak Dijast* 9.8 (December 2005): 2-3.

Third—and, again, much like the stories and "Islamic Page" columns in his magazine—the editor takes for granted a Muslim audience for his essay as he highlights the motif of Islamic solidarity. He does so by sounding the theme of Pakistani patriotism (note his praise of President Musharraf); but this is a patriotism that is framed entirely in religious terms, as a pan-Islamist nationalism (*Musulman-e qawm* is the phrase 'Alamgir favors: "the Muslim nation"/"the Muslim people").

One omission is worth noting. He praises Pakistanis for helping fellow Pakistani Muslims but says nothing about the massive amounts of humanitarian aid offered by the United States and other foreign nations. This reminds me of something I noticed in my visit to Pakistan in December 2005, barely two months after the earthquake. Several Pakistani friends told me of a TV show that aired shortly after the quake. The show featured several mullahs who stood ready to take live on-air questions on religious topics from a studio audience. Frequently, my friends noted, the mullahs disagreed vehemently with each other in answering questions.

One audience member spoke up and addressed the mullahs, mentioning TV news footage showing American helicopters and members of the U.S. military delivering food and blankets to quake survivors in Azad Kashmir.

The audience member's question was this. These Americans are *kafirs*, and normally infidels can safely be expected to be condemned to hellfire in the afterlife. But given the generosity of these foreigners in helping Pakistani Muslims after the earthquake, isn't there at least a possibility Allah will reward them with paradise?

The mullahs were unanimous and swift in their reply. True, they said, Allah will reward the Americans and other foreigners for their aid. But the reward will be solely in terms of material blessings in this lower worldly life. Paradise is out of the question. Unbelievers, they said, are barred from heaven, regardless of how many good deeds they do.

On Being Pelted With Slippers, Or, The Hazards of Public Speaking: The Uses of Piety in Fright Digest and the Arabian Nights

Several Lahori Muslims to whom I showed my copies of *Fright Digest* pointed out the very pragmatic function served by the *Islami Safhah* section of the magazine. Essays entitled "The Islamic Page" disarm critics. After all, a Pakistani magazine that features cover art showing gorgeous young women with fangs dripping blood is bound to rouse charges that its stories are frivolous and lewd. "Readers," as one Lahori friend said to me with a smile, "can point to the *Islami Safhah* section and say, 'See? This is a good Muslim publication'."

Displaying conspicuous piety to keep stories from being banned is a stratagem with a long history. The Quran itself (31.6-7) expresses displeasure with those who recite "frivolous stories," because of their potential for distracting listeners from the recitation of the word of Allah. Throughout the medieval era many Muslim religious scholars displayed a similar hostility to "frivolous stories." In response, professional story-tellers (known in Arabic as *qussas*) defended themselves via a technique we can recognize from the pages of *Fright Digest*: they incorporated 100% Islamic elements into their narratives.

Many of these *qussas* performed before large audiences in the court-yards of urban mosques, and they were generally careful in their choice of subject matter. They often began by quoting Quranic verses, especially those concerning Judgment Day, hellfire, and the need to prepare for the afterlife. The *qussas* then illustrated these verses with vivid anecdotes about well-known figures from Islamic scripture.

Religious authorities were forced to acknowledge the popularity of these performances but warned against their doctrinal weakness. Many storytellers fabricated *hadiths*, falsely ascribing utterances to the prophet Muhammad. Others, influenced by Sufi mysticism, mingled wine poetry and love stories with their discourses on the quest for union with the Divine.

The educated feared the sway over mosque crowds held by the *qussas*. To take one example: the thirteenth-century author Ibn al-Jawzi tells what happened to a famous Quran scholar, 'Amir al-Sha'bi, when he unwisely interrupted a storyteller to correct the speaker's faulty *hadith* citation concerning the angelic trumpet of Judgment Day. The mosque crowd immediately got angry. Encouraged by the storyteller, people in the audience pelted al-Sha'bi with sandals and slippers until he acknowledged the entertainer as correct. Interrupting a good tale is risky business.[37]

Ibn al-Jawzi understood the implications of such power over the masses. Himself a scholar and preacher employed by the caliphal government in Baghdad, he was careful not to condemn the *qussas* as a class. Instead he drew attention to the storytellers' potential for educating commoners in their faith. But he insisted that the *qussas* meet strict

37. David Pinault, "Story-Telling," in Julie Scott Meisami and Paul Starkey, eds., *Encyclopedia of Arabic Literature* (London: Routledge, 1998), vol. 2, 735-37.

standards of behavior and education: training in Islamic law and scripture; moral integrity and the ability to resist the temptation to extract
money from the audience; and the willingness to hold gatherings and
offer their distinctive combinations of story-cum-sermon only after being
given permission by the government.[38]

The pressure to justify narrative entertainment via conspicuous piety
can be seen at work in medieval Islam's most notorious story collection,
the *Arabian Nights*. In the pre-modern era and even in recent years,
arbiters of Islamic identity have tried to suppress publication of the
Nights because of its stories' alleged "immorality, debauchery, and per-
version."[39] But any careful reader of the *Nights* could point out that in
fact many of its tales were composed so as to highlight orthodox Islamic
themes.

A good example is a narrative called *Madinat al-nahas* ("The City of
Brass"). At one level it is an adventure story. The hero, an emir known as
Musa ibn Nusair, is commissioned by the caliph 'Abd al-Malik to search
the Sahara for magic bottles from the time of King Solomon. En route he
and his companions encounter jinns, enchanted statues, eerily abandoned
desert palaces, and a lost city of the sands, where death-traps await the
unwary.

But at another level the tale is structured so as to illustrate Islamic
doctrine. The abandoned city and palaces encountered by Musa and his
friends contain poetic inscriptions warning travelers of the evanescence
of life and the need to prepare for the pilgrimage to the afterlife:

> Look carefully, O man, at what you see here,
> and be on your guard before you leave on your journey.
> Prepare for yourself good provisions (*wa-qaddim al-zad min khair*)
> with which you may cross the desert,
> For everyone now dwelling in a home must one day depart.[40]

Of course these "good provisions" are not food in the ordinary sense but
rather good works in preparation for judgment by God at the end of life's
journey.

Thus Musa's travels through the desert become a dramatized enact-
ment of one of the Quran's dominant metaphors: human existence as a
journey towards the afterlife. Islamic scripture contains a prayer in which
believers entreat Allah to "guide us along the straight path." Moral

38. Pinault, "Story-Telling," vol. 2, 735.
39. Pinault, *Story-Telling Techniques in the Arabian Nights*, 1-4.
40. 'Abd al-Rahman al-Safati al-Sharqawi, ed., *Alf laylah wa-laylah* (Cairo:
Bulaq, 1835), vol. 2, 48.

conduct is described in terms of traversing a bridge, a way, a "path of God." Immoral conduct is understood as being "led astray."[41]

In other words, *Arabian Nights* stories such as "The City of Brass" function simultaneously as adventure tale and sermon-as-entertainment—a reliable way of ensuring the survival of a story that must endure the gaze of potentially hostile Muslim critics in a piously Islamic environment.[42]

"The gaze of potentially hostile Muslim critics" is also a feature of the Taliban-and-Deobandi-inflected environment in many parts of Pakistan today. No wonder, then, that the Pakistani magazine *Khofnak Dijast* shares thematic elements with the *Arabian Nights*. Some of *Khofnak's* phrasing is very similar to that of "The City of Brass." The "Islamic Page" column cited above from the March 2004 issue talks about the need for preparing *akhirat ke lie zad-e rah* ("traveling provisions for the journey to the afterlife")—a demonstration of how both the medieval and twenty-first-century texts have been influenced by the Quran and its metaphors.

Thus in their emphasis on action and exotic adventure, in their indulging of popular tastes while invoking the vocabulary of conventional piety, both the *Arabian Nights* and Lahore's *Fright Digest* can be said to belong to the genre of Islamic pulp fiction.

41. Quran 1.6-7.
42. On the genre of Arabic sermon-as-entertainment, see Pinault, *Story-Telling Techniques in the Arabian Nights*, 233-37.

THE POLITICS OF JOGGING:
WOMEN'S STATUS IN PAKISTAN

Marathons, Morality, and the Red Mosque

For several of my visits, I rented a room in a private home in one of the wealthier neighborhoods of Lahore. My landlady was a middle-aged Punjabi I'll call Fatima Sahiba. The daughter of a senior airforce officer, she displayed the easy confidence of the well-born (in Pakistan's social hierarchy, the military outranks religion and business). Tall and attractive, with a taste in clothes that ran to bright colors and fine fabrics, she was unmarried and glad to be so ("I don't want a husband telling me do this, do that"). Servants and idlers up and down the street gossiped about my presence. She shrugged it off.

Fatima liked her evening walks. Sometimes, if I got back to my room before dark, after a long day of interviews and shrine visits and getting stuck in traffic, I'd hear a knock on my door and find her housekeeper inviting me to share Fatima Sahiba's promenade. I was tired but knew she liked company for her outings.

Usually we'd hike the circuit at the Polo Ground. The track looped around a pond, and the smell of water on the air was good after the day's heat. Bats emerged into the lamplight and flitted overhead. We walked at a leisurely pace, making way for occasional runners, earnest men who came puffing by in zippered-up Adidas suits. But women, too, used the track. One night we passed a couple, a prayer-capped graybeard marching with stiff dignity beside a diminutive burqa-shrouded figure. Frequently we were overtaken by clusters of women—some college-aged, others older—striding purposefully, elbows pumping. Once in a while I'd see a solitary woman. In all cases they dressed modestly—traditional *kameez-shalwar* (tunics and baggy trousers) and *dupattas* (diaphanous shawls) that barely covered their heads—but their faces and hair were unconcealed and veiled only by the night.

I told Fatima I was impressed to see unescorted young women out and about on the track. "This is Lahore," she reminded me, "not some tribal backwater." She said proudly this was a cosmopolitan city and here women could move about as they pleased.

But when it involves women, jogging in Pakistan acquires a political edge. In April 2005 stick-wielding men attacked female participants in a coed road race held in the Punjabi town of Gujranwala. The assailants belonged to the MMA, the Islamist political coalition that specializes in the policing of public morality. "Since gaining control of the provincial government in the North-West Frontier Province [in 2002]," according to news reports, "the MMA has banned music and dancing in public, torn down advertising billboards featuring women, and introduced gender segregation on college campuses." An MMA spokesman explained why his group had disrupted the race: "Marathons are not objectionable—as long as the menfolk and womenfolk run separately." According to other MMA adherents, "Women runners should race separately, and indoors."[1]

A few weeks after the attack in Gujranwala, municipal authorities in Lahore caved in to the Islamists by banning "mixed-gender races." Human-rights activist Asma Jahangir joined with other social justice advocates to defy the ban by organizing a "symbolic one-kilometre mini-marathon" in Lahore that involved both male and female participants. Jahangir indicated that the event's purpose was to condemn violence against women in Pakistan and criticize "the lack of state protection for women wishing to participate in public sports events in the face of interference by Islamist groups." The race had barely begun before local police stepped in to break it up. Amnesty International's report on the incident notes that police officials claimed "they had intended to protect the demonstrators against Islamist attack." Lahori police notions of protection involved assaulting the runners and targeting the women for public humiliation: police officers slapped women and pulled them about by their hair. Jahangir's clothes were torn from her back.[2]

Jahangir is the most outspoken and courageous defender of women's rights in Pakistan today, so her involvement in the marathon guaranteed nationwide interest. Progressives and Islamists alike continue to refer to "mixed-gender races" as something emblematic in their divergent visions of the country's future.

1. Declan Walsh, "Mullahs Target Women Runners," *The Guardian*, April 12, 2005 (www.guardian.co.uk); "Pakistani Women Race Peacefully," *BBC News*, January 29, 2006 (http://news.bbc.co.uk).

2. "Pakistani Women Race Peacefully"; "Pakistan: Peaceful Rally of Human Rights Defenders Stopped by Police, Participants Arrested," *Amnesty International*, May 16, 2005 (http://web.amnesty.org).

The issue surfaced in one of the most violent incidents to trouble Pakistan in the summer of 2007—the storming of Islamabad's Lal Masjid (also known as the Red Mosque). The Lal Masjid's leaders, two brothers named Maulana Abdul Aziz and Abdul Rashid Ghazi, had organized the students in their madrasa into "Taliban-style vigilante squads." Their goal was the imposition of shari'ah throughout Pakistan; their tactic, kidnapping alleged prostitutes and Chinese masseuses, harassing video shop clerks, and raging against pleasures they deemed unislamic.

In July 2007 government troops besieged and overran the Red Mosque. More than one hundred persons died in the fighting, including Abdul Rashid Ghazi. In an interview Ghazi had condemned Musharraf's government for the kinds of public behavior it tolerated: "Vulgarity has been promoted—women running in marathons, brothels, pornography in CD shops... All these things have been accumulating in the minds and in the hearts of the people of Pakistan."[3]

In lieu of "women running in marathons," the Red Mosque's leadership offered its own vision of appropriate female behavior. The most notorious image from the Red Mosque affair was the sight of dozens of female students from the Jamia Hafsa (the mosque's madrasa for women), clad in enveloping black robes, wearing *niqabs* (face-veils that permit only the eyes to be seen), and wielding five-foot bamboo sticks. These *niqabis* (as they were called in the Pakistani press) frequently led the charge in raids on Islamabad's video shops and massage parlors. Some of them boasted they were ready to die as martyrs in suicide attacks.[4]

Of the many commentators on the Red Mosque showdown, the most perceptive is a U.S.-based attorney named Rafia Zakaria. In her analysis she focused on Jamia Hafsa's female students and how they were taught to accept a concept "deeply embedded in the fabric of Pakistani society... the belief that women are the source of '*fitna*' [discord/civil war] and the cause and basis for all strife and corruption." Women who internalize such notions "choose and ratify their own oppression if they want to be good Pakistani and Muslim girls." Modern Western concepts of feminism and women's liberation are rejected as foreign and unislamic. The Jamia Hafsa students illustrate this mentality, says Zakaria, in their religious conviction that "they are eliminating the *fitna*-producing element of their femaleness by donning *burqas*. They have adopted the

3. William Dalrymple, "Letter from Pakistan: Days of Rage," *The New Yorker* (July 23 2007): 26-35.
4. "Pakistani Women Threaten Suicide Attacks," *Contingency Today*, May 15, 2007 (www.contingencytoday.com).

violence of men and happily embraced the fundamentalist doctrine that justifies their own subjection."[5]

Zakaria argues that many Pakistani Muslims supported these *burqa*-clad students in their anti-vice rampage, and she analyzes the public-relations strategy used by the Red Mosque's leaders in deploying veiled females on violent missions in the name of Islam: "The stratagem divides women into two falsely constructed moral categories: the 'good' face-less, nameless women courageously wielding sticks against the 'bad' prostitutes, foreigners, and other 'fallen' women who must be saved and brought to the right path by their *niqabi* sisters." This, Zakaria says, is the moral vision that has seduced so many Pakistani Muslims—"the construction of simplistic moral binaries where all good women are militant *niqabis* and all bad women are prostitutes," a way of thinking that seductively promises to resolve the vexing problems of modernity with a slogan and a length of bamboo.[6]

But my landlady in Lahore moved in a different world, one that mixed traditional piety with a Western-inflected lifestyle. Fatima Sahiba drove her own car. Whenever she started the engine she touched the little Quran she kept on the dash and breathed a good-luck *Bismillah*: "In the name of Allah." Evenings we sat in her living room and watched old Disney films and other Hollywood fare. When the sunset call to prayer sounded from the neighborhood mosque, she kept her eyes on the TV but lifted the *dupatta* from her shoulders up over her head as a mark of devotion.

One night we drove to a party at the home of well-to-do family friends. I remember a spacious lawn sheltered behind a high brick wall that was topped with jagged glass—designed to keep impoverished Lahore from climbing in. The host presided over a drinks table featuring whisky and gin. But at first I paid no attention to the guests; I was busy getting acquainted with the household's pair of dogs—big friendly slobbering Labrador retrievers.

The dogs followed me across the lawn to where Fatima stood talking with a stern young man in a suit and tie. She started to introduced me to him—an accountant named Asad Something; I didn't catch it all—when the Labs thrust their muzzles among us in a bid for attention.

Fatima sprang back in alarm. I said I didn't think they'd hurt anyone. Asad—who'd also backed away—informed me I was missing the point.

5.   Rafia Zakaria, "The 'Anti-Woman' Pakistani Woman," *Daily Times* (Lahore), April 29, 2007 (www.dailytimes.com.pk).

6.   Rafia Zakaria, "Faceless, Yet Famous," *Daily Times* (Lahore), July 7, 2007 (www.dailytimes.com.pk).

"If one of them touches you, it makes you *najis* [ritually impure]." He sipped a virtuous orange juice in lieu of a Dewar's and quoted a saying of the Prophet: "No angel will enter a house where there's a picture or a dog."

The View from Cooco's Café: Nightlife, Romance, Talibanization

It was Fatima Sahiba who introduced me to my favorite dining spot in Lahore: Cooco's Café. A massive crumbling building four stories tall, it's located among the crowded alleys of the walled Old City. We always preferred a table on the rooftop terrace, with its view of the Shah Alam Gate and the minarets and bulbous domes of the seventeenth-century Badshahi Mosque.

Startling was the best word for Cooco's décor. In a marble alcove in the vestibule stood a statue of the Hindu monkey god Hanuman. The restaurant's walls were lined with paintings of quasi-abstract nudes and fat *tavayif* (dancing girls/prostitutes) that posed lounging on divans. (A waiter told me the paintings were all the work of the café's owner, Iqbal Hussain, a man with stories to tell—as will be revealed later—about both Hanuman and the *tavayif*.) Floral-motif tilework—copper-orange, sunburst-yellow—decorated the stairwell. Near the stairs on the roof was more statuary from a variety of faiths—a Virgin Mary, a Shiva accompanied by the sacred Nandi bull, a Bodhisattva in the ancient Greco-Buddhist style of Gandhara.

Equally remarkable was the discovery that Cooco's provided a thriving nightlife venue for dating. Each time I visited I saw clusters of young men and women, teens and undergraduates. Couples sat alone together in unsupervised bliss. They held hands and laughed in the dark and sang along to the music of Punjabi pop stars.

Fatima watched me studying the scene one night and said, "If the *maulvis* [mullahs] came to power in Lahore, all this would go. Plus I'd have to cover my head all the time. That's why," she added, "I support Musharraf. He keeps the *maulvis* from taking power with their shari'ah. They'd suffocate us women."

I sampled mullahs-in-power on my trips to Peshawar. There the MMA's religious coalition has ruled since 2002. As noted above, the MMA has curbed the playing of music and mandated gender segregation on university campuses. In December 2005, at the invitation of the University of Peshawar's history department, I gave a lecture to a hall full of undergraduates. I asked whether both male and female students would be allowed to attend and the history chairman said certainly.

And both males and females did attend—although they were segregated from each other at either side of the hall. Over fifty women showed up, every one of them veiled in either a *burqa* or *niqab*. This taught me something. When an audience is faceless, it's hard to gauge how much of what one says sinks in.

Nevertheless young women were getting an education in Peshawar—although this may be imperiled if recent trends worsen. News reports in 2006 and 2007 documented the ever-increasing Talibanization of the NWFP. Concomitant with the Taliban's resurgence in southern Afghanistan in recent years has been the rise of what is known as the "Pakistani Taliban" in the Tribal Areas along the Afghan–Pakistani border. In tribal regions such as North Waziristan, the Taliban have imposed their own bleak version of shari'ah. But even more alarming has been the deployment of Taliban "mobile units" from Waziristan to regions in the NWFP such as Swat and Bannu. There they've forbidden a range of activities they consider unislamic: singing at weddings, selling music cassettes, shaving off beards.[7]

Symptomatic of this Talibanization in the NWFP has been the rise of a Pakistani cleric named Maulana Fazlullah. Head of a group called *Tehreek-e Nifaz-e Shariat-e Muhammad* ("Movement for Implementing Muhammad's Shari'ah"), he controls a horde of armed and militant seminary "students." He preaches openly in the NWFP and in March 2007 successfully defied attempts by government forces to arrest him.[8]

Fazlullah's movement loudly condemns education for girls. "For months, using a pirated radio channel," reported the *Christian Science Monitor*, "Fazlullah had warned locals against sending their girls to school, calling it un-Islamic and a violation of purdah." The *Monitor* quoted one of Fazlullah's pronouncements: "A woman has been asked to remain behind the four walls of the house. Men have been given preference by God." (The latter sentence is a paraphrase of Quran 4.34: "Men are providers for women, insofar as Allah has preferred the one over the other.")[9]

In 2006 and 2007 Islamist militants bombed several girls' schools in the NWFP and intimidated families into keeping their daughters at home

7. Carlotta Gall and Ismail Khan, "Taliban and Allies Tighten Grip in Northern Pakistan," *The New York Times*, December 11, 2006; Barbara Plett, "Pakistan Faces the Taliban's Tentacles," *BBC News*, May 22, 2007 (http://newsvote.bbc.co.uk).

8. David Montero, "Pakistan Losing Territory to Radicals," *Christian Science Monitor*, May 29, 2007 (www.csmonitor.com).

9. David Montero, "Pakistani Girls' Schools in Radicals' Sights," *Christian Science Monitor*, May 31, 2007 (www.csmonitor.com).

and away from any classroom. A sad trend, given that—as noted by *Christian Science Monitor* reporter David Montero—"Pakistan has one of the highest rates of female illiteracy in South Asia, at about 60 percent." In Pakistan's Tribal Areas things are worse—only one percent of the female population can read.[10]

The groundwork for Talibanization in Pakistan and institutionalizing the oppression of women was laid in the 1970s by the dictator General Zia ul-Haq. To please fundamentalist clerics Zia sponsored a nationwide Islamization program. Its most infamous component: the Hudood ("religious penalties") Ordinances, which were enacted in 1979.

Particularly disastrous for women was the ordinance on sexual activity, which criminalized *zina* (adultery and fornication). The Hudood Ordinance mandated shari'ah punishments of public whipping and stoning for *zina*. Rape cases, to be tried in Islamic courts as a religious offense, were among the crimes subject to judgment under the Hudood laws. Under the terms of the *zina* Hudood Ordinance, if a rape victim wanted justice against her assailant, she had to produce four witnesses to the rape who were adult male Muslims known for their piety. If a victim came forward and failed to offer the requisite qualified witnesses, she was liable to prosecution as an adulteress or fornicator, based on the grotesque logic that she had admitted to engaging in illicit sex.[11]

This happened to rape victims on numerous occasions. "Women's groups used such cases to highlight the morbid injustice of the Hudood laws," reported Pakistani attorney Abira Ashfaq. She cited "the 1983 case of Safia Bibi, a blind 16-year-old girl who was raped by the sons of a wealthy landowner and was sentenced to three years in prison, 15 lashes, and a fine." Safia Bibi ultimately was released on appeal. Other women were not so lucky. Hundreds endured imprisonment or public lashings.[12]

The Hudood Ordinance criminalizing *zina* legitimized additional abuses. If the accused rapist claimed innocence and four pious male Muslim witnesses weren't forthcoming, he would go free. But pregnancy in the victim constituted proof of her guilt. Such "was the case of Jehan

10. Montero, "Pakistani Girls' Schools in Radicals' Sights."

11. Ian Talbot, *Pakistan: A Modern History* (New York: St Martin's Press, 1998), 275-77. If the alleged rapist was non-Muslim, then the ordinance allowed testimony from non-Muslims.

12. Emma Duncan, *Breaking the Curfew: A Political Journey Through Pakistan* (London: Arrow Books, 1989), 222-23; Abira Ashfaq, "Reform in Pakistan: Real Change, Or a Band-Aid?," *Peacework Magazine* (American Friends Service Committee), January 2007 (www.peaceworkmagazine.org).

Mina, a 13-year-old raped by her uncle and cousin. She too was convicted of *zina* after becoming pregnant."[13]

The traditional expectation in Pakistan was that rape victims would commit suicide rather than dishonor their families by drawing attention to what had happened to them. Mukhtaran Mai refused to conform. A victim of legally endorsed sexual brutality, she went public with the violence she'd undergone. *New York Times* correspondent Nicholas Kristof helped bring her story to the world's attention. She is a Punjabi peasant, sentenced to gang-rape in 2002 by her village council in retaliation for a supposed offense by her brother. "After four men raped her," reported Kristof, "she was forced to walk home nearly naked before a jeering crowd. She then defied tradition by testifying against her attackers... She is also campaigning against honor killings, rapes and acid attacks that disfigure women."[14]

The Hudood Ordinances embodied this culture of pervasive misogyny. Gender, religion, and social class all played a role in determining those who would suffer most because of the *zina* legislation. A human-rights advocate working with women imprisoned under the Hudood laws noted that "a large number of the women I spoke to held for *zina* crimes at the Karachi Jail in 2004 had suffered domestic violence, were not literate, and worked the most menial jobs."[15]

Religious identity is also a factor in sexual violence. The *Human Rights Monitor*, a report published annually by the Pakistan Catholic Bishops Conference, has documented numerous cases where young Hindu and Christian women—many of them employed as servants in Muslim households—have been raped and beaten by Muslim employers and neighbors. Frequently the assailants were released because the victims couldn't produce the requisite number of witnesses stipulated by the Hudood laws. The *Human Rights Monitor* comments on the coercive social function of sexual violence in Pakistani society: "This humiliation would remind non-Muslim labourers of their infinite subjugation to their masters and Muslim compatriots."[16]

After years of advocacy by human-rights groups, in November 2006 Pakistan's parliament amended the Hudood Ordinances by enacting the Women's Protection Bill. The new legislation makes rape subject to

13.   Ashfaq, "Reform in Pakistan."
14.   Nicholas Kristof, "A Free Woman," *The New York Times*, June 19, 2005.
15.   Ashfaq, "Reform in Pakistan."
16.   Emmanuel Yousaf Mani, ed., *Human Rights Monitor 2005* (Lahore: National Commission for Justice and Peace, 2005), 53-62; *idem, Human Rights Monitor 2006* (Lahore: National Commission for Justice and Peace, 2006), 84-91.

adjudication under Pakistan's civil code rather than shari'ah. Hence the Islamic requirement of four male Muslim witnesses is abolished. Victims unable to produce sufficient witnesses are no longer automatically liable to prosecution for adultery or fornication. Consensual sex outside marriage, however, remains a criminal offense.[17]

Women's groups hailed the new legislation as a partial victory but said the Hudood Ordinances should be abolished altogether. The religious parties were furious. MMA representatives denounced the amendments to the Islamic Hudood as "part of an American agenda." The new bill, according to MMA leader Fazlur Rahman, would turn Pakistan into a "free-sex zone."[18] Such talk is reminiscent of the rhetoric of Abu'l 'Ala Mawdudi, founder of the Jamaat-e Islami (the most prominent of the parties comprising Pakistan's MMA). In his writings Mawdudi warned Muslims of "that satanic flood of female liberty and licence which threatens to destroy human civilization in the West."[19]

Resistance to clerical attempts to dominate Pakistan come in many forms. One form resistance takes is art. An example is a 2006 exhibition called "Karkhana: A Contemporary Collaboration" (*karkhana* means "workshop"). The works in this show were created by a half-dozen Pakistani artists, most of them women, all of them graduates of Lahore's National College of Arts. Their art bristles with political themes challenging Pakistan's networks of authority. An example: an untitled watercolor from 2003 depicting a row of bearded mullahs, pious and somber, garbed in prayer caps and long clerical robes. They stare at a woman shrouded in a *burqa*. The line of mullahs emanates sobriety, control, and order—except for one unruly thing. From beneath each cleric's robe protrudes the hairy hindquarters and hooves of a goat.[20]

To close this chapter, another example of resistance, this one an anecdote from Cooco's Café. In March 2004 I happened to visit on an evening when Iqbal Hussain, the proprietor, was present. A waiter introduced us. Seated at an outdoor table in the alley in front of his restaurant, Iqbal

17. "Musharraf Signs Women's Bill," *Dawn* (Pakistan), December 2, 2006 (www.dawn.com).

18. Syed Shoaib Hasan, "Strong Feelings Over Pakistan Rape Laws," *BBC News*, November 15, 2006 (http://newsvote.bbc.co.uk); "The Location of Honor," *Asian Human Rights Commission*, February 12, 2007 (http://www.ahrchk.net).

19. Abu'l 'Ala Mawdudi, "Political Theory of Islam," in J. Donohue and J. Esposito, eds., *Islam in Transition: Muslim Perspectives* (2d ed.; New York: Oxford University Press, 2007), 265.

20. Some of these artists' collaborative work is available in an exhibition catalogue: Hammad Nasar, ed., *Karkhana: A Contemporary Collaboration* (Ridgefield, CT: Aldrich Contemporary Art Museum, 2005).

was enjoying the night air. Every passer-by seemed to know him and paused to chat.

We talked about his paintings of *tavayif*. Born in Heera Mandi (the "Diamond Market" locality of Lahore's Old City, famous for its prostitutes), Iqbal is the son and brother of dancing girls. He paints the life he knows, that he grew up with, that he refuses to be made ashamed of despite the morality-mouthings of Lahori mullahs.[21]

I asked about the café's décor, the Hindu statues and Blessed Virgins and Bodhisattvas. He said he got them from all over the Old City and beyond. Many of the artifacts came from buildings that have stood empty and abandoned since Partition. "I see myself as rescuing these pieces from destruction."

What about my favorite artwork, the statue in the alcove on the ground floor, the monkey god Hanuman? That, he said, he'd retrieved from an old *haveli* (palace) in the city.

Then he told me a story about this Hanuman. He used to display the figure out on the street by the entrance, to serve as a kind of greeter for customers. But one night a group of mullahs came up to him where he sat and said, "This is a Muslim city. Take that thing inside." They said otherwise they'd have him killed.

Iqbal shrugged and said to me, "What could I do? I sit outside here in the alley all the time. Very easy for someone on a motorbike to come by and shoot me."

So for now the monkey god stays inside. I hope it survives. It's a vestige of Pakistan's pluralist legacy—a legacy that one day might be freed to come out from behind closed doors and back onto the street.

21. For a study of the Old City's *tavayif*, see Louise Brown, *The Dancing Girls of Lahore* (New York: Fourth Estate, 2005).

11

THE GRECO-BUDDHIST PAST:
THE PESHAWAR MUSEUM
AND PAKISTAN'S PRE-ISLAMIC HERITAGE

Few buildings have functioned simultaneously as a dance hall and a showcase for ancient artifacts. Pakistan's Peshawar Museum has done both.

When it first opened a hundred years ago, the Victoria Memorial Hall (as it was then called) served as a social center for officials and soldiers of Britain's Indian Empire. But it also displayed recently excavated Greco-Buddhist statues from India's Northwest Frontier. Party-goers could pause between dances to admire the massive stone Buddhas and Bodhisattvas that lined the walls of the central ballroom. A second-floor balcony above the ballroom provided seating that allowed onlookers to admire the dancers and sculptures below or gaze upward at the coffered ceiling with its intricate leaf-and-flower pattern.

The Indian Empire is gone, and Peshawar is now part of Pakistan. But the balcony and coffered ceiling are still there, as is the old ballroom, which is now the main hall of the Peshawar Museum.

Today the museum's collection includes coins, manuscripts, Kashmiri shawls, and folk art from South Asia and Iran. But the Peshawar Museum is especially known for its Gandharan art—the largest such collection in the world. The term Gandhara refers to a land that in antiquity extended from Kabul (in what is now Afghanistan) to the Indus River valley of the Punjab. Gandhara formed the heart of the Indo-Greek empire ruled by successors of Alexander the Great, who conquered the region in the fourth century BC. Later, the invading Kushans of Central Asia established control over the area in the first centuries of the Common Era. At that time, Gandhara formed part of the Silk Road linking China with Rome. Artisans and craftsmen from the Mediterranean joined the merchants and other travelers who ventured along this route.

In Gandhara, a style of sculpture and carving evolved that combined the iconography of the Indian subcontinent with the canons of Greco-Roman portraiture. The result: a unique and Hellenized form of Buddhist statuary.

Afghanistan's Kabul Museum once boasted a superb collection of Gandharan art. Then came 1996 and the militant-Islamist rule of the Taliban. Despising Afghanistan's pre-Islamic heritage as pagan, Taliban zealots systematically vandalized Kabul's archaeological holdings. They did the same elsewhere in Afghanistan as well, destroying the colossal cliff-face Buddhas of Bamiyan in March 2001.

Luckily, Gandharan art survives elsewhere, most famously in Pakistan's *'Aja'ib-Gher* ("Wonder-House"), otherwise known as the Lahore Museum. Anglo-Indian author Rudyard Kipling had a special affection for this place—his father worked there as curator. In his celebrated novel *Kim*, Kipling described the Lahore Museum's Gandharan artifacts: "In the entrance-hall stood the larger figures of the Greco-Buddhist sculptures done, savants know how long since, by forgotten workmen whose hands were feeling, and not unskillfully, for the mysteriously transmitted Grecian touch."[1]

Less well known, but far more extensive, is the Gandharan collection at the Peshawar Museum. I had the opportunity to see this collection in 2002 and again in 2005, while taking a break from my research on Shia rituals. In touring the museum's old ballroom-*cum*-display hall, I saw that the explanatory texts accompanying a number of the objects indicated that many pieces had been donated to the museum in the days of the Indian Empire by the Queen's Own Corps of Guides.

How the Guides acquired these objects is a story in itself. The Corps of Guides (the first unit in the British Army to be issued khaki uniforms instead of conspicuous scarlet) was created in mid-nineteenth century India especially for reconnaissance and "collecting trustworthy intelligence beyond, as well as within, our borders," as reported in Colonel G. J. Younghusband's history, *The Story of the Guides*. Captained by British officers, the Guides recruited tribesmen from throughout the Northwest Frontier—Afridis, Khuttucks, and Yusufzai Pathans, among others. The headquarters of the Guides was situated close to the old Afghan–Indian border, in the village of Mardan—which also happened to be just a few miles from the ruins of Gandharan sites such as Jamal Garhi, Takht-i-Bahi, and Shahbaz Garhi.[2]

---

1. Rudyard Kipling, *Kim* (New York: Dell, 1959), 10.
2. Col. G. J. Younghusband, *The Story of the Guides* (London: Macmillan & Co., 1908), 4.

A number of officers of the Guides and Royal Engineers chose to use their leave-time excavating for Greco-Buddhist artifacts at these sites. Their boyhood education in classical studies endowed them with an enthusiasm (attested in the memoirs of various officers serving in India at that time) for any traces of Greco-Roman antiquity they might encounter in the ruins of Alexander's Asian empire.[3]

Some finds they donated to the British Museum in London; others found a home in the Guides' mess hall in Mardan. There the artifacts shared space with other trophies in the dining room—heads of ibex and Marco Polo sheep, banners and swords taken in battle, and prizes for triumphs in polo. In his history of the Guides, Colonel Younghusband describes the Mardan dining hall as it looked a century ago: "The present mess is full not only of historical mementoes, as is only natural, but also of archaeological treasures." He goes on to say of the Gandharan artifacts:

> The archaeological treasures consist of sculptures and friezes of Greco-Buddhist origin, illustrating incidents in the life of Buddha, while the statues represent the life of Gautama and some of his disciples. Most of these are still in perfect preservation... They were all discovered, many years ago, within a few miles of the mess, and are naturally preserved with the greatest care. Savants from even so far afield as France, Germany, and America have journeyed to see them.[4]

Nowadays amateur treasure-hunting of this sort is widely condemned. But it might be worth keeping in mind something told me by Pakistani scholars I met in Peshawar. To this day, many tribesmen and peasants in the NWFP still consider it an act of piety, if by chance they unearth a Gandharan figurine while plowing fields or planting crops, to smash the thing at once (after all, the Urdu term for idolatry is *but-parasti*—"Buddha-worship"—a less-than-flattering evocation of the region's pre-Islamic heritage). The only exception: if a looter is in the neighborhood and is ready with cash, the find might survive to appear on the illicit-antiquities market in Peshawar and abroad. In this light the Guides' careful preservation of such treasures at Mardan and subsequent donation of the artifacts to the Peshawar Museum seem perhaps not quite so bad after all.

Among the Corps of Guides' donations now on display at the Museum is a sculpted panel depicting a scene from the life of Siddhartha. The Buddha-to-be, accompanied by his attendant Vajrapani, is on his way to

---

3. See, for example, Francis Yeats-Brown, *The Lives of a Bengal Lancer* (New York: Viking, 1930), 41-42.

4. Younghusband, *The Story of the Guides*, 188-90.

Bodhgaya (where he will sit in meditation until he attains enlighten-ment). On the way he meets a grass-cutter, who humbly presents a gift to Siddhartha of all he has to offer: a sheaf of mown grass (which the Buddha will use as a seat while he meditates). Sculptures such as this, illustrating the stages of Siddhartha's spiritual evolution, were meant to be viewed by pilgrims and other worshippers at public shrines along Gandhara's Silk Road.

The Buddhist iconography in this work is unmistakable—Siddhartha's elongated earlobes, his halo and piled-up knot of hair (signifying spiri-tual knowledge). But even more remarkable are the marks of classical Greco-Roman influence: the toga worn by Siddhartha and the portrayal of Vajrapani. The latter figure, known as "the Thunderbolt Wielder," was revered in the Gandharan era as a chastiser of sinners and protector of devotees in need. Here his beard, muscled figure, and club-like weapon raised in a clenched fist all suggest the hero Hercules.[5]

Also showing influence from the Mediterranean world is a pair of sculpted Buddha portraits, both from Sahri Bahlol (a Gandharan site that was excavated by the Archaeological Survey of India from 1906 to 1926). The forehead of one, a pedestal-mounted sculpture, bears a gouge-mark that once held a gemstone signifying the "third eye" (representing the Buddha's state of "enlightened perception"). The facial features of both Sahri Bahlol sculptures, together with the carefully articulated drapery of the second Buddha's garment, however, are reminiscent of Hellenistic and Roman depictions of the god Apollo.

The main hall of the Peshawar Museum is crowded with panels repre-senting scenes from the Buddha's earthly life. One shows Siddhartha's father, turbaned and shaded by a parasol, leading a procession (including an elephant bearing a royal howdah) to welcome his son home after young Siddhartha's victory in an athletic contest. The elephant and line of celebratory figures recall Roman artwork depicting the god Dionysus and his triumphal march through India.[6] Worth noting here is the historian Arrian's remark that when Alexander reached Nysa (in the Kabul Valley region, near the present-day Afghan city of Jalalabad), his troops took the presence of ivy growing on nearby Mount Merus as an auspicious legacy of the ecstatic god's conquest of the region.[7]

    5.   Roy C. Craven, *Indian Art* (London: Thames & Hudson, 1976), 90-91; Robert E. Fisher, *Buddhist Art and Architecture* (London: Thames & Hudson, 1993), 48.
    6.   See, for example, the "Sarcophagus with the Triumph of Dionysus," a Roman artifact of the second century AD on display at the Walters Art Museum in Balti-more (www.thewalters.org/works_of_art/itemdetails.aspx?aid=21).
    7.   Arrian, *The Campaigns of Alexander* (trans. Aubrey de Sélincourt (Harmonds-worth: Penguin, 1971), 255-56.

On all the occasions I visited, I had the Peshawar Museum pretty much to myself. The few visitors I saw were local residents, who confined themselves to the newly installed manuscript gallery featuring exquisite hand-calligraphed texts of the Quran and Persian poetry. Museum staff members informed me that funding for this gallery was provided by the U.S. Embassy—a well-placed goodwill gesture.

While in Peshawar I asked whether foreigners often visit the museum. I was told that occasionally Japanese tourists turn up here on "Buddhist heritage tours." And in December 2005, the *Frontier Post*, one of Peshawar's local newspapers, published a photo of a "friendship delegation" from China posing in the main hall for snapshots beside various Gandharan Buddhas. But in general, the foreign tourist presence is low— understandable, given the volatile politics along the Afghan–Pakistani frontier.[8]

Dr. Ihsan Ali, Director of Archaeology and Museums for the North-West Frontier Province, hopes to find ways to attract more tourists. On my most recent visit to the Museum, in December 2005, Dr. Ali took me on a tour of a freshly constructed building that will house the museum's Islamic and ethnological collections. The transfer of these objects from the main building, he explained, will permit the display of more Greco-Buddhist material (over three-quarters of the museum's four thousand-plus Gandharan artifacts are currently locked away in outdoor storage sheds). The goal is to foster an appreciation for pre-Islamic culture that might help safeguard Peshawar's collection from the fate suffered by the Kabul Museum and the Buddhas of Bamiyan.

In January 2007 the museum marked its hundredth anniversary with conferences, speeches, and celebrations in the main hall. The old ball-room once again echoed with the sound of festivity and life. I think the vanished dancers and party-goers of a century ago would have approved.

8. "A Friendship Delegation From China," *The Frontier Post* (Peshawar), December 15, 2005.

12

THE HAZARDS OF BEING A FREE-THINKER:
PRINCE DARA SHIKOH AND THE PROSPECTS
FOR RELIGIOUS PLURALISM
IN TWENTY-FIRST-CENTURY PAKISTAN

Introduction: Degradation, Pity,
and a Final Gift from a Prince in Disgrace

Delhi, September 8, 1659. Crown prince Dara Shikoh, son of Shah Jahan, has been defeated in battle and captured by his rival and bitter enemy— his own brother, Aurangzeb. The latter has had court mullahs publish decrees against Dara, who has penned speculative treatises claiming both Hinduism and Islam to be valid pathways to God. The result: a fatwa declaring Dara a *kafir* and apostate from Islam—a ruling that targets the captive for death.

But first Aurangzeb wants to humiliate his brother. He orders him paraded through the city by elephant. Dara rides chained at the ankles, dressed in dirty clothes. Eyewitness François Bernier, a French physician present in the Delhi bazaar, describes the prisoner as "seated on a miser- able and worn-out animal, covered with filth"—a mockery of Dara's once-royal status. Mounted guards with drawn swords force a path through the crowds. Another traveler's account refers to the procession as "a melancholy spectacle, creating compassion in all those who saw him."[1]

If the new emperor hopes by this degradation to turn the commoners against Dara, he's miscalculated. "Piercing and distressing shrieks" rise up from the crowd as the prince passes in chains; there are "men, women, and children wailing," according to Bernier's account, "as if some mighty

---

1. François Bernier, *Travels in the Mogul Empire AD 1656–1668* (trans. Archibald Constable; Delhi: Low Price Publications, 1999), 98; W. E. Begley and Z. A. Desai, *The Shah Jahan Nama of 'Inayat Khan* (Delhi: Oxford University Press, 1990), 559; Niccolao Manucci, *Storia do Mogor* (trans. William Irvine; Delhi: Oriental Books, 1981), vol. 1, 336-37.

calamity had happened to themselves." For Dara Shikoh—known for his generosity to the poor, a donor to Hindu and Muslim shrines alike, a friend to pundits, mystics, freethinkers, and wanderers—is popular in Delhi.[2]

He recognizes in the crowd a fakir who cries out to him. Exhausted though he is, Dara—impulsive as ever—makes his last gift: a travel-stained cashmere shawl, which he takes from his shoulders and flings to the beggar. But guards snatch it away. A prisoner, they shout, has no right to bestow anything.[3]

Finally the procession halts before the royal palace. Here the captive, helpless and exposed to the sun, is made to linger for hours, awaiting the pleasure of the victorious Aurangzeb, who will decide at his leisure how best to dispose of this heretic-prince.

The Uses of Moghul History (i): Portraits of Dara Shikoh in Pre-Partition India

The power struggle between Aurangzeb and Dara Shikoh offered a grim cautionary tale for writers in early twentieth-century India who supported Mahatma Gandhi's attempt to bridge Muslim–Hindu communal differences to achieve independence from Britain. French orientalist Louis Massignon and Muslim scholar A. M. Kassim published an article in 1926 entitled "A Seventeenth-Century Attempt at Forming a Muslim–Hindu Coalition: The Mystical Humanism of Prince Dara." These scholars were fascinated by the career of Dara Shikoh, who is celebrated—or infamous, depending on one's point of view—for his attempt to harmonize Hindu and Muslim religious concepts. Massignon and Kassim contextualize their study of Dara Shikoh's thought in the opening paragraph of their 1926 essay:

> The political crisis that is presently obstructing the national unification of India, hindering the great spirit of social reconciliation that since 1917 had united Hindus and Muslims in a community of sufferings endured together and in shared admiration for an apostle like Gandhi, evokes for us another moment of crisis: that which, in the middle of the seventeenth century, put an end to the generous efforts of an enlightened prince, Dara Shikoh.[4]

2. Bernier, *Travels in the Mogul Empire*, 99.
3. Manucci, *Storia do Mogor*, vol. 1, 336-37.
4. Louis Massignon and A. M. Kassim, "Un essai de bloc islamo-hindou au xviième siècle: l'humanisme mystique du prince Dara," *Revue du monde musulman* 63 (1926): 1.

According to Massignon and Kassim, Aurangzeb's success in wresting the Moghul throne from Dara Shikoh had dreadful consequences for the "Muslim–Hindu coalition" envisioned by Massignon and Kassim in the 1920s. According to these scholars, Dara Shikoh's defeat caused "all the national hopes of India to vanish for more than two centuries."[5]

The enlisting of Dara's intellectual legacy in the service of the independence struggle can also be seen in the writings of Kalika-Ranjan Qanungo, who in 1935 published a biography of the prince:

> I feel that at this moment, when the unity of India depends on a new attempt at the mutual comprehension of the two spiritual elements (Hinduism and Islam), attention can legitimately be paid to the figure of Dara Shukoh, who attempted in the seventeenth century what Kabir and Akbar had done before in the fifteenth and sixteenth respectively.[6]

In the preface to the second edition of this same biography in 1952, Qanungo goes further in linking the theme of Indian nationalism with the life of a Muslim prince who had been condemned as an apostate for attempting to reconcile Muslim and Hindu religious thought:

> The independence of India has been as much favourable to the memory of Akbar and his worthy great-grandson Dara, as to our own happiness, for only a free and secular State like India to-day can truly appreciate the worth of these two liberal thinkers. In their own times both of them were looked down upon by the orthodox ulema as infidels, or at best as Hindu-ised Moslems. The lives of these two statesmen prove that our future is hopelessly dark if the spirit of India is not unchained from bondage to bigotry and dogmatic theology, whether Hindu or Muslim. Our patriots should remember that the path of Akbar or Dara is not for cowards, but only for men who are prepared to sacrifice their personal gain and popularity in the pursuit of their honest convictions.[7]

The interpretation of Dara Shikoh by Massignon, Kassim, and Qanungo, whereby they envisioned him as an advocate of humanistic religious pluralism in the context of Indian secular nationalism, can be found more recently in a verse drama authored by Gopal Gandhi and published in Delhi in 1993. Entitled *Dara Shukoh: A Play*, Gandhi's drama focuses on the last years of Dara's life, when he struggled against his brother Aurangzeb in an unsuccessful bid to succeed their father Shah Jahan as ruler of the Moghul empire. The closing scenes depict Prince Dara in jail awaiting execution. Rather than indulge in self-pity or lament his own

5. Massignon and Kassim, "Un essai de bloc islamo-hindou," 1-4.
6. Kalika-Ranjan Qanungo, *Dara Shukoh, Volume 1: Biography* (2d ed.; Calcutta: S. C. Sarkar & Sons Ltd., 1952), vii-viii.
7. Qanungo, *Dara Shukoh*, v.

death, Dara is depicted by the playwright as having the gift of foresight, of seeing the long-term consequences of Aurangzeb's triumph, and of predicting the end of the Moghul dynasty because of the failure of future Moghul emperors to understand or respect the diverse populations over whom they reign:

> It is they [the Moghul rulers of the future] who will grieve,
> When forlorn, forsaken,
> They run through history's sieve…
> For no other reason than
> Their never having tried
> To get under India's skin,
> Inside her wondrous soul,
> Never trying to win
> Her trust, which is her all.[8]

Gandhi then has Dara in his jail cell go on to predict the 1947 Partition of India and its attendant communal violence:

> What is truly tragic
> Is we are ensuring
> Our future will be sick,
> Vengeful, unforgiving
>
> Will hatch a reaction
> Much worse than our action.
> The future will pay
> For the present's delay,
>
> Its failure of role
> To see, understand
> India's textured whole
> And stay Division's hand.
>
> We were meant to unite
> Those we have taught, now, to fight.
> That is my true regret.
> The rest, my fate, I can forget.[9]

The Uses of Moghul History (ii):
Pakistani Portraits of Dara Shikoh and Aurangzeb

Pakistani representations of Dara Shikoh—especially those published in the years immediately following the creation of Pakistan—have tended to be much less uniformly positive than what one finds in India. In 1957

8. Gopal Gandhi, *Dara Shukoh: A Play* (New Delhi: Banyan Books, 1993), 180.
9. Gandhi, *Dara Shukoh: A Play*, 180-81.

A. Aziz, a member of Pakistan's National Assembly, wrote a book called *Discovery of Pakistan*, which chronicles the political and social developments that led to the creation of Pakistan. In his preface Aziz states, "This book...exposes the threads which have woven the structure of the myth known by the terminology Hindu, and lays naked the hands which have seated the Brahman [priest] on the pedestal of *Bharata Varsha* [the nation of India]." The book's dedication is "to the victims of Brahmanism." Hinduism is depicted as the religion of priestly oppressors crushing the inhabitants of the subcontinent.[10]

Further context for evaluating Aziz's appraisal of Dara Shikoh can be gained by noting his depiction of Dara's great-grandfather, the emperor Akbar the Great. (Akbar, through his creation of the syncretistic *din-e ilahi* or "divine religion," is often represented as Dara's predecessor and model in showing a sympathetic interest in Hinduism and other non-Muslim faiths.) "Islam's decadence in India," asserts Aziz, "set in with Akbar, the Great Pagan." This is how Aziz characterizes early twentieth-century scholarship that depicted Akbar in a favorable light: "[I]n the days of pre-partition India, Akbar was presented by some writers as a deity installed on a pedestal to be worshipped with bell and brass."[11]

Aziz dismisses Dara Shikoh's study of Hinduism as a political trick: "In the hope of engaging to his side the inclination of Rajputs and Brahmanic people in the coming contest for the throne of Delhi, Dara... eagerly employed his time in flirting with Brahmanism." Aziz interprets Dara's sympathy for Hindu thought as a symptom of anti-Muslim sentiment. "Dara forgot," notes Aziz with apparent satisfaction, "that his childish criticism of Islam would alienate the sympathies of his own people." Worth remarking here is the unspoken assumption on Aziz's part, that the only persons to be regarded rightfully as Dara's "own people" are the Muslims of the subcontinent (an assumption far different from the pluralistic vision espoused in Gopal Gandhi's drama). Aziz contrasts Dara with Aurangzeb, "the ablest son of Shah Jahan," and Aziz lavishes praise on Aurangzeb for his competence, modesty, and orthodox piety.[12]

More balanced than Aziz's assessment is a work published in 1964 entitled *Muslim Civilization in India*. The author, S. M. Ikram, was at one time a member of Pakistan's Civil Service and a visiting professor of international affairs at Columbia University. Ikram acknowledges that

10. A. Aziz, *Discovery of Pakistan* (2d ed.; Lahore: Sh. Ghulam Ali & Sons, 1964 [1st ed. 1957]), vii.

11. Aziz, *Discovery of Pakistan*, 62.

12. Aziz, *Discovery of Pakistan*, 79-80.

Dara "seems to have been a center of an entire literary, spiritual, and intellectual movement" in India.[13] But he weakens any positive impression a reader might acquire of Dara by piling one negative reference atop another. After remarking on the prince's "arrogance and tactlessness," Ikram refers to a claim by the traveler Bernier that Dara arranged the killing of Shah Jahan's prime minister. This constitutes evidence, says Ikram, "that he [Dara] was not the paragon of virtue his partisans would have him." Likewise Ikram asserts of Dara: "[H]is interference with Aurangzeb's efforts to extend the empire in the south shows his inability to rise above personal enmity."[14]

Ikram's portrait of Dara's brother Aurangzeb, on the other hand, is highly laudatory. He acknowledges the negative effect on Hindus of Aurangzeb's policies of reimposing the *jizya* (the discriminatory tax on non-Muslims) and "ordering the destruction of newly built Hindu temples." But he describes Aurangzeb's administrative decrees as "reforms which could make his dominion a genuine Muslim state." Concerning Aurangzeb's military campaigns, Ikram says, "He greatly enlarged the Mughal empire and much of what he accomplished has endured. A large part of what is East Pakistan today was either conquered or consolidated during his reign." Ikram then concludes his chapter on Aurangzeb with this assessment: "Aurangzeb can be seen not as the instigator of policies that led to ruin but as the guardian of the Islamic state in India." Thus Ikram's portrait depicts Aurangzeb not only as the forerunner of present-day Islamist shari'ah -minded politicians but also as virtually a founding father of the nation of Pakistan (at least in the version in which it still existed in 1964). The portrait seems calculated to appeal to Pakistani national pride.[15]

A much more sensationalistic approach to the life and execution of Dara Shikoh appears in a popular-format book published in Lahore in 1971 entitled *Unique Trials for Virtue and Vice*. Authored by one Masud-ul-Hasan, the book offers capsule histories of famous trials and death penalties imposed on various personages over the centuries, ranging from Socrates and Jesus Christ to Joan of Arc and Louis the Sixteenth.

Hasan's chapter on the death of Dara Shikoh can best be appreciated by looking first at what the author says concerning the trial and execution of two other Muslims. One is famous: Husain ibn Mansur al-Hallaj, the tenth-century Sufi who went about crying *Ana al-haqq*, "I am the divine

---

13. S. M. Ikram, *Muslim Civilization in India* (New York: Columbia University Press, 1964), 188.

14. Ikram, *Muslim Civilization in India*, 187.

15. Ikram, *Muslim Civilization in India*, 188, 198-99, 208.

Truth!," and who was put to death in Baghdad for his allegedly blasphe-mous outcries. The other is not quite so famous: Ghazi Ilm Din, a young man sentenced to death in Lahore in 1929 for killing a Hindu publisher who had issued a book Muslims considered offensive.

Concerning the caliphal Islamic state's execution of Hallaj, Hasan has this to say: "The announcement that al-Hallaj had become God was blas-phemy... He was tried, and he held that he was the Truth. This was heresy, for it implied incarnation." Hasan concludes his description of Hallaj's trial by quoting the verdict on Hallaj's heterodox faith issued by the eleventh-century Sufi master Data Ganj Bakhsh al-Hujwiri: "'There-fore, although he is dear to my heart, yet his path is not soundly estab-lished on any principle, and his state is not fixed in any position, and his experiences are largely mingled with error.'" The use of this quotation is an astute stratagem on Hasan's part. Data Ganj Bakhsh is Pakistan's best-known Sufi saint, a figure whose tomb in Lahore is an object of veneration for pilgrims from the Punjab and the entire country. The criticism by Data Ganj Bakhsh is used to corroborate Hasan's own verdict—"blasphemy" and "heresy"—as the author aligns himself with the defenders of Islamic orthodoxy.[16]

Hasan's chapter on the trial and execution of Ghazi Ilm Din in 1929 further illuminates the author's viewpoint concerning Islam. He justifies Ilm Din's murder of a Hindu publisher on the grounds that the latter had published "a scurrilous book against the Holy Prophet of Islam." Because of this offense, Hasan sees Ilm Din's act of violence as having been both necessary and praiseworthy: "The story of the trial and martyrdom of Ghazi Ilm Din is a story of love and sacrifice—a youth offering his life for the vindication of the honour of the Holy Prophet of Islam." Because the government had not punished the Hindu publisher with the rigor such a person deserved, Hasan argues, self-sacrificing individuals like Ilm Din were forced to take direct action. "The Muslims had waited in vain for the courts to do justice," says our author, "and under the circumstances there was nothing left for the lovers of Islam, but to take the law in their own hands."[17]

Hasan's judgment of Hallaj and Ghazi Ilm Din provides perspective for appreciating his assessment of Dara Shikoh. According to Hasan, when Aurangzeb and Prince Murad first began to challenge Dara's claim to the throne, Shah Jahan advised against the use of force in dealing with this incipient rebellion. Other Muslim noblemen, says Hasan, also tried

---

16. Masud-ul-Hasan, *Unique Trials for Virtue and Vice* (Lahore: Unique Publications, 1971), 13-14, 17.

17. Hasan, *Unique Trials for Virtue and Vice*, 63, 68.

to prevent civil war. What then caused the outbreak of this fratricidal conflict between Muslims? Hasan asserts, "The Hindu nobles were of the view that the rebel princes should be dealt with once for all with force. Dara Shikoh fell in with the advice of the Hindu councillors." As in his chapter on the execution of Ghazi Ilm Din, Hasan draws attention to the supposed presence of Hindu provocateurs and troublemakers as the source of problems for the Muslim community.[18]

Given his preoccupation with the notion of Hindu conspiracies, it is not surprising that our author foregoes any serious examination of Dara Shikoh's mystical speculations. Instead he recapitulates the charges brought against Dara that demonstrated how the prince's faith had been contaminated by his study of Hinduism. Hasan gives particular attention to the notion that Dara regarded the *Vedas* as the original source of Islamic scripture. Here is Hasan's judgment on Dara's attempt to reconcile the Hindu and Muslim scriptural traditions: "In howsoever mystical language, abstruse and enigmatic he might have expressed the idea [*sic*], in ultimate analysis it meant that the Quran was not the word of God, and was based on the *Vedas*. That shook the very foundation of Islam. This was heresy and *kufr* [unbelief] in unmistakable terms."[19]

Thus it is with a complete lack of sympathy that Hasan recounts the murder of Dara Shikoh following the fatwa issued by Aurangzeb's ulema finding him guilty of apostasy.

This theme of the threat to Islam posed by Hindu influence on Dara Shikoh's thought recurs in numerous Pakistani texts that deal with the conflict between the rival Moghul brothers. One example is a book by Moinul Haq entitled *Ideological Basis of Pakistan in Historical Perspective*, published in 1982 by the Pakistan Historical Society. The book's preface states:

> For students of history, particularly in the universities and colleges of Pakistan, the study of the ideological background of Pakistan in its historical perspective is indispensable, because they are likely to get confused in this regard by western concepts of nationalism and nationhood which in most cases form the basis of modern states. On the contrary, in Islam the basis of *ummah* [the Muslim community] is common religious belief.[20]

Haq's emphasis on the importance of "common religious belief" for building national identity helps explain his hostility to Dara Shikoh. His

18. Hasan, *Unique Trials for Virtue and Vice*, 39.
19. Hasan, *Unique Trials for Virtue and Vice*, 42.
20. S. Moinul Haq, *Ideological Basis of Pakistan in Historical Perspective, 711– 1940* (Karachi: Pakistan Historical Society, 1982), v.

text offers nothing on the content of Dara's intellectual lifework—nothing, that is, except the remark that Aurangzeb would never have felt it necessary to seize the throne for himself "if Shahjahan had been only fair to him and taken the necessary steps to stop Dara from making a joke of the Islamic principles. Where Islam was concerned, Awrangzib [*sic*] was not prepared for a compromise."[21]

Referring to Aurangzeb by his throne-name 'Alamgir, Haq asserts that the reign of this pious and uncompromising emperor delayed the subsequent rise of Hindu political power: "It was only when the disintegration of the Moghul Empire had set in after 'Alamgir's death that the Maratha Peshwa conceived the idea of establishing *Hindu pad padshahi* (Hindu rule)."[22]

Discussion of Aurangzeb's rule in terms of a perceived threat from Hinduism also appears in S. F. Mahmud's *Concise History of Indo-Pakistan*, published in Karachi in 1988. The book's back-cover advertisement-copy announces that this text is "intended for secondary school and college level students." Mahmud's representation of the conflict between Aurangzeb and Dara Shikoh is preceded by an unflattering description of Akbar's *din-e ilahi*, a description not calculated to soothe present-day Pakistani communal anxieties:

> Akbar appeared to favor the Hindus more than the Muslims… The encouragement of the Hindus gave a great impetus to the ideas of Hindu nationalism which were rising in India… His virtual anti-Muslim policy…also started a reaction among the Muslims in favor of orthodoxy, which culminated in the reign of Aurangzeb.[23]

Worth noting here is the anachronistic transposition of "Hindu nationalism" to sixteenth-century Moghul India.

In characterizing Aurangzeb's reign Mahmud gives particular attention to the ruler's piety: "He learned the Quran by heart and gave all his sons and daughters a sound education in Islamic studies… He never missed any observance of Islam, whether praying, fasting, or almsgiving." Our author says very little about Dara Shikoh except to note his "unorthodox views about the Quran," his assertion that the Hindu *Upanishads* were "equally sacred" in comparison with Islamic scripture, and his subsequent execution for apostasy.[24]

21. Haq, *Ideological Basis of Pakistan*, 22.
22. Haq, *Ideological Basis of Pakistan*, 110.
23. S. F. Mahmud, *A Concise History of Indo-Pakistan* (Karachi: Oxford University Press, 1988), 144.
24. Mahmud, *A Concise History of Indo-Pakistan*, 161-63.

Considerably more interest in the prince-mystic's religious thought is displayed in Muhammad Salim's *Dara Shikoh: ahwal o afkar* ("Dara Shikoh: Life-Circumstances and Ideas"), published in Lahore in 1995. Salim offers individual chapters on Dara's Sufi treatises, his poetry, and his translation of the *Upanishads*. Nevertheless the book's preface makes clear the politically driven nature of Salim's interest. He claims that hitherto "there has been no analysis of what would have become of the map of India had [Dara] been vested with the crown of sovereignty." Salim announces that his book will include such an analysis.[25]

The partisan quality of Salim's analysis comes through most clearly in a chapter entitled *Shakhsiyat aur mazhab* ("Personality and Religion"). Here is how he describes the changes in Dara's personality and moral character that occurred as a result of exposing himself to Hindu scripture: "Along with learning Sanskrit, he began the study of the sacred books of the Hindu religion, especially the *Upanishads*. A feeling of his own greatness became fixed in his mind, and he began to believe that along with being a prince, he was someone upon whom rested the divine favor of God."[26]

Of particular interest to Salim is how Dara's study of Hinduism affected his understanding of Islam: "Dara Shikoh had the habit of interpreting the holy Quran and the *hadith* according to his own personal inclination. But in reality, after all his encounters with pundits, yogis, and Hindu renunciants, and after studying the *Upanishads* and the Hindu science of idols, his manner of thought had become completely altered."[27]

From Salim's point of view, the study of Hinduism had a corrupting influence on Dara Shikoh, and this influence had powerful and dire political implications:

> The Hindus were the largest community in India. They were attracted to him because of his ideas and deeds. They had the notion that when Dara Shikoh sat on the throne, they would regain the favor and influence they had acquired during the time of Akbar... Not only Aurangzeb but also Shah Jahan's Muslim emirs considered Dara Shikoh unacceptable as successor to Shah Jahan because he had become so influenced by Hinduism that he abandoned ritual prayer, Ramadan fasting, sharia, and other divine precepts mandated by God. From his thoughts and deeds it had become clear that if he gained the throne, all kinds of new interpretations of Islam would arise, a blow would be struck against the beliefs of Muslims, and the reign of Akbar would return.[28]

25.   Muhammad Salim, *Dara Shikoh: ahwal o afkar* (Lahore: Maktabat-e Karvan, 1995), vii-viii.

26.   Salim, *Dara Shikoh: ahwal o afkar*, 159.

27.   Salim, *Dara Shikoh: ahwal o afkar*, 160.

28.   *Salim, Dara Shikoh: ahwal o afkar*, 162-63.

After this alarmist scenario, Salim quotes Muhammad Iqbal, whom Pakistanis revere as their nation's intellectual progenitor: "The seed of heresy fostered by Akbar grew forth and sprouted within the cunning temperament of Dara." Salim then asserts, "There is no doubt that if Dara Shikoh had become emperor, Islam in India would have been shrouded by the cloak of Hinduism."[29] Thus his analysis is dominated by a perception of Dara's religious inquiries as a threat to both the Islamic faith and Muslim political domination of the subcontinent.

My next text is from a very different source—an Urdu-language leaflet recently distributed in Pakistan by a group that calls itself al-Muhajiroun Harakat al-Khilafah (a title that could be translated as "the pious emigrants of the caliphate movement"; the term "muhajiroun" evokes early Islamic history and those faithful Muslims who followed the prophet Muhammad's lead in emigrating from pagan Mecca to found a Muslim community in Medina). Like other pan-Islamic partisans of the nineteenth and twentieth centuries, members of the Muhajiroun deride the concept of national boundaries as unislamic and call for the reunification of the *ummah* under the global leadership of a caliph. The group is militant and confrontational in its politics (to take one example: in 2003, on the occasion of the second anniversary of the September 11 terrorist attacks, the Muhajiroun website issued a statement praising the hijackers as the "Magnificent 19"). Based in London (where they are now banned), the Muhajiroun have been active in Lahore and elsewhere in Pakistan.[30]

The Urdu Muhajiroun leaflet I referred to is entitled *Pakistan meyn jashan-e kufr kyon* ("Why are there pagan festivals in Pakistan?"). I found a stack of copies of this leaflet in March 2002 in the vestibule of the Shah Faisal mosque in Islamabad. The text was authored by the Muhajiroun headquarters office in Lahore. The leaflet condemns President Pervez Musharraf for permitting the observance of two "pagan festivals" in Pakistan—Valentine's Day and the annual spring festival known as Basant. Basant is famous in Lahore (as it is across the border in India) as an occasion for the sport of *patang-bazi* (kite-flying). The Muhajiroun condemn *patang-bazi* as a frivolous activity unworthy of Muslims. Such condemnations are not unknown elsewhere in the Islamic world; consider the banning of kite-flying in Afghanistan under Taliban

29. Salim, *Dara Shikoh: ahwal o afkar*, 163.

30. The Muhajiroun's statement about September 11 and the "Magnificent 19" can be found in an article entitled "Bush & Blair Choke on the Fallout From September the 11th," at the Muhajiroun website: http://www.almuk.com/obm/pr/2003/911.html.

rule.[31] But I draw attention to this leaflet in the present context because of the way in which the Muhajiroun make use of Moghul history to justify their hostility to the sport:

> The historical background of Basant is connected with a Hindu who behaved with arrogant rudeness toward the dignity of the pure Prophet. Aurangzeb, the ruler of the Islamic government at that time, proclaimed the sentence of death against that individual. The Hindu who insulted the pure Prophet's dignity was fond of *patang-bazi* and was very skilled at flying kites. On the yearly anniversary date of his execution, Hindus celebrate a festival in this man's honor, and they give this festival the name Basant.[32]

Thus the strategy used by the Muhajiroun to discourage Pakistani Muslims from pursuing this popular sport is to link it with Hinduism and past insults to the prophet Muhammad. The figure invoked as the guardian of Muslim honor and the chastiser of Hindu villains is the Moghul emperor Aurangzeb—a role consistent with the portrayals we have seen in Pakistani historical accounts, where Aurangzeb rescues Islam from the corrupting Hindu influence introduced by Akbar and perpetuated by Dara Shikoh.

The Uses of Moghul History (iii):
Evaluations of Dara Shikoh and Aurangzeb
in Pakistani School Textbooks

On my most recent visit to Lahore, in December 2005, I stopped by Ferozsons, the city's best bookshop, to see what titles were in print and available to the Pakistani public on Moghul history and the Dara Shikoh–Aurangzeb conflict.

The two publications I found that were the most nearly even-handed in their treatment of the brothers' rivalry were textbooks for students. One was a history of Pakistan published by the Karachi branch of Oxford University Press. Its author, Farooq Naseem Bajwa, received a PhD in international relations from the London School of Economics. Bajwa says nothing about Dara's most interesting legacy—his fascination with Hinduism and attempts to merge Quranic and Vedantic teachings—and instead limits himself to the observation that "Dara lacked a military

31. For the banning of kite-flying by the Taliban in Afghanistan, see Ahmed Rashid, *Taliban: Militant Islam, Oil, and Fundamentalism in Central Asia* (New Haven: Yale University Press, 2000), 217-19.

32. *Pakistan meyn jashan-e kufr kyon* (leaflet distributed by the Lahore office of al-Muhajiroun Harakat al-Khilafah).

temperament and was more interested in Sufism than administration."[33] The other school textbook is by a former Pakistani government minister, Wali-ur-Rehman. Like Bajwa, Rehman spends little time on Prince Dara, noting merely he was "a Sufi and a religious eclectic who had translated the *Upanishads* into Persian." Rehman criticizes Aurangzeb for his "harsh treatment" of his family—to seize the throne Aurangzeb not only murdered Dara but killed his other brothers and imprisoned his own father, Shah Jahan, for life—but nonetheless Rehman seems impressed by the winner in this dynastic dispute: "Aurangzeb was the superior in both military talent and administrative skills. Aurangzeb easily outclassed his brothers in the bid for power."[34]

Another book I found at Ferozsons, Shaykh Muhammad Ikram's *Raud-e kauthar*, an Urdu-language cultural history of Moghul India, offers more detail than the other texts on Dara Shikoh's intellectual work. Ikram concedes one benefit of the prince's translations of Hindu scriptures into Persian: "Some Muslims began to understand that not all Hindus were idolaters who gave their gods human attributes and vulgar human qualities; some were pure-minded, selfless, sincere ascetics." But he concludes his discussion as follows: "Like-minded individuals used to call Dara Shikoh 'a reviver of the faith and the community,' but Muslims will certainly find unacceptable the fact that he kept company with Hindu yogis and holy men."[35]

Much harsher in its treatment of Dara is an undergraduate textbook by a professor at Lahore's Aitchison College named Muhammad Tariq Awan. After praising Aurangzeb as "a pious man" and "a practicing Muslim," Awan has this to say about Dara's religious writings: "He wanted to impress the Muslims with his sainthood, but...he shocked them by stating that the Prophet practiced the control of breath...in the cave of Hira and meditated...in the same way as the Hindu yogis did. In this work, Dara Shikoh unfolded...his proclivities for Hinduism." Judgmental is the best word to describe Awan's assessment of *Majma' al-bahrain* ("The Mingling of the Two Oceans," Dara's treatise on Quranic and Vedantic scriptures, which triggered the fatal fatwa from Aurangzeb's clerics): "In *Majma' ul-Bahrain*, 1655, he brought Islam (the

33. Farooq Naseem Bajwa, *Pakistan: A Historical and Contemporary Look* (Karachi: Oxford University Press, 2002), 51.

34. Wali-Ur-Rehman, *Indo-Pak History 712–1815* (Lahore: AN Publishers, 2004), 87.

35. Shaykh Muhammad Ikram, *Raud-e kauthar: islami hind aur pakistan ki mazhabi aur 'ilmi tarikh-e 'ahd-e moghuliyyah* (Lahore: Idarat-e thaqafat-e islamiyyah, 2005), 447, 453.

religion of monotheism) on level with Hinduism (the faith of idol-wor-shippers) and failed to find any difference between the two, implying therefore that one could attain salvation by following either of the two religions." Given the attitudes towards Hinduism prevalent in Pakistan today, Awan's textbook seems calculated to ensure that Muslim students find Dara repugnant.[36]

Even more partisan is a book that a clerk at Ferozsons enthusiastically recommended. It's an elementary-school text published in Lahore called "First Steps in Our History." The author, a "Dr. Kh. Abdul Haye," announces his didactic approach in the preface: "History is like a drama in which the great heroes...leave a permanent mark on the minds of those who read it... It is for us to keep burning brightly the torch which our forefathers had lit."[37]

Haye's textbook criticizes Dara's ancestor Akbar for promulgating a religious policy that amounted to coddling Hindus: "Akbar thought that since most of his people in the empire were Hindus, he should try to keep them in good humour. He therefore abolished many taxes that they did not like to pay." Haye says nothing about Dara's spiritual writings but offers a damning thumbnail character assessment: "Dara...was a good man, but he was rather lazy and weak." Aurangzeb, however, comes off as a beacon of piety and manly virtue: "Aurangzeb was a God-fearing ruler... He had great love for learning, but he was not a timid book-worm. He turned out to be a great scholar and brave soldier... For his own livelihood he earned small sums of money sewing [prayer] caps and copying the Holy Quran."[38]

Professors I interviewed at the University of Peshawar's history department said most Pakistanis today are altogether ignorant of Dara Shikoh and his life. This was my impression, too. I drew a blank men-tioning his name in casual talk with mechanics, rickshaw drivers, and streetside vendors. "Common folk who have heard of him," said one history professor, "think of Dara as a heretic who favored Hindus."

Zahid Ali, a University of Peshawar history lecturer who happens to be Shia, asserted there's a sectarian divide in how Pakistanis view their Moghul past. In detailed emails he sent me on the subject he wrote that Pakistani Sunnis—who are much more familiar with Aurangzeb's name than with Dara's—view Aurangzeb as a "true follower of Islam, a

36. Muhammad Tariq Awan, *History of India and Pakistan* (Lahore: Ferozsons, 1994), 394-96.

37. Kh. Abdul Haye, *First Steps in Our History: Book 2* (Lahore: Ferozsons, 1990), vi.

38. Haye, *First Steps in Our History*, 44, 61, 64.

mujahid and a great saviour of the faith...when great odds and challenges were posed by Hindus." Shias, Zahid argued, tend to be much more conversant with the details of Islamic history. "Hope you will agree with me," he wrote, "if I say that a Shia individual knows and is aware and is more conscious of the past and is vigilant in the present he/she lives in and is more fearful of the future. The reasons are easy to understand."[39]

My correspondent briefly reviewed the recurrent persecution of the Shia minority by the Sunni majority. The result of such persecution: "The Shias had to and have to be conscious of the affairs around [them]." For their own survival, Zahid wrote, Pakistani Shias have had to develop a more finely tuned and accurate awareness of the realities of Islamic history than that possessed by Sunnis.

"With me," he concluded, "and the majority of those Shias in touch with history, Aurangzeb's era was a repetition of those of Umayyads, Abbasides, and Ottomans, where Shias had been persecuted, tortured, killed and exiled... They [the Shias of Aurangzeb's time] in no way could opt and support the cause of Aurangzeb, who had no liking for the faith they professed and had no mercy on them. On the other hand Dara-shikoh was a proclaimed secular and had made it very clear that nobody [would] be treated or harassed in the name of blood, colour or faith."[40]

Syed Minhaj-ul-Hassan, the history department's chairman at the University of Peshawar, summarized for me the view of Aurangzeb among ordinary Pakistani Sunnis: "A pious simple man, the savior of Islam in India, the last good Moghul ruler." He also mentioned Aurang-zeb's reputation for stitching together his own prayer caps.

Worth noting here is a glimpse of Aurangzeb offered by a seventeenth-century Venetian adventurer, Niccolao Manucci. A teenaged soldier of fortune in Dara's army, he stayed at the doomed prince's side even as the latter's Muslim entourage deserted him. (Manucci's loyalty led Dara to weep and exclaim, "See, you others, the fidelity of this European Farangi lad.") Manucci had this wry observation about Aurangzeb's conspicuous piety: "He let it be known that he underwent severe penances and fastings; he allowed himself to be found in prayer or reading the Quran." Aurangzeb knew the worth of what today we'd call the photo op.[41]

On my visits to Pakistan I occasionally met men named Aurangzeb or 'Alamgir ("World-Seizer," Aurangzeb's throne-name) in honor of the triumphant Moghul. Not once did I encounter anyone named after Aurangzeb's vanquished philosopher-mystic brother—except in literature.

39. Zahid Ali, email communication, July 30, 2003.
40. Zahid Ali, email communication, December 4, 2003.
41. Manucci, *Storia do Mogor*, vol. 1, 294.

Mohsin Hamid's novel *Moth Smoke* features a protagonist called Darashikoh Shezad.[42] An unemployed dopehead adrift in late-twentieth-century Lahore, Hamid's fictional Darashikoh is a loser and ne'er-do-well. Loser though he is, the hero of *Moth Smoke*—much like his Moghul-era namesake—is an appealing character, perceptive, honest, and impulsive—even as he finds himself overtaken by ruin.

Conclusion: The Death of Dara Shikoh— and Prospects for the Revival of His Spirit

Delhi, September 10, 1659. After being paraded in chains through the city streets, Dara is forced into a prison cell. He knows he's unlikely to live long. With just a few hours of life remaining, he thinks of an old friend, a Flemish Jesuit named Henriques Buzeo, "much loved by the prince," according to Manucci, "…and well liked by all the nobles, who delighted in his conversation." Dara asks his guards to bring the priest. They refuse. Time has run out.[43]

Aurangzeb sends slaves to Dara's cell to kill him. But he resists. He's concealed a small knife in his pillow. No use: they fling him to the ground. Three men hold him down; a fourth decapitates him.

Aurangzeb orders the severed head brought to him on a tray. He contemplates it a moment and then has the head tossed to the floor. He gloats over his dead brother, stabbing the head three times with a sword and saying, "Behold the face of a would-be king." When the new emperor is done with this sport he turns and says, "Take him out of my sight."[44]

Whereupon Aurangzeb began a decades-long reign that is hailed today by Islamists for its pious orthodoxy but recalled with dismay by progressive-minded reformers for its violent intolerance towards non-Muslims (especially Hindus and Sikhs) and religious minorities (especially Shias).

In recent years some Pakistani Muslim authors have sought to extract from these Moghul brothers' rivalry lessons that might be applicable to the challenges facing twenty-first-century South Asia. Anthropologist and diplomat Akbar Ahmed has borrowed Samuel Huntington's "clash of civilizations" paradigm to question whether religious and nationalist conflict between India and Pakistan is inevitable. He identifies two forms of Islam in South Asian history, the "inclusivist" and "exclusivist," linking the first with Dara Shikoh and the second with Aurangzeb. The

42. Mohsin Hamid, *Moth Smoke* (Delhi: Penguin, 2000).

43. Manucci, *Storia do Mogor*, vol. 1, 215; vol. 2, 144.

44. Bernier, *Travels in the Mogul Empire*, 102; Manucci, *Storia do Mogor*, vol. 1, 340.

latter, says Ahmed, "drew the boundaries tightly around Islam." The triumphant emperor's legacy: "The next centuries saw the depletion of compassion, vitality and learning in Muslim society." Ahmed sees the ideological consequences of Aurangzeb's reign as Deobandism, the intellectual godfather of the Taliban. Whereas Dara Shikoh, according to Ahmed, sought to perpetuate the national policy promulgated by his great-grandfather Akbar: *sulh-e kull*, "universal reconciliation," a vision of state-sponsored religious tolerance. Ahmed sees *sulh-e kull* in South Asia today as threatened by terrorism, "religious prejudice," and "closed minds that exclude compassion."[45]

The divergent visions of Dara and Aurangzeb inspired a recent meditation on the Iraq war by a Pakistani writer for Lahore's *Daily Times*, Syed Mansoor Hussain. His essay is entitled "The Poisoned *Iftar*" (*Iftar* denotes the meal eaten at sunset to celebrate the end of the islamically mandated daylong fast during Ramadan).

Hussain begins with a confession. "For years I have felt bad as a Muslim." He explains why: "Sectarian violence, Muslims killing each other even in mosques, intellectual backwardness." But a news item from October 2006 marked a low point for Islam: the report that "dozens of Muslim policemen were…poisoned in Baghdad as they broke their fast. Poisoning an *iftar*? Is this what we have come to, and become?"

Hussain extrapolates from Iraq's Muslim-on-Muslim killings to consider the condition of his own nation: "Even within a Pakistan awash in 'enlightened moderation' [a favorite slogan of Musharraf's administration], government policy as well as mainstream religious thought continues to support violence in the name of religion." He traces the origin of this vice to a moment in Moghul history:

> Emperor Akbar and his great-grandson, Dara Shikoh, attempted to make Islam more inclusive, at least in the context of India. Their detractors saw this as heterodoxy and all attempts at inclusiveness ended completely with the death of Dara Shikoh and his entire family at the hand[s] of his brother.[46]

A harsh indictment. But the fact that Dara Shikoh's life continues to inspire thoughtful responses to current events seems to me a hopeful sign. The murdered prince will not have died altogether in vain if he helps revive in Pakistan the imperiled tradition of pluralism.

---

45. Akbar S. Ahmed, "Search for a Muslim Ideal in South Asia: The Path to Inclusion," *Zaman Daily Newspaper Online* (Istanbul), September 11, 2005 (www.zaman.com).

46. Syed Mansoor Hussain, "The Poisoned *Iftar*," *Daily Times* (Lahore), October 16, 2006 (www.dailytimes.com.pk).

BIBLIOGRAPHY

Abdallah, Osama. "Are Tattoos Allowed in Islam?" www.answering-christianity. com/tattoos.htm.

Ahmad, Munir. "Convert or Die? Pakistani Christians Seek Help." *Associated Press*, May 18, 2007. http://news.aol.com.

Ahmed, Akbar S. *Jinnah, Pakistan and Islamic Identity: The Search for Saladin*. London: Routledge, 1997.

Ahmed, Khaled. "Pakistani Madrassas and Apostatisation of the Shia." *Friday Times* (Lahore), December 16, 2005.

'Alamgir, Shahzada. "Ya Allah rahm farma!" *Khofnak Dijast* 9.8 (December 2005): 2-3.

'Ali, Mir Ahmed, ed. *Karbala-wale: nauhajat-e anjuman-e parwaneh-ye shabbir*. Hyderabad, India: Maktab-e turabia, 1989.

Anonymous. *Qur'at al-Qur'an ya'ni fal-nama-ye Qur'an-e majid*. Lahore: Idara-ye Raushna'i, 2001.

'Arabani, Ghulam Mustafa. "Khofnak Tota." *Khofnak Dijast* 8.15 (February 2005): 132-34.

Attar, Farid ud-Din. *The Conference of the Birds*. Afkham Darbandi and Dick Davis, trans. Harmondsworth: Penguin Books, 1984.

Awan, Muhammad Tariq. *History of India and Pakistan*. Lahore: Ferozsons, 1994.

Aziz, A. *Discovery of Pakistan*. 2d ed. Lahore: Sh. Ghulam Ali & Sons, 1964.

Bajwa, Farooq Naseem. *Pakistan: A Historical and Contemporary Look*. Karachi: Oxford University Press, 2002.

Beg, Rajab 'Ali. *Fasana-ye 'aja'ib*. Lahore: Ferozsons, n.d.

Begley, W. E., and Desai, Z. A., eds. *The Shah Jahan Nama of 'Inayat Khan*. Delhi: Oxford University Press, 1990.

Benedict XVI. "Faith, Reason, and the University." University of Regensburg, Sept. 12, 2006. www.vatican.va/holy_father/benedict_xvi/speeches/2006/september.

Bernier, François. *Travels in the Mogul Empire AD 1656–1668*. Trans. Archibald Constable. Delhi: Low Price Publications, 1999.

Bonner, Raymond. "Two Americans Killed in Attack on Pakistan Church." *The New York Times*, March 18, 2002.

Brown, Louise. *The Dancing Girls of Lahore*. New York: Fourth Estate, 2005.

Burkert, Walter. *Creation of the Sacred: Tracks of Biology in Early Religions*. Cambridge: Harvard University Press, 1996.

Carrington, Charles. *Rudyard Kipling: His Life and Work*. London: Macmillan & Co., 1955.

Chaudhry, Muhammad Harun. "Haqiqi khawf-e Khoda aur andesha-ya akhirat." *Khofnak Dijast* 7.11 (March 2004): 4.

Clarke, L., ed. *Shi'ite Heritage: Essays on Classical and Modern Traditions*. Binghamton: Global Publications, 2001.

Collins, Larry and Lapierre, Dominique. *Freedom at Midnight*. New York: Avon Books, 1975.

Dalrymple, William. "Letter from Pakistan: Days of Rage." *The New Yorker*, July 23, 2007: 26-35.

Deeb, Lara. "Living Ashura in Lebanon: Mourning Transformed to Sacrifice." *Comparative Studies of South Asia, Africa and the Middle East* 25.1 (2005): 122-37.

Donohue, John, and John Esposito, eds. *Islam in Transition: Muslim Perspectives*. 2d ed. New York: Oxford University Press, 2007.

Duncan, Emma. *Breaking the Curfew: A Political Journey Through Pakistan*. London: Arrow Books, 1989.

Ewing, Katherine Pratt. *Arguing Sainthood: Modernity, Psychoanalysis, and Islam*. Durham: Duke University Press, 1997.

Fallon, S. W., ed. *A New Hindustani-English Dictionary*. Benares: Medical Hall Press, 1879.

Al-Faqeeh, Mufti Abdulla. "Tattoos in Islam." Fatwa No. 8383, www.islamweb.net.

Felix, Qaiser. "84-Year-Old Christian Accused of Blasphemy to Force Him to Sell Land." *Asia News*, May 10, 2007. www.asianews.it.

—"New Apostasy Bill to Impose Death on Anyone Who Leaves Islam." *Asia News*, May 9, 2007. www.asianews.it.

Gandhi, Gopal. *Dara Shukoh: A Play*. New Delhi: Banyan Books, 1993.

Gascoigne, Bamber. *A Brief History of the Great Moguls*. New York: Carroll & Graf, 2002.

Ghauri, Aamir. "Demolishing History in Pakistan." *BBC News World Edition*, December 5, 2002. http://news.bbc.co.uk.

Gill, Jerry H. *Mediated Transcendence: A Postmodern Reflection*. Macon, GA: Mercer University Press, 1989.

Gottschalk, Peter. *Beyond Hindu and Muslim: Multiple Identity in Narratives from Village India*. New York: Oxford University Press, 2000.

Green, Roger L., and Alec Mason, eds. *The Readers' Guide to Rudyard Kipling's Work*. Canterbury: Gibbs & Sons Ltd., 1961.

Griffith, F. L., and Herbert Thompson, eds. *The Leyden Papyrus: An Egyptian Magical Book*. New York: Dover, 1974.

Hamid, Mohsin. *Moth Smoke*. Delhi: Penguin, 2000.

Haq, S. Moinul. *Ideological Basis of Pakistan in Historical Perspective, 711–1940*. Karachi: Pakistan Historical Society, 1982.

Hasan, Masud-ul. *Unique Trials for Virtue and Vice*. Lahore: Unique Publications, 1971.

Hasrat, Bikrama Jit. *Dara Shikuh: Life and Works*. 2d ed. Delhi: Munshiram Manoharlal, 1982.

Haye, Kh. Abdul. *First Steps in Our History*. Lahore: Ferozsons, 1990.

Hinge, Helle. "Islamic Magic in Contemporary Egypt." *Temenos* 31 (1995): 93-112.

Hirsi Ali, Ayaan. *The Caged Virgin: An Emancipation Proclamation for Women and Islam*. New York: Free Press, 2006.

Huart, Claude, and Louis Massignon. "Les Entretiens de Lahore." *Journal Asiatique* 209 (1926): 285-334.

Husain, Amir. "Qabr ka khawf." *Khofnak Dijast* 4.8 (December 2000): 2.

Ikram, Shaykh Muhammad. *Muslim Civilization in India*. New York: Columbia University Press, 1964.

—*Raud-e kauthar: islami hind aur pakistan ki mazhabi aur 'ilmi tarikh-e 'ahd-e moghuliyyah*. Lahore: Idarat-e thaqafat-e islamiyyah, 2005.

John, Asher. "Shantinagar Christians Getting Threatening Letters." *Daily Times* (Lahore), June 23, 2007. www.dailytimes.com.pk.

Kennedy, Charles H., ed. *Pakistan: 1992*. Boulder: Westview Press, 1993.

Khamenei, Seyyed 'Ali. *'Ashura: bayyanat-e rehbar-e mu'azzam-e inqilab-e islami*. Qom: Daftar-e tablighat-e islami, 1994.

—*Istifta'at ke jawabat hissa-ye davvom: mu'amalat*. Qom: Nur mataf, 2002.

Khan, Aamer Ahmed. "Sipah-e-Sahaba Pakistan." *The Herald* (Karachi) 25.6 (1994): 35.

Khan, Muhammad Wali Ullah. *Lahore and Its Important Monuments*. 2d ed. Karachi: Department of Archaeology and Museum, 1964.

Khan, Shahnawaz. "Drenched in Red." The Daily Times (Lahore), March 15, 2006. www.dailytimes.com.pk.

—"Weeklong Janamasthamy Comes to an End." *The Daily Times* (Lahore), August 17, 2006. www.dailytimes.com.pk.

Kipling, John Lockwood. *Beast and Man in India* London: Macmillan & Co., 1891.

Kipling, Rudyard. *A Kipling Pageant*. New York: Halcyon House, 1942.

Kurzman, Charles, ed. *Liberal Islam: A Sourcebook*. New York: Oxford University Press, 1998.

Lane, E. W. *Manners and Customs of the Modern Egyptians*. London: J. M. Dent & Sons, 1908.

Latif, Syed Muhammad. *Lahore: Its History, Architectural Remains and Antiquities*. Lahore: Syed Muhammad Minhaj-ud-Din, 1956.

Lesser, Robert, ed. *Pulp Art: Original Cover Paintings for the Great American Pulp Magazines*. New York: Castle Books, 1997.

Lubow, Arthur. "Tokyo Spring! The Murakami Method." *The New York Times*, April 3, 2005.

Mahdi, Muhsin, ed. *The Thousand and One Nights (Alf layla wa-layla) from the Earliest Known Sources*. 2 vols. Leiden: E. J. Brill, 1984.

Mahmud, S. F. *A Concise History of Indo-Pakistan*. Karachi: Oxford University Press, 1988.

Malik, Hafeez, ed. *Pakistan: Founders' Aspirations and Today's Realities*. Oxford: University Press, 2001.

Mani, Emmanuel Yousaf, ed. *Human Rights Monitor 2005: A Report on the Religious Minorities in Pakistan* (Lahore: National Commission for Justice and Peace, 2005).

—*Human Rights Monitor 2006: A Report on the Religious Minorities in Pakistan*. Lahore: National Commission for Justice and Peace, 2006.

Manucci, Niccolao. *Storia do Mogor*. Trans. William Irvine. 4 vols. Delhi: Oriental Books, 1981.

Maqsud, 'Ali Javid. *Yeh matam kayse ruk ja'ay: nauhe*. Hyderabad, India: Maktab-e turabia, n.d.

Marcotty, Thomas. *Dagger Blessing: The Tibetan Phurpa Cult*. Delhi: B. R. Publishing, 1987.

Massignon, Louis and Kassim, A. M. "Un essai de bloc islamo-hindou au xviième siècle: l'humanisme mystique du prince Dara." *Revue du monde musulman* 63 (1926): 1-14.

McNeill, William H. and Waldman, Marilyn Robinson, eds. *The Islamic World*. Chicago: University Press, 1973.

Metcalf, Barbara Daly. *Islamic Revival in British India: Deoband, 1860–1900*. Princeton: University Press, 1982.

Miller, Barbara Stoler, trans. *The Bhagavad-Gita: Krishna's Counsel in Time of War*. New York: Bantam, 1986.

Momen, Moojan. *An Introduction to Shii Islam*. New Haven: Yale University Press, 1985.

Montero, David. "Pakistani Girls' Schools in Radicals' Sights." *Christian Science Monitor*, May 31, 2007.

—"Pakistan Losing Territory to Radicals." *Christian Science Monitor*, May 29, 2007.

Moon, Penderel. *Divide and Quit: An Eye-Witness Account of the Partition of India*. Delhi: Oxford University Press, 1998.

Nadhir, Minwar. "Purana mandir." *Khofnak Dijast* 6.11 (March 2003): 160-65, 172.

Nasar, Hammad, ed. *Karkhana: A Contemporary Collaboration*. Ridgefield, CT: Aldrich Contemporary Art Museum, 2005.

Nasr, Vali. "The Revival of Shia Islam." Speech presented to the Pew Forum on Religion and Public Life, July 24, 2006. http://pewforum.org/events/index.php?EventID=120.

Nelson, Victoria. *The Secret Life of Puppets*. Cambridge: Harvard University Press, 2001.

Oates, Joyce Carol. *Haunted: Tales of the Grotesque*. New York: Penguin, 1995.

Parimi, Mukhtar 'Ali. "Dozakh ki ag aur andhera." *Khofnak Dijast* 6.1 (May 2002): 3.

Parwana, Qaysar Jamil. "Ayat al-kursi ki barakat." *Khofnak Dijast* 7.11 (March 2004): 65.

—"Khofnak jinnat." *Khofnak Dijast* 7.11 (March 2004): 90-96.

Pinault, David. *Horse of Karbala: Muslim Devotional Life in India*. New York: Palgrave, 2001.

—*The Shiites: Ritual and Popular Piety in a Muslim Community*. New York: St. Martin's Press, 1992.

—"Story-Telling." In Meisami, Julie Scott and Starkey, Paul, eds., *Encyclopedia of Arabic Literature* (London: Routledge, 1998): vol. 2, 735-37.

—*Story-Telling Techniques in the Arabian Nights*. Leiden: E. J. Brill, 1992.

Pinney, Thomas, ed. *Kipling's India: Uncollected Sketches 1884-88*. New York: Schocken Books, 1986.

Propp, Vladimir. *Morphology of the Folktale*. Bloomington: Indiana University, 1958.

Qanungo, Kalika-Ranjan. *Dara Shukoh*. 2d ed. Calcutta: S. C. Sarkar & Sons Ltd., 1952.

Al-Qazwini, Zakariyya ibn Muhammad. *'Aja'ib al-makhluqat wa-ghara'ib al-mawjudat*. Cairo: Mustafa al-Babi al-Halabi, 1966.

Rashid, Ahmed. *Taliban: Militant Islam, Oil, and Fundamentalism in Central Asia*. New Haven: Yale University Press, 2000.

Rehman, Wali-Ur. *Indo-Pak History 712–1815*. Lahore: AN Publishers, 2004.

Roof, Wade Clark. "Pluralism as a Culture: Religion and Civility in Southern California." *Annals of the American Academy of Political and Social Science* 612 (2007): 82-99.

Salim, Muhammad. *Dara Shikoh: ahwal o afkar*. Lahore: Maktabat-e Karvan, 1995.

Sharif, Ja'far. *Islam in India or the Qanun-i-Islam*. Trans. G. A. Herklots. London: Curzon Press, 1972.

Al-Sharqawi, 'Abd al-Rahman al-Safati, ed. *Alf laylah wa-laylah*. 2 vols. Cairo: Bulaq, 1835.

Shinakeh, Shabnam Daoud. "Panj qabron ki chashmdid-e halat ne gonahgar ko tawba par amada kar diya." *Khofnak Dijast* 6.7 (November 2002): 4.

Sivan, Emmanuel. "Sunni Radicalism in the Middle East and the Iranian Revolution." *International Journal of Middle East Studies* 21 (1989): 1-30.

Talbot, Ian. *Pakistan: A Modern History*. New York: St. Martin's Press, 1998.

Todorov, Tzvetan. *The Poetics of Prose*. Ithaca: Cornell University Press, 1977.

Vallette, Paul, ed. *Apulée: Apologie*. Paris: Société d'édition "Les Belles Lettres," 1924.

Walbridge, Linda S. *The Christians of Pakistan: The Passion of Bishop John Joseph*. London: Routledge, 2003.

Williams, Alex. "Up to Her Eyes in Gore, and Loving It: Young Women Bond with Horror Films." *The New York Times*, April 30, 2006.

Woodcock, Martin. *Collins' Birds of India*. London: Harper Collins, 1980.

Yeats-Brown, Francis. *The Lives of a Bengal Lancer*. New York: Viking, 1930.

Younghusband, Col. G.J. *The Story of the Guides*. London: Macmillan & Co., 1908.

Zakaria, Rafia. "The 'Anti-Woman' Pakistani Woman." *Daily Times* (Lahore), April 29, 2007. www.dailytimes.com.pk.

—"Faceless, Yet Famous." *Daily Times* (Lahore), July 7, 2007. www.dailytimes.com.pk.

Zaman, Muhammad Qasim. "Sectarianism in Pakistan: The Radicalization of Shii and Sunni Identities." *Modern Asian Studies* 32 (1998): 689-716.

INDEX